The Serpent in Samuel

The Serpent in Samuel

A Messianic Motif

BRIAN A. VERRETT

foreword by Jason S. DeRouchie

RESOURCE *Publications* · Eugene, Oregon

THE SERPENT IN SAMUEL
A Messianic Motif

Resource Publications
An Imprint of Wipf and Stock Publishers
199 W. 8th Ave., Suite 3
Eugene, OR 97401

www.wipfandstock.com

PAPERBACK ISBN: 978-1-7252-5984-3
HARDCOVER ISBN: 978-1-7252-5983-6
EBOOK ISBN: 978-1-7252-5985-0

Manufactured in the U.S.A.   02/10/20

To my beautiful wife, Ang.
Thank you for helping me hope in a future
without the serpent and its thorns.

To New Creation Church.
The God of peace will soon crush Satan under your feet.
The grace of our Lord Jesus Christ be with you (Rom 16:20).

Contents

FIGURES

FOREWORD

ONE OF SCRIPTURE'S EARLIEST narratives portrays evil entering the world in the form of a serpent (Gen 3:1). Following mankind's sin in the Garden, God first cursed the serpent more than every other beast, noted that he would have offspring, and promised that a male descendant of the first woman would one day overcome the evil one through suffering (Gen 3:14–15). The story begins here. . . . The end of the story tells us that this dragon—God's greatest enemy, "that ancient serpent, who is called the devil"—would seek to destroy the promised royal, eschatological male child who was "to rule all the nations with a rod of iron" (Rev 12:3–5). Nevertheless, "the salvation and the power and the kingdom of our God and the authority of his Christ" would triumph through tribulation, and those associated with God and his Christ would also conquer the evil one "by the blood of the Lamb and by the word of their testimony" (12:10–11). The God of peace would indeed crush Satan under their feet (Rom 16:20). While God in Christ has bound the serpent for a time, in the end the sovereign one will fully defeat him and throw him into the lake of fire for eternal punishment (Rev 20:2, 10).

These are Scripture's bookends, and between them the Bible uses the serpent as a recurring motif. In this carefully researched study, Brian Verrett identifies how the biblical author of Samuel was one who employed serpent language, imagery, and concepts to heighten hope in the coming messianic king. Other scholars have rightly identified various characters in Samuel as "serpents," be they Goliath, Nahash (king of the Ammonites), Hanun, Absalom, or Amasa. Nevertheless, Verrett is the first of whom I am aware who uses careful literary analysis and biblical theology to show how the author intentionally employs what can truly be called a serpent motif in order to present the offspring of David as the promised offspring of the woman from Genesis 3:15 who will defeat the serpent and reign as king in the new creation.

Following his introductory chapter, Verrett identifies key words, images, and concepts associated with the serpent in Genesis 3 and then uses a canonical approach to biblical theology to identify how a serpent motif pervades all of Scripture (ch. 2). In this chapter, Verrett helpfully notes that Genesis 3:15 not only promises the defeat of the serpent but also foresees a restored new creation. He then takes two chapters to exegete the key texts in Samuel where others have seen the serpent, and he effectively argues for the pervasiveness of this idea in the book (chs. 3–4). Chapter 3 carefully looks at the book's description of Goliath's armor and death and Habakkuk 3:13–14's interpretation of David's victory in order to show that the narrator indeed viewed this giant warrior as a serpent. Chapter 4 then overviews those named or associated with "Nahash" (the Hebrew term for "serpent") in Samuel and notes how the book consistently portrays them as serpentine if they stand against Israel. The final three chapters show how all the serpentine passages in Samuel are united lexically and conceptually, consistently portray the "serpent" character opposing the protagonist, and work together to communicate a unified message. Chapter 5 relates the different serpent stories together. Chapter 6 demonstrates how 2 Samuel 7:11b–17 foresaw the promised offspring of David to be the serpent slayer. And chapter 7 argues that 2 Samuel 23:1–7 explicitly links this messianic Davidic son's reign over the new creation with his victory over the serpent.

Just weeks after Jesus Christ's death, burial, and resurrection, Peter boldly proclaimed that, along with Moses, "all the prophets who have spoken, from Samuel and those who came after him, also proclaimed these days" (Acts 3:24; cf. 3:18). In this well-researched study, Verrett identifies for us how the book of Samuel utilizes the serpent motif to foretell the triumph of the Messiah over the serpent as the means for initiating the new creation. This study models careful exegetical and theological method for the glory of Christ and the good of his church, and I am thrilled that it is now published. May its message nurture living hope in the living Messiah who has triumphed through tribulation and whose new creational kingdom is inaugurated and will be consummated.

Jason S. DeRouchie, PhD
Research Professor of Old Testament and Biblical Theology
Midwestern Baptist Theological Seminary

ACKNOWLEDGEMENTS

THIS BOOK WOULD NEVER have seen the light of day if it were not for many wonderful people. My deepest gratitude extends to my wife, Ang, and my three children, Lydia, Abigail, and Luke. Thank you all for supporting me as I wrote this book. I love you all dearly with the love of Jesus.

Thank you, Dr. Jason DeRouchie, for overseeing this revised ThM thesis from the beginning. Without your guidance, I would not have known how to start this project. Your encouragement along the way motivated me to continue to do the best I could. You are a godly man who has sacrificially served me. I must also thank Drs. Brian Tabb and Jim Hamilton for their critique of a previous form of this book. Without your constructive criticism, I know this book would be far less helpful than it is now. For all who took the time to read and endorse this book, thank you. May the Lord bless each of you for this act of kindness. Also, thank you, Wipf and Stock, for kindly agreeing to publish this book.

Besides these, I would also like to express my deep appreciation to Drs. Jason Meyer and Michael B. Shepherd. You both were the first to begin to teach me how to cherish and understand the Bible. I would not be who I am today if I had not previously known you. The Lord has used you mightily in my life, and for this grace I am eternally grateful.

Last of all, I'd like to thank my heavenly Father for sustaining me as I wrote this book. May glory abound to him through the knowledge of his Son.

ABBREVIATIONS

AT	Author's translation
ANE	Ancient Near East
BHS	Biblia Hebraica Stuttgartensia
CSB	Christian Standard Bible
ET	English Translation
ESV	English Standard Version Bible
HALOT	Koehler, Ludwig, Walter Baumgartner, and Johann Jakob Stamm. *The Hebrew and Aramaic Lexicon of the Old Testament,* translated by M. E. J. Richardson. Study Edition 1. Leiden: Brill Academic, 2001.
LT	Lucianic text
LXX	Septuaginta
LXX^B	Septuagint Codex Vaticanus
LXX^A	Septuagint Codex Alexandrinus
LXX^L	Septuagint Codex Lucianic
MT	Masoretic Text
NASB	New American Standard Bible
NET	New English Translation Bible
NETS	New English Translation of the Septuagint
NIV	The New International Version Bible
NLT	The New Living Translation Bible

NRSV   New Revised Standard Version Bible

NT   New Testament

OG   Old Greek

OT   Old Testament

1

INTRODUCTION

ALLUSIONS TO GEN 3 abound throughout the Old Testament and New
Testament (hereafter OT and NT). As John L. Ronning has demonstrated,
one of these allusions from Gen 3 that permeates the Bible is to the serpent.[1] James Hamilton has also shown that the serpent's defeat is a major
theme in Scripture.[2]

Some have suggested that the joint book of 1 and 2 Samuel (hereafter
Samuel) cast particular characters as serpents in order to allude to Gen 3.
The Samuel narrative refers to Nahash, the king of the sons of Ammon on
multiple occasions.[3] As some recognize, Nahash (נחש) means "snake."[4]
Given the biblical authors' tendency to imbue names with meaning, could
these references to Nahash be allusions to Gen 3? Furthermore, 1 Sam 17:5

---

1. Ronning, "The Curse on the Serpent," 143–373.

2. Hamilton, "The Skull Crushing Seed of the Woman," 30–55.

3. Both the MT and the OG reference the name "Nahash" in 1 Sam 11:1, 2; 12:12;
2 Sam 10:2; 17:25, 27. In 1 Sam 11:10, the OG (Old Greek) mentions Nahash by name
and the MT does not. In this instance, the difference is marginal in that the OG clarifies
what is already sufficiently clear in the MT. The OG says, "And the men of Jabesh said
to Nahash, the Ammonite, 'Tomorrow we will go out to you,'" while the MT says, "And
the men of Jabesh said, 'Tomorrow we will go out to you.'" Notably, 4QSam[a] mentions
Nahash by name two additional times between 1 Sam 10:27—11:1. For more on this
material within 4QSam[a] see Whiston, *The Works of Josephus*, 156–57; Tsumura, *The
First Book of Samuel*, 303; Firth, *1 & 2 Samuel*, 130; Decker, "Multivalent Readings of
Multivalent Texts," 412–16; Eves, "One Ammonite Invasion or Two," 308–26.

4. See Auld, *I & II Samuel*, 123; Bergen, *1, 2 Samuel*, 135; Catastini, "4Q Sama: 11
Nahash il 'Serpente,'" 17–49.

says that Goliath's armor is scaly (קשקשים)—a word always used for the skin of a sea creature.[5] According to most, David then crushes Goliath's forehead with a stone.[6] He then falls with his face—and therefore mouth—to the ground immediately before David decapitates his head. Perhaps the text intends to allude to Gen 3 when God's judgment falls on a scaly foe whose mouth is on the ground and who dies from a strike to his head.

1.1. PREVIOUS SCHOLARSHIP IDENTIFYING SERPENTS WITHIN SAMUEL

As mentioned, scholars have identified various characters as "serpents" within Samuel. These characters are Goliath, Nahash (the king of the Ammonites), Hanun, Absalom, and Amasa. What follows is a brief survey of their various arguments for identifying these characters as being serpentine.

1.1.1. Goliath as a Serpent in Samuel

Ronning is one who has argued that the Samuel narrative presents Goliath as a serpent.[7] Ronning points out that Goliath has "scale" (קשקשים) armor and that the word "scale" is used for sea creatures. The only other person to have "scaly" skin is Pharaoh in Ezek 29:3–4, and this text presents Pharaoh as a sea monster. Ronning understands the connection between קשקשים and sea creatures to suggest that Goliath is serpentine. Ronning finds further support of Goliath's serpent identity in 1 Sam 17:5–6. In these verses the narrator mentions four times that his armor and weaponry is bronze (נחשת), which Ronning suggests is a wordplay with "serpent" (נחש). Finally, in 17:4 Goliath, the Philistines' "champion," is literally the "in betweens-man" (איש־הבנים).[8] Ronning posits that Goliath's unusual title alludes to the four times that "between" (בין) is used in Gen 3:15.

---

5. See Lev 11:9, 10, 12; Deut 14:9, 10; Ezek 29:4.

6. Ariella Deem has argued that David's stone sunk into Goliath's greave in "And the Stone Sank into His Forehead," 349–51. Since Deem has made her argument, others continue to understand מצח to refer to Goliath's forehead. See Bergen, *1, 2 Samuel*, 197. Still others—like Johanna W. H. van Wijk-Bos—remain agnostic on the issue (see *Reading Samuel: A Literary and Theological Commentary*, 99). For more on whether David's stone struck Goliath's greave or head see section 3.2. and its subsections below.

7. All of the information within this paragraph from Ronning comes from "The Curse on the Serpent," 296–97.

8. The word "champion" is how the ESV renders the Hebrew phrase איש־הבנים. Unless noted otherwise, all biblical citations will come from the ESV.

Hamilton's conclusions about Goliath agree in large measure with Ronning's. After demonstrating that the bruising of the serpent's skull is a prominent theme throughout the OT, he argues that Goliath's crushed skull is an allusion to the serpent from Gen 3:15.[9] Peter Leithart too believes that the author of Samuel signals that Goliath is a serpent by detailing his scale armor and crushed head.[10]

1.1.2. Nahash, the King of the Sons of Ammon, and Hanun as Serpents in Samuel

Ronning has interpreted Nahash, the king of the sons of Ammon, and his son, Hanun, to be serpents. Ronning understands Nahash to be a serpent based on the Ammonite king's name, Nahash, which means serpent.[11] He then suggests that when Hanun humiliates David's servants by uncovering their nakedness, he is acting like Ham and the serpent of Gen 3, which associates Hanun with the offspring of the serpent.[12] Alessandro Catastini also argues that one should interpret Nahash as a "serpent," but Catastini differs from Ronning in that he interprets Nahash as a serpent against the backdrop of mythical deities seen in extra-biblical ANE literature instead of against previous biblical literature.[13] Leithart also understands Nahash and Hanun to be serpentine; Israel's new Adam-like kings must crush the heads of their adversaries.[14] Ronning, Hamilton, and Leithart also all link these victories over serpents within Samuel to the messianic hope because they interpret Gen 3:15 to anticipate a royal eschatological deliverer who will defeat the serpent.

1.1.3. Absalom and Amasa as Serpents in Samuel

Ronning has also understood Absalom and Amasa to be serpentine. The evidence that Ronning adduces from within Samuel to show that Absalom is serpentine is four-fold. He suggests that Absalom's murder of Amnon reveals that Absalom has adopted the serpent's view of God, namely that God

---

9. Hamilton, "The Skull Crushing Seed of the Woman," 30–55.

10. Leithart, *A Son to Me*, 97, 100.

11. Ronning, "The Curse on the Serpent," 310.

12. Ronning, "The Curse on the Serpent," 310.

13. Catastini, "4Q: 11 Nahash il 'Serpente,'" 17–49.

14. Leithart, *A Son to Me*, 81, 97, 233.

is one who withholds that which is good.[15] Besides this, Absalom's murder of Amnon harkens back to Cain's murder of Abel. Since Cain is the seed of the serpent, this aligns Absalom with the serpent's seed.[16] Absalom also deceives Israel. This reminds Ronning of the serpent's deception.[17] Lastly, Absalom is serpentine because he affiliates with and appoints Amasa, who is serpentine, over his army.[18]

In Ronning's estimation the key text in determining that Amasa is serpentine is found in 2 Sam 17:25. Many have observed the textual difficulties between 2 Sam 17:25 and 1 Chr 2:13–17 noting that in 2 Sam 17:25 Nahash is Abigail's father and Amasa's grandfather while in 1 Chr 2:16–17 Jesse, the father of king David, is Abigail's father and Amasa's grandfather. To reconcile this, some have suggested that Abigail is David's half-sister because David's mother was married to Nahash prior to marrying Jesse.[19] Others have suggested that the Masoretic Text's (hereafter MT) translation may contain an error, though they note that there "is no reliable textual witness to contradict it."[20] Ronning concludes that the text identifies a man named Nahash as Abigail's father because Amasa, Abigail's son, has joined Absalom's rebellion. Aligning with Absalom demonstrates that Amasa is of the seed of the serpent since he shows enmity against David.[21] Thus, Amasa's father (i.e., grandfather) is named serpent, and Amasa is his offspring. According to Ronning, Amasa aligning with the serpent is ironic because Shobi, the son of Nahash of Ammon, brought aid to David two verses later in the form of beds and various foods as David and his men fled from Absalom (2 Sam 17:27).[22]

1.2. LITERARY CRITICISM WITHIN SAMUEL

While the scholars mentioned above have suggested that Samuel contains multiple serpentine characters based primarily on biblical theological links, many other scholars have utilized literary-criticism on Samuel. As a result, they have identified many motifs within Samuel.

---

15. Ronning, "The Curse on the Serpent," 314.

16. Ronning, "The Curse on the Serpent," 144–45, 314.

17. Ronning, "The Curse on the Serpent," 314.

18. Ronning, "The Curse on the Serpent," 314.

19. Hertzberg, *I and II Samuel,* 57.

20. McCarter, *II Samuel,* 392.

21. Ronning, "The Curse on the Serpent," 315.

22. Ronning, "The Curse on the Serpent," 314–15.

1.2.1. Selected Literary Critics

K. L. Noll notes that "the 1980s and early 1990s saw a virtual explosion of literary-oriented scholarship into the book of Samuel."[23] J. P. Fokkelman is one of these scholars. He employed literary criticism on all of Samuel and 1 Kings 1–2. His work focuses on repetition at the micro-structural level within the MT.[24] Moshe Garsiel has also concentrated on the MT, but unlike Fokkelman, Garsiel elucidates broader comparative structures, and he does so only within 1 Samuel.[25] Some of these literary strategies are comparisons between Eli and the parents of Samuel,[26] defeat under Eli and victory under Samuel,[27] and the use of the verb "ask" [שאל] with respect to Samuel, David, and Saul.[28]

Robert Polzin is similar to those above in that he works from the MT, and he employs literary criticism, but he differs from them because he performs a literary study of the Deuteronomic history within Samuel. His stance on textual criticism is also worth noting. He believes that "the similarities between one witness and another are so overwhelmingly greater than their often important differences that a law of diminishing returns takes effect the further one proceeds."[29] In the end, Polzin believes that "the more time and effort one puts into establishing the text, the less crucial successive effort will be for matters of global interpretation."[30]

Robert Alter's praised translation and commentary on Samuel also gives preference to the MT. He chose to "follow the Masoretic Text as long as it made some sense, even if a seductive variant beckoned from the Septuagint or elsewhere."[31] Like those listed above, Paul Borgman agrees that Samuel should be read as a literary whole.[32] When this is done, the reader can discern in Samuel a "dozen or so broad patterns of repetition governing the narrative's progress."[33] Johanna W. H. van Wijk-Bos writes in this same stream of scholarship. She states, "I follow many contemporary scholars,

23. Noll, *The Faces of David*, 14.

24. Fokkelman, *King David*; Fokkelman, *The Crossing Fates*; Fokkelman, *Throne and City*; Fokkelman, *Vow and Desire*.

25. Garsiel, *The First Book of Samuel*.

26. Garsiel, *The First Book of Samuel*, 33–35.

27. Garsiel, *The First Book of Samuel*, 35–37.

28. Garsiel, *The First Book of Samuel*, 72–74.

29. Polzin, *Samuel and the Deuteronomist*, 1.

30. Polzin, *Samuel and the Deuteronomist*, 1.

31. Alter, *The David Story*, xxvi.

32. Borgman, *David, Saul, and God*.

33. Borgman, *David, Saul, and God*, 3.

such as Robert Polzin, Robert Alter, and especially J. Fokkelman."[34] She wrote her literary-theological commentary on Samuel by concentrating on the MT. She says, "In principal, I only emend the Masoretic reading when the Hebrew is incomprehensible and in such cases have leaned on the Qumran or the Septuagint versions or both."[35]

1.2.2. Selected Literary Motifs

Many have written articles about Samuel's various motifs. Some of these motifs are beauty,[36] displaced husbands,[37] food provisions,[38] the exodus,[39] and ancestral allusions to the patriarchs in Genesis.[40]

Another prominent motif is how Samuel presents Saul as a foil to David. Kevin Rayfield McGill has done one such study with respect to 1 Sam 18.[41] While considering 1 Sam 16:1—18:5 Borgman in passing says that "in the contrast between how [David and Saul] handle fear, and in the differences in how each uses the sword and spear, we come to clearer insight about David's character, with Saul as foil."[42]

Likewise, Garsiel demonstrates that Saul and David are compared in many ways. Three of these comparisons are David's anointing,[43] appearance at court,[44] and secret anointment as king.[45] In similar fashion, V. Philips Long argues that the text of Samuel contrasts Saul and David's kingly selections. He writes, "David was Yahweh's choice in a way that Saul, given in response to the people's request, was not."[46] Polzin sees things similarly when he says, "The Deuteronomist contrasts God's choice of David with Saul's."[47]

34. van Wijk-Bos, *Reading Samuel*, 15.
35. van Wijk-Bos, *Reading Samuel*, 14.
36. Avioz, "The Motif of Beauty in the Books of Samuel and Kings," 341–59.
37. Kessler, "Sexuality and Politics," 409–23.
38. Gilmour, "Reading a Biblical Motif," 30–43.
39. Runions, "Exodus Motifs in First Samuel 7 and 8," 130–31.
40. Biddle, "Ancestral Motifs in 1 Samuel 25," 617–38.
41. McGill, "The Foil Relationship of David and Saul in 1 Samuel 18."
42. Borgman, *David, Saul, and God*, 51.
43. Garsiel, *The First Book of Samuel*, 108.
44. Garsiel, *The First Book of Samuel*, 108–10.
45. Garsiel, *The First Book of Samuel*, 110–11.
46. Long, *The Reign and Rejection of King Saul*, 93.
47. Polzin, *Samuel and the Deuteronomist*, 157.

Mark George argues that an additional contrast between David and Saul is
the moral uprightness of David's heart.[48]

1.3. THE WAY FORWARD

As shown above, many scholars recognize that the book of Samuel employs
various motifs. Others have argued that Samuel regularly uses serpentine
language, imagery, and concepts. Given the book of Samuel's penchant for
employing various motifs, could the repeated use of serpentine language
be yet another motif working its way through the book? What would be
the significance of this motif within the book of Samuel? In addition, how
does Samuel's use of this potential motif compare to other places within the
OT that contain serpentine language and imagery? Also, does the author
of Samuel understand his serpent references to be a motif within a larger
theme, and if the author does, what theme might that be?

1.3.1. Thesis

To my knowledge, no one has answered all of these questions from Samuel.
On account these unanswered questions, this book investigates (1) whether
Samuel contains a serpent motif and (2) what the probable significance of
this motif might be. My thesis is that the Samuel narrative contains a serpent motif and that this motif's significance within Samuel is to present the
seed of David as the promised seed of the woman from Gen 3:15 who will
defeat the serpent and reign as king in the new creation.

1.3.2. Methodology

Methodologically speaking, this book divides into two parts. In the first part
(chapter 2), we will employ a canonical approach to biblical theology in
order to determine if there is a serpent motif that runs through the OT and
NT.[49] In this endeavor I will follow the tri-partite division of the Tanak as
represented by the *BHS*. This biblical theology is not intended to be exhaustive. Rather, its aim is merely to be thorough enough to warrant a consideration of Samuel's possible serpent motif.

In order to better ensure that our biblical-theological findings are
accurate, we will first develop a paradigm to discern serpent allusions by

48. George, "Yhwh's Own Heart," 442–59.
49. Klink and Lockett, *Understanding Biblical Theology*, 125–40.

noting those words, images, and concepts that the text associates with the serpent in Gen 3. These words and their serpentine associations will provide the framework to conduct the biblical-theological survey in the hopes of reaffirming that there is a serpent motif that runs through the OT and NT. We will also pay close attention to those words within the broader semantic range of "serpent" (נחש).[50]

In the second part of this book (chs. 3–7), we will employ literary-criticism within Samuel to determine if Samuel contains a serpent motif and what that potential motif's significance might be. The type of literary criticism we will employ is similar to those mentioned above (i.e., Alter, Fokkelman, Garsiel, Wijk-Bos, Long) in that we will "focus on the text, not on the author or the reader"[51] as it is within its "final context as a literary whole."[52] Tremper Longman III understands this specific type of literary criticism to be a "kind of formalism or New Criticism."[53] While our focus will be on the MT, we will consider alternate readings when they may affect this book's argument.

In chapters 3–4 we will investigate whether or not Nahash, Goliath, Absalom, and Amasa are serpentine as the previously mentioned scholars have suggested. Upon determining that the Samuel narrative repeatedly casts certain characters as serpents, we will have established that Samuel does contain a serpent motif. This is the case because a motif is simply a "recognizable pattern or unit."[54] In this case, the recognizable pattern would be the Samuel narrative repeatedly casting characters as serpents.

Once we have established that Samuel does contain a serpent motif, in chapters 5–7 we will attempt to demonstrate that the different serpentine passages work together to communicate a unified, coherent message. To do this we will point out lexical and conceptual similarities between those passages containing serpent language. We will also see that Samuel consistently uses serpentine language to describe those who oppose whoever the main protagonist is within the flow of Samuel. Furthermore, our reading

---

50. Ronning identifies those words within the broader semantic range of נחש to be אפעה, לויתן, עכשוב, פתן, צפע, צפעוני, רהב, שרף, שפיפון. See "The Curse on the Serpent," 146. We should also recognize that תנין is related to serpentine language because it works closely with serpentine terms on more than one occasion (cf. Exod 7:9; Isa 27:1; 51:9).

51. Longman, "Literary Approaches to the Old Testament," 100.

52. Longman, "Literary Approaches to the Old Testament," 98.

53. Longman, "Literary Approaches to the Old Testament," 100.

54. This definition comes from Bernard Aubert's *The Shepherd-flock Motif in the Miletus Discourse*, 16. A motif is to be distinguished from a theme since a motif is an element within a broader theme. A motif is a thread, and a theme is the rope made of different threads.

of Samuel will demonstrate that these serpent texts are at similar structural locations within the narrative and that they affect the narrative's flow in the same way. If we are able to demonstrate the above, we will have warrant for identifying a serpent motif and suggesting its intended purpose.

2

BIBLICAL THEOLOGY
OF THE SERPENT

THIS CHAPTER WILL SURVEY the serpent motif within Scripture by employing biblical theology. Due to this book's emphasis on Samuel, this biblical-theological survey of the serpent will not be exhaustive. Rather, the aim of this chapter is to demonstrate that both the OT and NT contain a serpent motif that derives from Gen 3. Before demonstrating that both the OT and NT contain a serpent motif, we will develop a paradigm to determine allusions to the serpent by noting those words, images, and concepts that the text associates with the serpent in Gen 3. These words and their serpentine associations will provide the framework to complete our biblical-theological survey of the serpent.

2.1. THE SERPENT OF GENESIS 3

A brief overview of the serpent's dealings will enable us to create a list of key words, images, and concepts that better equip us to know when a text may or may not be alluding to the serpent. We will consider (1) the serpent's identity along with the identity of the serpent's seed and the woman's seed, (2) the serpent's insurrection, and (3) the Lord's judgment upon the serpent, man, woman, and humanity. At the end of all of these sub-sections, we will summarize our findings.

2.1.1. The Serpent's Identity

Scholars have disputed the identity of the serpent for years. Michael Rydelnik claims that there are four different views on the matter: (1) naturalistic, (2) symbolic, (3) *sensus plenior*, and (4) messianic.[1] We will now explain each of these views, and then we will adopt the messianic interpretation.

The naturalistic view understands the serpent to be a mere serpent. Claus Westermann represents this view. For Westermann, the curse on the serpent "is clearly an etiological motif."[2] Predictably then, he understands the serpent's seed to be literal serpents and the woman's seed to be humans. Westermann summarizes his understanding of the passage by saying, "The enmity will work itself out by humans and the serpent continually . . . trying to kill each other."[3]

We can describe the symbolic and *sensus plenior* views together. John H. Walton represents the symbolic view, and Gordon J. Wenham argues for the *sensus plenior* view.[4] Wenham states that "the serpent symbolizes sin, death, and the power of evil,"[5] and that its offspring are "the powers of evil."[6] Likewise, Walton understands the serpent as a mere serpent and its seed as serpents. Still, the serpent and its seed are symbolic of a greater reality. The woman's seed is humanity. Hence, Walton concludes, "The verse is depicting a continual, unresolved conflict between humans and the representatives of evil."[7]

Naturally, the messianic view focuses more on the identity of the woman's seed than the serpent. It understands the seed of the woman to be the royal eschatological deliverer, which later texts understand to be the Messiah. On the other hand, it understands the serpent to be God's greatest enemy, whom Scripture later refers to as "the adversary" (הַשָּׂטָן), hereafter called Satan. With most critical scholars, Westermann disagrees with this view. He says the messianic reading is unlikely because "it is beyond doubt that זרע is to be understood collectively" and because Gen 3:15 "occurs in the context of a pronouncement of punishment (or of a curse). It is not

---

1. Rydelnik, *The Messianic Hope*, 131–35.

2. Westermann, *Genesis 1–11*, 259.

3. Westermann, *Genesis 1–11*, 259.

4. Wenham differs from Walton because Wenham believes that "a messianic interpretation may be justified in the light of subsequent revelation, a *sensus plenior*" (*Genesis 1–15*, 81), whereas Walton does not.

5. Wenham, *Genesis 1–15*, 80.

6. Wenham, *Genesis 1–15*, 81.

7. Walton, *Genesis*, 226.

possible that such a form has either promise or prophecy as its primary or even as its secondary meaning."[8]

Both of Westermann's arguments fail. First, one cannot separate judgment from promise or prophecy. Jesse R. Scheumann captures this well: "Westermann . . . makes a false dichotomy between judgment and promise. Properly speaking, the serpent receives a promise of judgment: his head *will* be crushed."[9]

Concerning Westermann's second objection, it is by no means beyond doubt that זֶרַע refers to a collective offspring. Collins has demonstrated that "when *zera'* denotes a specific descendant, it appears with singular verb inflections, adjectives, and pronouns."[10] In Gen 3:15, הוּא finds its antecedent in זֶרַע. Collins's syntactical work demonstrates that the woman's seed is a single, male descendant. Collins concludes, "We might wonder if the singular *hû'* in Genesis 3:15 is used precisely in order to make it plain that an individual is being promised."[11] Building on Collins's work, T. Desmond Alexander has argued that Gen 22:17 and 24:60 anticipate a single, male, eschatological deliverer.[12]

Walton dismisses Alexander and Collins's work when he writes, "There are examples in which singular pronouns are used even though 'seed' means posterity (Gen. 22:17; 24:60, discounting as special pleading T. D. Alexander's attempt to argue that they do not refer to posterity)."[13] Walton's argument fails to account for the fact that Moses could add plural pronouns when he wanted to demonstrate that he wrote about a collective seed.[14] Walton also fails to account for texts like Ps 72:17. This text seems to allude to Gen 22:18 and apply Genesis's seed language to the coming Messiah.[15]

In addition, Walton fails to recognize that in texts like Gen 22:17 when God says that he will "surely multiply [Abraham's] offspring as the stars of heaven," this does not necessitate a plural offspring. On the contrary, a singular interpretation of "offspring" is natural. This is so because Walton apparently misunderstands how the word "multiplies" (רבה) operates within Genesis. Within Genesis, when a particular human "multiplies," it does not

8. Westermann, *Genesis 1–11*, 260.

9. Scheumann, "A Biblical Theology of Birth Pain and the Hope of the Messiah," 16, (emphasis his).

10. Collins, "A Syntactical Note (Genesis 3:15)," 144.

11. Collins, "A Syntactical Note (Genesis 3:15)," 145.

12. Alexander, "Further Observations on the Term 'Seed' in Genesis," 363.

13. Walton, *Genesis*, 225.

14. DeRouchie and Meyer, "Christ or Family as the 'Seed' of Promise?," 38.

15. See Hossfeld and Zenger, *Psalms 2*, 218.

mean that more of that human comes into existence. On the contrary, when a human "multiples," it simply means that the human has children (cf. 1:28; 6:1; 9:1, 7; 16:10; 17:2). For example, in Gen 17:2 God tells Abram that he will "multiply" (רבה) him greatly. By this the Lord means that he will give Abram descendants so that he will become "a father of a multitude of nations" (v. 4). Likewise, in Gen 22:17 when God promises to "multiply" (רבה) Abraham's offspring as the stars of heaven, God is promising that one day Abraham's singular offspring will have numerous descendants. This singular seed will have descendants who are as many as the stars of heaven (cf. Isa 53:10; 54:1–3).

As stated before, the messianic view understands the serpent to be God's greatest enemy (cf. Rev 12:9). In the Prophets section below, we will argue that Isaiah understands the serpent in Gen 3 to be God's greatest enemy, and at the end of this book we will see that Samuel presents God's greatest enemy as the serpent of Gen 3.[16] It follows then that we understand the seed of the serpent to be humans who follow in the ways of God's greatest adversary by opposing God and his people (cf. Matt 13:38; 23:15; John 8:44; Acts 13:10; 1 John 3:10).

Now we should seek to understand how the seed of the woman relates to other individuals or groups within Scripture who experience the enmity of the serpent. We will see in the second half of this chapter that the serpent's seed regularly expresses enmity against the Lord's people. This effectively places the Lord's people parallel to the coming royal eschatological deliverer from Gen 3:15. We understand the nature of this parallel relationship that exists between the seed of the woman and anyone who experiences the enmity of the serpent's seed to be typological. The seed of the serpent's hostility against the Lord's people is a type or foreshadowing of future hostility against the eschatological royal deliverer. Likewise, when the people of the Lord defeat the seed of the serpent, we understand this to be a foreshadowing or a type for when the seed of the woman will defeat the serpent. We will see below that the OT frequently casts individuals and groups as the seed of the woman in anticipation of the ultimate fulfillment of Gen 3:15 when the eschatological royal deliverer will defeat evil and the serpent.

Lastly, how do the serpent and his seed relate to each other? In Gen 3:15 God states that he set enmity between the serpent and the woman. He also set enmity between the serpent's offspring and the woman's offspring. One

---

16. That the serpent can speak also makes it unlikely that it is just a mere snake. Within the Pentateuch, the only other animal that is capable of speaking is Balaam's donkey, and it could only speak because the "LORD opened [its] mouth" (Num 22:28). If within the Pentateuch an animal can only speak because of a supernatural influence, it is worth asking who or what is influencing the serpent?

would then expect God to say to the serpent, "The woman's offspring will bruise your offspring's head, and your offspring will bruise his heel," but the text breaks the previous parallelism. Rather than the woman's seed bruising the serpent's seed, the woman's seed bruises the serpent itself. Why does the woman's offspring bruise the serpent's head and not the heads of the serpent's offspring? Sailhamer insightfully suggests, "Though the 'enmity' may lie between two 'seeds,' the goal of the final crushing blow is not the 'seed' of the snake but rather the snake itself. . . . In other words, it appears that the author is intent on treating the snake and his 'seed' together, as one."[17] The serpent and his seed cannot be separated. On account of this unity, one can say that the defeat of the serpent's seed anticipates the day when the seed of the woman will decisively defeat the serpent.

2.1.2. The Serpent's Insurrection

Being the Lord's greatest enemy, it is no surprise that the serpent is fundamentally one who opposes God. The serpent manifests his opposition toward God through the following actions: questioning God's word, lying about and contradicting God's word, tempting the woman, deceiving the woman, and exercising authority over the first man and woman. We will now consider each these actions.

After the narrator introduces the serpent as being shrewder than any of the other animals that the Lord had made (v. 1a), in Gen 3:1b the serpent immediately questions what God had previously said in 2:16–17: "Did God actually say, 'You shall not eat of any tree in the garden?'" In response, the woman tells the serpent that she and her husband may eat of any tree except for the tree in the midst of the garden, which she claims she is prohibited from even touching (vv. 2–3).[18]

The serpent then escalates his opposition against God by not merely questioning his word but by contradicting it by lying. God told the first man that in the day he eats from the tree of knowledge with respect to good and evil he "shall surely die" (2:17). In contrast, in 3:4 the serpent tells the woman, "You will not surely die" (לֹא־מוֹת תְּמֻתוּן).[19] The serpent then speaks a half truth

17. Sailhamer, *The Pentateuch as* Narrative, 107.

18. On the first woman saying that God has prohibited her from touching the tree see Wenham, *Genesis 1–15*, 73.

19 Scholars disagree as to whether the serpent is saying that it is not certain that the woman will die or that it is certain that the woman will not die. One's interpretation of the serpent's words depends upon whether one sees significance in the serpent placing a negation (לֹא) before the infinitive absolute instead of before the verb, which is the normal syntax. Some commentators understand this deviation from the standard

to the woman that God has tried to prevent her from eating the fruit because he is attempting to keep her from being like God who knows good and evil.[20]

By listening to the serpent's instruction, the serpent tempted the woman.[21] She "saw that the tree was good for food, and that it was a delight to the eyes, and that the tree was to be desired (חמד) to make one wise, [so] she took of its fruit and ate" (3:6).[22] Though God had made every tree so that it would be "desirable" to gaze upon (2:9), the woman's desire is different. She does not desire the fruit for food, but for wisdom. The serpent has effectively tempted her to desire to know good and evil and be like God.[23]

When the Lord God finally asks the woman what she has done, the woman replies, "The serpent deceived me, and I ate" (v. 13). Here we see that deception is another of the serpent's actions. As Hamilton writes, "The serpent, so to speak, fed her a line, presented an attractive proposal, and she bought it."[24] Not only does the serpent question and contradict God's word, but it also seeks to deceive God's people. On account of this deception the woman rebelled against the Lord.[25]

Lastly, the serpent exercised authority over the first man and woman. God made humanity in his image and likeness (1:26, 28). Theologians have long disputed what the image of God is.[26] With that said, the present author

---

syntax to mean that the serpent is negating the certainty that the infinitive absolute indicates. In this reading, the serpent tells the first woman that it is not certain that she will die if she eats the forbidden fruit (see Walton, *Genesis*, 205). Others understand the serpent to be directly contradicting God's previous words in the starkest terms (Waltke, *Genesis*, 91). Either way, the serpent contradicts the Lord's warning that eating from the tree will certainly bring about death.

20. For the serpent uttering half-truths see Wenham, *Genesis 1–15*, 74. For the various opinions on what it means to "know good and evil" see Hamilton, *The Book of Genesis*, 163–66; Walton, *Genesis*, 213–17.

21 Admittedly, the text does not explicitly say that the serpent tempted the woman. The main word for "tempt/test" (נסה) does not appear in this passage. However, one must not fall prey to the "word equals concept" fallacy. Because of the serpent's words, the woman "desired" or "coveted" (חמד; cf. Exod 20:17; Deut 5:21) the wisdom she thought could be gained from eating of the tree. What is desiring or coveting that which is prohibited except for temptation?

22. We will see below that one way the OT regularly alludes to Gen 3 is by repeating the key words from Gen 3:6: "saw" (ראה), "good" (טוב), "desired" (חמד), and "took" (לקח).

23. Matthews, *Genesis 1–11:26*, 238.

24. Hamilton, *The Book of Genesis*, 194.

25. Within the text, there is no indication that the serpent deceived the man as it deceived the woman. He apparently joined the rebellion understanding what he was doing (cf. 1 Tim 2:13–15).

26. Wenham provides the five main interpretations regarding what it means for God to make mankind in his image. These interpretations of the image of God are as follows: (1) understanding the "image" to refer to man's natural abilities and the "likeness" to

finds Walton's definition most accurate: "The image is a physical manifestation of divine (or royal) essence that bears the function of that which it represents; this gives the image-bearer the capacity to reflect the attributes of the one represented and act on his behalf."[27] For God to make humanity in his image fundamentally means for man to represent his heavenly rule on earth by reigning as kings and queens over creation.[28]

Despite humanity's call in 1:26 to exercise royal authority over "every creeping thing that creeps on the earth," humanity did not exercise this authority over the serpent. Instead, humanity listened to the serpent, and by listening to the serpent, humanity failed to listen to God's command to rule over the animals. G. K. Beale succinctly summarizes this dynamic when he writes, "[The first man] allowed the serpent to 'rule over' him rather than 'ruling over' it."[29] By submitting themselves under the rule of the serpent, the first man and woman failed to act as vice-regents of the Lord. Instead they acted as vice-regents of the serpent, which now appears kingly on account of his authority over those bearing the royal image of God. Though still made in God's image (i.e., called to exercise dominion over creation on God's behalf), humanity finds itself under the authority of the serpent without a proper domain being exiled away from the garden (cf. Luke 4:5–6; 1 John 5:19).[30]

In sum, the serpent is one who opposes God. It does this by questioning, lying about, and contradicting God's word, tempting and deceiving the Lord's people, and exercising authority over humanity. Throughout the remainder of our study, any of these actions may allude back to the serpent.

---

refer to supernatural graces; (2) the mental and spiritual faculties that man shares with his creator; (3) man's physical resemblance; (4) man's calling to be God's representative on earth; (5) man's ability to relate to God (see Wenham, *Genesis 1–15*, 29–31).

27. Walton, *Genesis*, 131.

28. Both Wenham and Hamilton are in basic agreement with Walton's definition. Wenham writes, "The strongest case has been made for the view that the divine image makes man God's vice-regent on earth" (*Genesis 1–15*, 31). Likewise, Hamilton says, "Thus, like 'image,' *exercise dominion* reflects royal language. Man is created to rule" (Hamilton, *The Book of Genesis*, 138, [emphasis his]).

29. Beale, *A New Testament Biblical Theology*, 46. In the same vein, Beale elsewhere writes, "Adam did not guard the Garden but allowed a foul snake to enter, which brought sin, chaos and disorder into the sanctuary and into Adam and Eve's lives. He allowed the serpent to rule over him rather than ruling over it and casting it out of the Garden" (see *We Become What We Worship*, 132).

30. Dempster agrees that the text presents the serpent as one who rules in humanity's stead as they are exiled. He speaks of the serpent as one who "has apparently won," and of Adam and Eve as people "who have lost their royal status and dominion" (see *Dominion and Dynasty*, 68). See below for additional evidence that the Lord expelling Adam and Eve from the garden is presented as an exile.

2.1.3. The Lord's Judgment

In response to the man and woman rebelling against the Lord's command because of the serpent's temptation, the Lord speaks judgment against the serpent, woman, and man (Gen 3:14–19). He then casts the man and woman out of the garden lest they take and eat from the tree of life and live forever (vv. 22–24). Though most of these judgments are not directed against the serpent, it is still important for us to analyze all of the judgments because they are all the result of the serpent leading the man and woman into rebellion against the Lord. For this reason, it is possible that later biblical authors may subtly allude to the serpent by employing language and imagery from the various judgments that the serpent's insurrection brought about.

2.1.3.1. The Serpent's Judgment

As we have seen, the serpent in Gen 3 opposed God by leading his vice-regents into rebellion against the Lord. In response to the serpent's actions, the Lord judged it first (vv. 14–15). God states that the serpent is cursed above all of the animals.[31] The essence of this curse is then explained. The serpent will crawl on its belly and eat dust (i.e., experience humiliation and subjugation).[32]

God's damning pronouncement continues. God will set hostility between the serpent and the woman and tension between the serpent's offspring (זרע) and the woman's offspring (זרע). The narrative then further explains the hostility between the serpent's offspring and the woman's offspring. Ultimately, the woman's offspring will bruise (שׁוף) the serpent's head, and the serpent will bruise (שׁוף) this offspring's heel. In this way the text sets the woman's offspring, the royal eschatological deliverer, in opposition against the serpent.

The stage is set for a showdown between these two. Dempster captures the significance of the serpent's defeat at the foot of the royal eschatological deliverer: "In the light of the immediate context, the triumph of the woman's seed would suggest a return to the Edenic state, before the serpent had wrought its damage, and a wresting of the dominion of the world from

---

31. Some like Hamilton (*The Book of Genesis*, 196–97) try to understand ארור + מן to communicate separation instead of a comparison. Thus, instead of "cursing" the serpent, God "banished" it away from all of the other creatures. This reading is unlikely. God punishes the serpent by humiliating it (forcing it to go on its belly and to eat dust) and by bruising its head, both of which explain the serpent's ארור. It is difficult to know how these two elements explain banishment. Nevertheless, even if Hamilton is correct that ארור + מן communicates a separation instead of a comparison, we should see the banishment itself as a form of God's curse on the serpent.

32. Hamilton, *The Book of Genesis*, 197.

the serpent."[33] For this reason, if a text speaks of the royal eschatological deliverer defeating the serpent or ending any of the effects that the serpent's insurrection brought about, then that text may well be envisioning "a return to the Edenic state."[34] Furthermore, since Eden was part of God's original creation, a return to a renewed Eden would entail a new creation.[35]

Thus, we learn why and how God cursed the serpent for his deceptive work. Fundamentally, the Lord's judgment against the serpent is that the royal eschatological deliverer will one day defeat the serpent and its offspring. Through this judgment the narrative associates many different images or concepts with the serpent's judgment. These images and concepts are imposing judgment or a curse against one who is hostile against the Lord's people, going on one's belly, eating dust, being trodden underfoot, and suffering a damaged head. A text mentioning any of these images or concepts may be alluding to the serpent.[36]

2.1.3.2. The Woman's Judgment

After judging the serpent for instigating the rebellion, the Lord then judges the woman (v. 16). The Lord's first judgment against the woman is multiplied pain in childbirth. It is no coincidence that God charged the man and woman to "be fruitful and multiply" (פרו ורבו; 1:28) and that the next time the word "multiply" (רבה) occurs is when God reproves the woman (3:16). Scheumann succinctly explains how these two verses relate: "Whereas

---

33. Dempster, *Dominion and Dynasty*, 68. That the remainder of the Genesis narrative is awaiting this individual who will bring about an Edenic state is evident from 5:29, which reads, "[Lamech] called his name Noah, saying, 'Out of the ground that the LORD has cursed this one shall bring us relief from our work and from the painful toil of our hands.'" By mentioning the curse on the ground Lamech is referring back to God's curse on the land in Gen 3:17–19 (see Sailhamer, *The Meaning of the Pentateuch*, 590–91). Lamech gives Noah the name he does in hope that Noah will remove the curse on the ground bringing it back to its Edenic state. In this way the author of Genesis presents Noah as a possible fulfillment to God's promise from Gen 3:15. This implies that Gen 3:15 speaks of a single, male offspring born of a woman who will restore the world to its previous Eden-like conditions. Kenneth Matthews agrees when he writes, "Yet the naming of Noah is preeminently optimistic. Lamech looks ahead to a future victory (as 3:15) and prays that Noah will be instrumental in achieving it" (*Genesis 1–11:26*, 317).

34. Dempster, *Dominion and Dynasty*, 68.

35. For a return to Eden being a new creation see Schreiner, *The King in His Beauty*, 339–40; Beale, "Eden, the Temple, and the Church's Mission in the New Creation," 1–31.

36. James M. Hamilton Jr. provides a similar list: broken heads, broken enemies, trampled enemies, enemies lick dust, and stricken serpents (see Hamilton, *God's Glory in Salvation through Judgment*, 77).

Adam and Eve were to 'be fruitful and *multiply*' (1:28), God would now 'greatly multiply pain' in being fruitful (3:16)."[37]

God's second judgment against the woman concerns her relationship with her husband. Prior to the man and woman's rebellion, they experienced peaceful relations, but after the rebellion God judges the woman saying, "Your desire shall be for your husband, and he shall rule over you" (Gen 3:16b). Though made to help her husband, the woman now desires to dominate the man prompting the man to assert his authority over the woman.[38] The picture is one of consistent contention and fighting. In Hamilton's words, "This is judgment."[39]

On account of the woman rebelling against the Lord under the serpent's influence, she must now suffer significant pain in pregnancy and relational conflict with her husband. As seen above, the only hope in overcoming these trying realities is found in the seed of the woman's ability to restore the now corrupted world into an Edenic state. Because the serpent was influential in prompting the woman to rebel against the Lord, it is conceivable that later texts may allude to the serpent by recalling the Lord's judgments against the woman. Key concepts that these texts could allude to are pain in pregnancy/child bearing and marital challenges arising from power struggles.

2.1.3.3. *The Man's Judgment*

Immediately after the Lord judged the woman for heeding the serpent's instruction, he judged the man. All of the man's judgments pertain to the ground. God's judgment against the man is that the ground is cursed. The result of this judgment is that the man's work will be exceedingly difficult. Before the man sinned, the man was expected to work.[40] God tasked him

37. Scheumann, "A Biblical Theology of Birth Pain and the Hope of the Messiah," 19, (emphasis his). John C. Collins—among others—has also noted this play on words between "multiply" (רבה) (Collins, *Genesis 1–4*, 169).

38. Not all agree with the interpretation above. For an essay supporting male headship, see Ortland, "Male-Female Equality and Male Headship: Genesis 1–3," 95–112. See also Collins, *Genesis 1–4*, 141–47. For an essay supporting egalitarianism see Hess, "Equality With and Without Innocence," 75–95.

39. Hamilton, *God's Glory in Salvation through Judgment*, 79.

40. Sailhamer disagrees that work preceded the fall. He argues that since the Pentateuch uses the words "work" (עבד) and "keep" (שמר) together to signify priestly service (cf. Num 3:7–8), the narrative presents the man as a priest and not a worker of the ground or garden. Thus, Sailhamer suggests that in Gen 2:15 God charged the man, "to worship and obey" instead of "to work it and keep it" (Sailhamer, *The Pentateuch as Narrative*, 100–01). Though Sailhamer is right to notice that Genesis presents the

to "work and keep" (לעבדה ולשמרה) the ground (אדמה; 2:15).[41] After the rebellion occurred, the man would only eat of the ground in pain (3:17) having to work with "thorns and thistles" (v. 18a) instead of an earth that would "sprout vegetation, plants yielding seed, and fruit trees bearing fruit" (1:11).[42] Finally, at the end of the man's labor he would die and return to the dust from which he was taken (3:19). Hamilton summarizes the Lord's judgment against the man: "The land will no longer cooperate with man in his efforts at cultivation, and eventually man's body will return to the dust from which he was taken: he will die."[43]

As was true regarding the woman, so too the man rebelled against the Lord under the influence of the serpent. Therefore, it is possible that later texts may allude to the serpent by recalling the man's judgment he received from the Lord. We have already seen that the hope of the passage is that the seed of the woman will return humanity and the world back to their Edenic-like existence by ending the man's thorn-riddled suffering. Critical

---

man as a priest serving in a temple, this does not necessitate that the man had no work before sin entered the world. As a priest's work in the temple was a form of worship to the Lord, so the first man's work in the garden was the means by which he was supposed to honor and worship the Lord. It is likely that the narrator's intention in comparing the man to a priest had less to do with saying the man had no work and more to do with presenting the garden as a temple (see Beale, *The Temple and the Church's Mission*, 77).

41 It is unlikely that in Gen 2:15 God specifically charged the man to work and keep the "garden" (גן). The pronominal suffixes attached to the end of לְעָבְדָהּ and וּלְשָׁמְרָהּ are feminine singular and גן is masculine. HALOT understands every usage of גן to be masculine except for Gen 2:15; see Koehler, et al., *HALOT*, 1:198. A better option is to see God charging the man to work and keep the "ground" (אדמה). Three reasons suggest this reading: (1) אדמה—which appears in 2:9—is the closest possible feminine singular antecedent. (2) The intervening texts (2:10–14) are offline background information. This background information is signaled by the noun first clause in verse 10. Also note that the *wayyiqtol* in verse 9 is picked back up in verse 15 because there are no *wayyiqtol* verbs in verses 10–14. This further suggests that verses 10–14 are offline. (3) The next time the verbal root of עבד occurs is when God sends the man out of the garden to work the ground (לעבד את־האדמה) in Gen 3:23. If אדמה is the antecedent for the third feminine singular suffixes in the phrases לעבדה ולשמרה, then the man was supposed to work and keep all of the ground—which includes but is not limited to the garden. This implies that the "ground" would eventually become a garden as humanity continued to bear fruit and multiply.

42. Gerhard von Rad nicely captures how man's pre and post rebellion work compare: "Work was ordained for man even in Paradise (ch. 2:15). But that [work] makes life so wretched, that it is so threatened by failures and wastes of time and often enough comes to nothing, that its actual result usually has no relation to the effort expended— *that* the narrator designates as a dissonance in creation which is not accounted for by God's original ordinance." See von Rad, *Genesis*, 94–95, (emphasis his).

43. Hamilton, *God's Glory in Salvation through Judgment*, 80.

words and images that could evoke this serpentine scene are pain in work, ground, dust, thorns, or thistles.

2.1.3.4. *Humanity's Judgment*

Though the man and woman each received gender specific judgments, two judgments applied equally to them both. The Lord judged both the man and woman with exile and death. The narrative casts the man and woman's departure from the garden as an exile through a series of word plays. God created the man and woman naked (עָרוֹם), and they felt no shame (2:25). Because of the serpent's craftiness (עָרוּם), the man and woman disobeyed. The result is that they were no longer comfortable in their original na- kedness (עֵירֹם; 3:7). In other words, the man and the woman felt shame. Concerning the play on words between "craftiness" (עָרוּם) and "nakedness" (עֵירֹם), John H. Sailhamer states:

> There is a difference in meaning between עָרוֹם ("naked") in 2:25 and עֵירֹם ("naked") in 3:7. Although both terms are infrequent in the Pentateuch, the latter is distinguished by its used [*sic*] in Deuteronomy 28:48, where it depicts the state of Israel's exiles who have been punished for their failure to trust and obey God's word. . . . In distinguishing the first state of human nakedness from the second, the author has introduced a subtle yet percep- tible clue to the story's meaning. . . . The man and the woman . . . came to know that they were . . . "under God's judgment."[44]

The man and woman's nakedness (עֵירֹם) is a link with Israel's future exile. This helps confirm that God drove the man and woman out of the garden as exiles (Gen 3:24).[45]

Within the Genesis narrative, this exile comes off as a death. This is the case because in Gen 2:17 the Lord told the man that "in the day that [he] ate of [the prohibited tree he] would die," and when the man and woman ate from the tree, the Lord exiled them outside of the garden. While it is true that the phrase "in the day" does not always refer to a twenty-four hour- period, it would also be a mistake to think that the death the Lord referred to in Gen 2:17 is about the man's physical death. This is the case because the phrase "in that day" implies "promptness."[46] It is difficult to understand how

---

44. Sailhamer, *The Pentateuch as Narrative*, 103.

45. For additional reasons for seeing the first man and woman's expulsion from the garden as an exile see Postell, Bar, Soref, *Reading Moses, Seeing Jesus*, 58–59.

46. Walton, *Genesis*, 174; Wenham, *Genesis 1–15*, 174.

the man dying hundreds of years later at the age of 930 qualifies as being prompt (Gen 5:5).

For this reason, it is better to understand the events that occurred when the man and woman sinned as being the death spoken of in Gen 2:17. Read in this way, death is coming under the judgment of God and being exiled away from his presence. Because the man and woman listened to the serpent's shrewd words, God exiled them after covering their shameful nakedness. This is death.[47]

The effects of the serpent's insurrection upon the world and humanity were dramatic. The only remedy that the passage presents is that one day the seed of the woman will defeat the serpent and restore all things to their pre-rebellion state. Key words and concepts associated with humanity's judgment are shame, nakedness, exile, and death.

2.1.4. Summary of the Serpent in Genesis 3

We began this section by considering the serpent's identity along with the identity of the serpent's seed and the woman's seed. We adopted the messianic interpretation which affirms that the seed of the woman is the royal eschatological deliverer (whom later Scripture calls "Messiah"), the serpent is God's greatest enemy, and the seed of the serpent are those who act like the serpent in opposing God and his people. In light of our findings below, we also suggested that frequently within the OT the seed of the serpent exhibits hostility against individuals or groups who are not the promised male deliverer from Gen 3:15. In these instances, we understand the text to be presenting those whom the serpent's seed oppose as a type or foreshadowing of the royal eschatological deliverer. In this way, the OT will regularly cast the people of the Lord as a type of the coming seed of the woman.

We next considered the serpent's actions. We understood the common denominator of all of his actions to be opposition against the Lord. In opposing the Lord, the serpent questioned, lied about, and contradicted God's word, tempted and deceived the woman, and exercised authority over the first man and woman, which makes the serpent appear as a royal figure since it "ruled" over the Lord's vice-regents. Regarding the temptation, we noted that Scripture may allude to this narrative by repeating key words such as "saw" (ראה), "good" (טוב), "desired" (חמד), and "took" (לקח).

---

47. It is not uncommon for the Bible to present exile as death. This is especially common in Deuteronomy. See Deut 4:26; 6:15; 8:19–20; 11:16–17; 28:20–24, 45–51, 61–64; 30:17–18. For an extended defense of Israel's exile as a death see Turner, *The Death of Deaths in the Death of Israel: Deuteronomy's Theology of Exile.*

We then analyzed the Lord's judgment against the serpent, woman, man, and humanity. Key words or concepts we uncovered while analyzing the Lord's judgment against the serpent were a judgment or curse against one opposing the Lord and/or his people, going on one's belly, eating dust, being trampled underfoot, and suffering a damaged head. Because this is the only judgment in which God directly addresses the serpent, there is a higher chance that an author would intend for a reference to this judgment to allude to the serpent than if the author alluded to the other judgments. Even so, we considered the other judgments because if it were not for the serpent's actions, the man and woman would not have rebelled, and the Lord would not have judged them.

For the woman's judgment we concluded that any pain associated with child bearing and relational conflict with one's husband arising from a power struggle may refer back to the effects brought about by the serpent's deception. Concerning the man's judgment, a critical concept that may allude to the serpent's insurrection in Gen 3 was painful work, and key terms were ground, dust, thorns, or thistles. Lastly, we decided that key words and concepts from God's judgment against humanity that came about from the serpent's insurrection were shameful nakedness, exile, or death.

We also sought to understand the implications of the Lord's promise to bring about the seed of the woman to defeat the serpent within Gen 3's larger context. Following Dempster we understood the promise of the coming seed to "suggest a return to the Edenic state, before the serpent had wrought its damage, and a wresting of the dominion of the world from the serpent."[48] On account of this, we decided that if a text speaks of the woman's seed conquering the serpent or ending any of the negative effects that came about from the serpent's insurrection, then that text could be envisioning a return to an Edenic state, which biblical theologians understand to be the new creation.[49]

2.2. BIBLICAL THEOLOGY OF THE SERPENT

Having observed the different words, images, and concepts from Gen 3 that may signal the presence of the serpent or his work in general, we will now consider how the Law, Prophets, Writings, and NT develop the serpent motif.

---

48. Dempster, *Dominion and Dynasty*, 68.

49. See Schreiner, *The King in His Beauty*, 339–40; Beale, "Eden, the Temple, and the Church's Mission in the New Creation," 1–31.

2.2.1. The Serpent in the Law

Within this section on the Law, we will consider how Genesis, Exodus, and Numbers present the serpent's seed.

2.2.1.1. The Serpent in Genesis

Scholars have identified different stories within Genesis that contain the serpent's seed. Two of these stories are Cain and Abel and Noah's flood.

2.2.1.1.1. THE SERPENT IN GENESIS 4

The present author argued that the interpreter should understand the serpent's seed figuratively. The serpent's seed are those who follow the serpent's God-defying ways. Though later biblical passages emphasize individuals and nations' hostility against the Lord and his people, it is worth asking if Genesis itself provides textual warrant for understanding the serpent's seed to be those who oppose the Lord and his people?

Genesis 4 presents Cain as the seed of the serpent and Abel and Seth as seeds of the woman. One can see that Abel and Seth are seeds of the woman because after Cain kills Abel, Adam knew his wife again, and this time she gave birth to Seth (שֵׁת). To this Eve replies, "God has set (שֵׁת) to me another seed (זֶרַע) in the place of Abel, for Cain killed him" (4:25b; AT). When Eve says that God "set" Seth to her as a "seed" (זֶרַע), the narrative identifies Seth as a seed of the woman. Seth is Eve's "seed," and Eve says that the Lord gave Seth as another seed "in the place of Abel." This implies that Abel too was Eve's seed. In this way, Genesis 4 identifies both Abel and Seth as seeds of the woman.

In contrast to Abel, Cain is the seed of the serpent. There are at least four lines of evidence that point in this direction. First, Cain clearly shows hostility against his brother Abel. Cain's hostile act of murdering Abel demonstrates that Cain is the serpent's seed because he displays the enmity from Gen 3:15 that exists between these two seeds. Second, unlike Abel and Seth, Eve does not call Cain her seed. When she gave birth to Cain, she oddly calls him a "man" (אִישׁ). By not calling him a "seed," the text is subtly demonstrating that Cain is not Eve's seed. Since there are only two seeds (i.e., the serpent's and the woman's), the reader can identify Cain as the serpent's seed.[50] Third, Cain acts similarly to the serpent. We noted above that the

50. Hamilton makes a similar point: "Eve had called the newborn Cain a 'man' (4:2), but she calls Seth an *offspring* (Heb. *zera'*, lit., 'seed'), which reminds one of the

serpent brought death (i.e., being exiled under God's judgment) into the world through his deception. In Gen 4 Cain brings physical death into the world by murdering Abel. Fourth, the Lord curses Cain similarly to how he cursed the serpent. To both Cain and the serpent he said, "Cursed are you" (ארור אתה; Gen 3:14; 4:11). Within Gen 4, Cain is the seed of the serpent, and Abel and Seth are seeds of the woman.[51]

2.2.1.1.2. THE SERPENT IN GENESIS 6–9

As time progresses, the effects of the serpent's insurrection increase through-out the world. After Eve "saw" (ראה) that the fruit was "good" (טוב), and she "took" (לקח) it, then God punished the man and woman. It is at this point that the division between the serpent and woman's seed occurs. Likewise, after the sons of God "saw" (ראה) that the daughters of men were "good" (טבת) and they "took" (לקח) them, the text presents another division among mankind.[52] On the one hand, God promised to punish all people because of their sin (6:5–7), and, on the other hand, God spares Noah because he is righteous (v. 9). On account of this division, the text parallels rebellious mankind with the offspring of the serpent and Noah with the seed of the woman. For this reason, Noah is a type of the seed of the woman.[53] Thomas R. Schreiner says, "The influence of the serpent was now becoming rampant on the earth so that the earth was filled with corruption. . . . The offspring of the woman after the flood is restricted to Noah and his family."[54] Waters flood the seed of the serpent, but the woman's typological seed finds refuge through the ark.

After sparing Noah from the flood, the text reintroduces creation language. Genesis 8:13 recalls 1:9 when it states that Noah safely lands on dry land (חרבו פני האדמה), and the mention of wind (רוח) in 8:1 recalls 1:2. God then repeats the same basic creation mandate to Noah and his family (9:1–3;

---

promise made to Eve in 3:15 about 'her seed.'" Hamilton, *The Book of Genesis 1–17*, 242, (emphasis his); cf. also Kline, *Kingdom Prologue*, 189.

51. This is not to say that either Abel or Seth is the promised one in Gen 3:15. Rather, the different seeds of the woman throughout the biblical testimony anticipate the coming seed who will crush the serpent's head (Num 24:17–24).

52. Identifying who the sons of God and daughters of man are is not essential for the present section. For a useful discussion that seeks to identify them see Gentry and Wellum, *Kingdom through Covenant*, 149–51.

53. See above for an additional reason that the text presents Noah as a type of the coming seed of the woman.

54. Schreiner, *The King in His Beauty*, 12.

cf. 1:28–30). The text presents humanity's new beginning as a new creation.[55] With the destruction of the serpent's seed comes a new creation.[56]

2.2.1.2. The Serpent in Exodus and Numbers

Throughout the remainder of the Pentateuch, the serpent's seed continues to emerge. We will now consider the development in both the exodus narrative and Balaam's oracles.

2.2.1.2.1. THE SERPENT IN THE EXODUS

Exodus begins by comparing Israel to the first man and woman. Israel was "fruitful (פרה) and increased greatly; they multiplied (רבה) and grew exceedingly strong, so that the land (ארץ) was filled (מלא) with them" (Exod 1:7). This recalls how the first man and woman were supposed to "be fruitful (פרה) and multiply (רבה) and fill (מלא) the earth (ארץ)" (Gen 1:28). Exodus also calls Israel God's firstborn son, just like Genesis presented the first man as God's son (Exod 4:22; cf. Luke 3:38).[57]

Because of Israel's rapid growth, Pharaoh sought to harm Israel. Pharaoh opposed Israel in three ways: (1) setting taskmasters over Israel to afflict them with heavy burdens (vv. 11–12), (2) making Israel work as slaves increasing their work load (vv. 13–14), and (3) attempting to murder Israel's new born baby boys (vv. 15–22). On account of the hostility that Pharaoh demonstrates against Israel coupled with the strong echoes of Gen 1, it is likely that the text presents Pharaoh and the Egyptians as the seed of the serpent and Israel as a collective seed of the woman.[58] As the serpent opposed the first man, God's son, in his attempts to fulfill God's creation mandate,

---

55. To see where original creation language is used in Noah's narrative see Gentry and Wellum, *Kingdom through Covenant*, 161–65.

56. Also, if "the sons of God" are the serpent's seed in Gen 6:1–5, and if they are doing evil against the woman's seed (i.e., the daughters of men), then the flood narrative would also explicitly display the seed of the serpent's hostility/enmity toward the woman's seed.

57. For a treatment on Adam as God's son see Beale, *A New Testament Biblical Theology*, 36.

58. Hamilton seems to agree with this assessment. He notes that Pharaoh is the serpent's seed in Gen 12:10–20 (Hamilton, *God's Glory in Salvation through Judgment*, 84). This encourages one to read Pharaoh and Egypt as the serpent's seed within Exodus because Gen 12:10–20 foreshadows Pharaoh's later opposition in Exodus against Israel (see Sailhamer, *The Pentateuch as Narrative*, 37–39).

so now Pharaoh opposes Israel, God's son, in its attempt to fulfill God's creation mandate. Pharaoh is the serpent's seed, and Israel is the woman's seed.

After the Lord proves that he is the true God by sending plagues against Egypt and Pharaoh (cf. Exod 5:2; 12:12), he delivers his people through Moses. In this exodus deliverance, familiar images from God's original creation and Noahic new creation emerge. After God pushes back the waters by "wind" (רוח; Exod 14:21; cf. Gen 1:2; 8:1), "dry ground" (חרבה; יבשה) appears and Israel crosses over (Exod 14:21–22; cf. Gen 1:10; 8:13), and the Egyptians drown in the sea (14:27; cf. Gen 7:20–21). By comparing Israel's deliverance to Noah's salvation and the drowning of the Egyptians to the drowning of the world during Noah's time, the text does three things. First, it presents Israel as the seed of the woman like Noah was. Second, it presents the Egyptians as the seed of the serpent like wicked humanity was during Noah's time.[59] Third, it presents Israel's exodus and Egypt's defeat as a new creation.

2.2.1.2.2. THE SERPENT IN ISRAEL'S WILDERNESS WANDERINGS

After Israel refused to enter the land the Lord promised them (Num 14), the Lord judged that generation by making them wander the wilderness for forty years until they died (v. 34). While wandering in the wilderness and immediately after defeating Arad (21:1–3), the Israelites set out from Mount Hor, and they spoke against God and Moses by complaining about their food and water provisions (vv. 4–5). The Lord punished Israel for speaking against Moses and the Lord by sending fiery serpents to bite and kill them (v. 6). After the people confessed their wrong doing (v. 7), God instructed Moses to set a fiery serpent on a pole, which was a battle standard (נס), so that everyone who would look at the serpent would live (v. 8). Moses then made a bronze serpent and placed it upon the battle standard. Those who looked at the raised serpent after being bit lived (v. 9).

Based in part on Jesus's comments in John 3:14–15, Ronning has understood this passage from Numbers to be part of the serpent motif that we

---

59. Subsequent Scripture sees Egypt's defeat as the defeat of a serpent (cf. Isa 51:9–10; Ezek 29:3; Ps 74:13–14). Also, one finds an additional link between Egypt's defeat at the exodus and the serpent's defeat by comparing Exod 7:12 and 15:12. In both of these verses the text uses the verbal root בלע, which means "to swallow." In Exod 7:12, Moses's staff/sea monster (תנין) swallows up the staves/sea monsters (תנין) of Pharaoh's magicians. In Exod 15:12 the earth swallows up Egypt as they chase Israel through the Red Sea. Egypt and its serpents suffered the same fate. They were swallowed up. This suggests that Exodus presents Egypt's destruction as a sea monster's destruction. The present author learned this through personal correspondence with Brian J. Tabb.

are tracing. In those verses Jesus says, "And as Moses lifted up the serpent in the wilderness, so must the Son of Man be lifted up that whoever believes in him may have eternal life." Ronning understands Jesus's comparison between the serpent and himself to mean that Jesus "receives the curse on the serpent on behalf of those he redeems, and who are in their natural state under that curse, so that they might partake of his victory over the serpent."[60] In Ronning's reading, when Jesus is lifted up (i.e., dies on the cross) as the serpent was lifted up, Jesus is able to remove the curse on those who suffer the judgment of the serpent.[61] The reason that they suffer the serpent's judgment is because they are its seed. Ironically, this would mean that God actually slays Christ, the serpent-slayer, as though he were the cursed serpent. Ronning notes a similar irony in Isa 53. There "the Lord's servant makes himself a guilt offering though he himself had done no wrong."[62] He became a serpent on the cross in that he bore the sin of the serpent's seed in order to save them.

While Ronning's interpretation is possible, it is not clear that Jesus's reference to Num 21:4–9 depends upon Gen 3:15. Jesus does not explicitly mention Gen 3. Also, none of the words, concepts, or images from our Gen 3 paradigm are present within Num 21:4–9 except that both of these texts mention serpents. Even this textual link is not without two key dissimilarities. In Num 21:4–9 God judges his people by means of serpents while in Gen 3 God judges the serpent. Moreover, in Gen 3 the serpent acts contrary to God's will, but in Num 21:4–9 the serpents fulfill God's will.[63] For these reasons, the present author does not understand Num 21:4–9 to be part of the serpent motif that derives from Gen 3. One need not think that every reference to serpents is an allusion to the serpent of Gen 3.[64]

2.2.1.2.3. THE SERPENT IN BALAAM'S ORACLES

As the exodus account repeated elements from the flood account, Balaam's oracles repeat elements from the exodus narrative. The Balaam account begins by alluding to material that began the exodus narrative (cf. Num 22:3, 6; Exod 1:7, 12). Also, as Pharaoh tried to destroy Israel in three successive attacks, so too Balak hired Balaam, and Balaam gave three sets of oracles aimed

60. Ronning, "The Curse on the Serpent," 359.

61. When applied to Jesus, John's gospel consistently uses the phrase "lifted up" to refer to the crucifixion (cf. John 8:28; 12:32, 34). See below for more information.

62. Ronning, "The Curse on the Serpent," 359.

63. See Heiser, "Why Would Jesus Compare Himself to a Snake."

64. For an explanation of Jesus's statement in John 3:14–15 see the excursus at this chapter's conclusion.

at Israel's demise (Num 23:4–12, 13–24; 25—24:25; cf. 24:10). Furthermore, just as the text used Pharaoh's third attack against Israel to introduce Israel's coming deliverer (cf. Exod 1:15—2:4), Numbers also introduces Israel's coming king during Balaam's third set of oracles (cf. Num 24:7–9, 17–19).[65]

Nevertheless, the exodus narrative and Balaam's oracles do present a major difference. In Exodus, God judged Egypt through Israel (a collective seed of the woman). In Balaam's oracles a royal, individual male—a star from Jacob and scepter from Israel—will break Moab's head (24:17). Numbers 24:9 alludes to material from Gen 12:3 and 49:10. In so doing, it shows that Balaam's royal individual is Jacob's Lion of Judah and that the blessing of Abraham will come through him (cf. Gal 3:14).[66] Hamilton is therefore correct to stress that this male individual is the future Messiah, the seed of the woman promised in Gen 3:15. He adds that while "the words used in Numbers [24:17] are not the words used in Genesis, . . . the image of the crushed head of an enemy is clearly invoked."[67] This helps confirm that the Pentateuch does understand the woman's seed to be the royal eschatological deliverer. This deliverer will crush the serpent's skull by trampling the temples of the serpent's seed.

Recognizing that the promised salvation in Balaam's oracles is a new exodus coming from the seed of the woman suggests three things. First, the prophesied royal eschatological deliverer in Num 24:7–9 and verses 17–19 is a "new Moses." As Moses brought salvation to God's people in Pharaoh's third attempt to undo Israel, so too it is during Balaam's third attempt to undo Israel that the text says this future deliverer will bring salvation to God's people. This suggests that Moses's rise and deliverance of Israel in Exodus foreshadows this "new Moses's" future rise and deliverance (cf. Deut 18:5–19; 34:10–12). Second, the Lord conquering Egypt through Moses foreshadows this "New Moses's" victory over his enemies. Since this "new Moses" is the seed of the woman from Gen 3:15 who defeats the serpent, this suggests that the Pentateuch itself understands Moses and Israel's victory over Egypt as a foreshadowing of when the royal eschatological deliverer would defeat the serpent by bruising its head (cf. Isa 51:9–10; Ezek 29:1–4; Ps 74:12–14). Third, Exodus presented the exodus deliverance that the Lord wrought through Moses as a new creation. This implies that the royal eschatological deliverer's new exodus will also bring about a new creation.[68]

65. For a defense of this reading see Sailhamer, *The Pentateuch as Narrative*, 41–44.

66. Hamilton, "The Seed of the Woman and the Blessing of Abraham," 263–64.

67. Hamilton, "The Skull Crushing Seed of the Woman," 34.

68. Because Balaam's fourth oracle in Num 24:15–24 will be fulfilled "in the latter days" (באחרית הימים; v. 14; cf. Jer 48:47), there is good reason to believe that a new creation will accompany this royal eschatological deliverer's victory over the serpent and

2.2.2. The Serpent in the Prophets

The serpent motif continues in the Prophets. Following traditional lines, this study divides the Prophets into the Former and Latter Prophets but gives greater focus to the Former in order to provide further warrant for investigating Samuel for a serpent motif.

2.2.2.1. *The Serpent in the Former Prophets*

Joshua, Judges, and Kings all contain a serpent motif derived from Gen 3. Since chapters 3–7 of this book will consider the serpent motif and its purpose within Samuel in detail, this chapter will not discuss Samuel's serpent motif.

2.2.2.1.1. THE SERPENT IN JOSHUA

The Joshua narrative presents the Gibeonites as the serpent's seed. Upon hearing what God did to Jericho and Ai through Joshua (Josh 9:3), the Gibeonites acted cunningly (ערמה) by pretending to be people who lived far away. After Joshua learns that these cunning people are the nearby Gibeonites, he asks, "Why did you deceive (רמיתם) us" (v. 22)? Because of the Gibeonite's cunning deception, Joshua then "curses" (ארור) them (v. 23). This pattern is reminiscent of Gen 3. There the serpent was "crafty" (ערום; Gen 3:1), and it "deceived" (v. 13; נשא) Eve. In response God "cursed" the serpent above all animals (ארור אתה מכל־הבהמה; v. 14).

Besides the shared concepts and language between Josh 9 and Gen 3, two additional pieces of evidence suggest that the episode in Josh 9 is a genuine allusion to Gen 3. First, Joshua's curse on the Gibeonites recalls Cain's curse, which in turn echoed the serpent's curse. God told Cain, "And now, cursed are you" (ועתה ארור אתה; Gen 4:11), and Joshua told the Gibeonites, "And now, cursed are you" (ועתה ארורים אתם; Josh 9:23; AT).[69]

Second, this would not be the first time that Israel commits a sin reminiscent of Gen 3 immediately after winning a crucial victory within the book of Joshua. After God conquered Jericho through Joshua (ch. 6), Israel entered into sin because Achan took forbidden items from Jericho

---

its seed. For a discussion on the "latter days," Num 24:17, and the new creation, see Beale, *A New Testament Biblical Theology*, 141–42.

69. The only difference between these two curses is that the "you" is singular in Gen 4:11 (אתה) and the "you" is plural in Josh 9:23 (אתם). For similar arguments independently reached suggesting that the Gibeonites are serpentine see Postell, *Adam as Israel*, 123–24.

(ch. 7). When Joshua asked Achan what he did, Achan answered, "When I saw (ראה) among the spoil a beautiful (טוב) cloak from Shinar, and two-hundred shekels of silver, and a bar of gold weighing fifty shekels, then I coveted them (חמד) and took them (לקח)" (v. 21).[70] The author of Joshua has copied the verbiage from the first woman's sin in the garden. David M. Howard says as much when he writes, "The same verbs are used of Eve."[71] By alluding to the first woman's sin, Joshua presents Achan's sin as a repeat of the first woman's sin from the garden.

Immediately after Israel defeated Jericho (ch. 6), Israel committed a Gen 3 sin (ch. 7). Likewise, immediately after Israel defeated Ai (ch. 8), they committed a Gen 3 sin by falling prey to the Gibeonites' deception (ch. 9). The present author understands the net effect of this pattern to show that Joshua's leadership is not capable of bringing Israel past the serpent's effects. Israel still needs the woman's seed to rescue them from the serpent's deceptive ways.

The Gibeonites are the seed of the serpent. Though they do not exhibit hostility against Israel, this is only because they knew they did not have the military might to defeat Israel (9:3–4). Israel was certainly supposed to demonstrate their hostility against the Gibeonites by destroying them (cf. Exod 23:32; 34:15). Instead of outright hostility, they deceive the Israelites like the serpent deceived the first woman, and for this reason they are cursed like the serpent was.

2.2.2.1.2. THE SERPENT IN JUDGES

Judges presents both Sisera and Abimelech as the serpent's seed. Sisera was the commander of Jabin's army. He battled against Israel, and expressed enmity against Israel. Thus, Israel collectively represents the woman's seed. Eventually, Jael drives a tent peg through Sisera's temple (רקה; Judg 4:21), and this kills him (5:26; cf. Num 24:8, 17). Sisera, the serpent's seed, is dead from a crushed skull.

Though Abimelech was Gideon's son, he is still the serpent's seed. Hamilton writes, "In some cases those who have their heads crushed are physically descended from Abraham, but by their actions they show themselves

---

70. Similar to how "hiding" (חבא; Gen 3:8, 10) was associated with the first man and woman's sin, Achan's sin was also hidden (טמונים; Josh 7:21). Just as God knew the first man and woman hid after sinning (Gen 3:9), so too Joshua apparently knew that Achan was hiding (תכחד) his sin (Josh 7:19).

71. Howard, *Joshua*, 197.

to be at enmity with those who are faithful to Yahweh."[72] Hamilton goes on to say, "Judgment falls on the seed of the serpent (Abimelech), however, [*sic*] when a woman throws a millstone on Abimelech's head (*rō'š*) and his skull (*gulĕggōlet*) is crushed (*rāṣaṣ*)."[73]

One can strengthen Hamilton's argument that Abimelech is the serpent's seed. Like the Gibeonite story, Abimelech's narrative contains Gen 3 language. The MT of 9:31 says that Zebul (Abimelech's officer) deceitfully (בְּתָרְמָה) sent messengers to Abimelech in order to inform Abimelech of an uprising.[74] The end result is that Abimelech's head is crushed, fulfilling Jotham's "curse" (קללת; v. 57). After Zebul "deceptively" sent messengers, Abimelech was "cursed" with a "crushed skull." This is reminiscent of the serpent, which, in the context of deception, God cursed to bear a death-blow to the head. The Lord judged Abimelech as he showed enmity toward Israel, the woman's collective, typological seed.

2.2.2.1.3. THE SERPENT IN 1–2 KINGS

The books of 1–2 Kings present the woman and the serpent's seed in primarily two ways. One way it does this is by presenting Solomon as the woman's seed. Beale has persuasively argued that 1 Kings presents Solomon as a new Adam.[75] As such, it is to be expected that Solomon would encounter the serpent.

Adonijah is most clearly presented as the serpent. He is introduced as one who sacrifices animals by the stone of Zoheleth (אבן הזחלת) "which might mean 'the Serpent-Stone'"[76] (1 Kgs 1:9; cf. Mic 7:17). Hamilton suggests that "Adonijah's crafty solicitation of help from Bathsheba (2:13–25) is like the serpent's temptation of Eve (Gen. 3:1–7)."[77] Unlike Adam, Solomon slays the serpent, Adonijah (1 Kgs 2:24–25). And whereas Adam failed to extend the sacred space due to his sin, Solomon "goes on to build the temple, establishing the presence of God among Israel and making the land

---

72. Hamilton, "The Skull Crushing Seed of the Woman," 35.

73. Hamilton, "The Skull Crushing Seed of the Woman," 35.

74. The *BHS* understands בְּתָרְמָה in Judg 9:31 to possibly be a corrupt form of בָּארוּמָה. It suggests this to match Abimelech's location in verse 41. Still, the *BHS* proposes emending to בַּת אֲרֻמָה. The LXX[A] has μετὰ δώρων (בְּתְרוּמֹת). Both J. Alberto Soggin and Daniel I. Block understands בְּתָרְמָה to be a *hapax* from רְמָה (cf. Josh 9:22). There is no pressing reason to emend text in this instance, and the LXX[B], Vulgate, and Syriac all agree with the MT. See Soggin, *Judges*, 187; Block, *Judges, Ruth*, 327.

75. Beale, *A New Testament Biblical Theology*, 65–72.

76. Gray, *I and II Kings*, 83. See also Ronning, "The Curse on the Serpent," 315.

77. Hamilton, *God's Glory in Salvation through Judgment*, 178.

the realm of life."[78] With these connections, Beale has also demonstrated that Solomon's temple is like a new Eden, which amounts to a new creation.[79]

A second way 1–2 Kings demonstrates a serpent motif from Gen 3 is by consistently mentioning the mother of each Judean king in his introduction (cf. 1 Kgs 14:21; 15:2, 9), but neglecting to mention the mothers of each Israelite king (cf. 15:25–26, 33–34). Scheumann has argued this difference signals a messianic hope. The promise of the seed of the woman is still alive in the southern kingdom because the promised seed of the woman will come through the Davidic offspring.[80] In Scheumann's words, "Frequently mentioning the Judaean mothers animates the hope that one of David's offspring would be the serpent-crushing offspring of the woman. The true Judaean line is marked by kings whose mother's names are given, literally marking them as offspring of the woman."[81] The southern kingdom being the woman's seed reveals that the northern kingdom is a "distinct, rival" line.[82] The northern kingdom is the serpent's seed and the two showed hostility against each other through consistent war (1 Kgs 15:6, 16). Also, the narrative presents individuals from the northern kingdom like Jezebel and Athaliah as trying to dilute the godly commitment of the southern kingdom.[83]

2.2.2.2. *The Serpent in the Latter Prophets*

Within this section on the Latter Prophets we will consider the serpent within Isaiah.

2.2.2.2.1. THE SERPENT IN ISAIAH

Isaiah has many verses containing words within the semantic range of נחש, and because of this, the book contributes much to the Bible's serpent motif.[84] Isaiah 27:1 and 65:25 are the most important to consider. In Isa 27:1, God will slay Leviathan, the fleeing serpent (נחש; ὄφιν), the dragon (התנין; δράκοντα) in the sea. God will kill this serpent as an act of final judgment.

---

78. Hamilton, *God's Glory in Salvation through Judgment*, 178.

79. Beale, *The Temple and the Church's Mission*, 32–38, 66–73.

80. See Scheumann, "Mothers of Offspring in 1–2 Kings," 37–56. For a defense that the seed of David is the promised seed of the woman see chapters 6–7 of this book.

81. Scheumann, "Mothers of Offspring in 1–2 Kings," 52.

82. Scheumann, "Mothers of Offspring in 1–2 Kings," 52.

83. Scheumann, "Mothers of Offspring in 1–2 Kings," 45–47.

84. See Isa 6:2, 6; 11:8; 14:29; 27:1; 30:6; 51:9; 59:5; 65:25.

This is evident from the events that surround this text. Michael B. Shepherd says, "This text is part of the conclusion to Isaiah 26, a passage that looks forward to a future resurrection for the people of God (cf., Dan 12:2) and a final judgment for the world in terms borrowed from the Genesis flood account (e.g., Gen 7:16)."[85] Catching the allusion to Noah's flood is important because a new creation followed Noah's flood.[86] Thus, if Isaiah contains a serpent that God judges in connection with the coming of a new creation, then we would have warrant to identify the serpent in Isa 27:1 as the serpent of Gen 3:15.

Isaiah 65:25 recalls the serpent (נחש) of 27:1,[87] adding now that it will eat the dust for food—a clear allusion to part of the serpent's curse in Gen 3:14. Furthermore, the text adds that this experience of God's judgment will be during the new creation (Isa 65:17). Because the serpent in Isa 65:25 is God's great eschatological enemy from Isa 27:1, and because the serpent in Isa 65:25 is the serpent from Gen 3, we can conclude that Isaiah understood the serpent in Gen 3 to be God's greatest enemy. The serpent from Gen 3 is

---

85. Shepherd, *The Text in the Middle*, 14. Shepherd is correct to see Isa 26:20 as an allusion to Gen 7:16. In both texts the Lord's people hide within closed doors until God's wrath finishes. Notice how in both texts God's people have to come (בוא) into a place of safety while God judges the world. God's people must hide behind (בעד) closed (סגר) doors to safely endure his wrath. Additionally, Isa 26:21b seems to allude to Gen 4:10; 6:13.

86. Isaiah 26:20 may also allude to the Passover narrative. Isaiah 26:20 tells God's people to enter their rooms until fury has passed over. This is reminiscent of how Israel waited in their houses until the Lord passed over Egypt killing every first born not protected by blood (Exod 12:23). The study has already demonstrated the connections between Noah's flood and the exodus narrative, and we will see this yet again when we consider Ps 74 below.

87. Not only does Isa 65:25 recall 27:1, but it also contrasts with 11:8. Isaiah 65:21 parallels 11:6–9:
- The wolf shall dwell with the lamb (Isa 11:6) // The wolf and the lamb shall graze together (Isa 65:25a)
- The lion shall eat straw like the ox (v. 7c) // The lion shall eat straw like the ox (v. 25b)
- The nursing child shall play over the hole of the cobra, and the weaned child shall put his hand on the adder's den (v. 8) // Dust shall be the serpent's food (v. 25c)
- They shall not hurt or destroy in all my holy mountain (v. 9a) // They shall not hurt or destroy in all my holy mountain (v. 25d).

Because of the similar elements, the difference between 11:8 and 65:25c is striking. The present author understands this broken parallel to correct a possible misunderstanding in the reader. Lest the reader think that in the age to come God's people will associate kindly to all serpents (11:8), the parallel demonstrates that the Lord will forever judge the serpent from the garden (65:25c). In the new creation, the Lord will make all things—even snakes (11:8)—new (65:17), and yet the Lord will forever judge the serpent from Gen 3 (Isa 65:25c). The broken parallelism further demonstrates that Isaiah says that the Lord will judge the serpent from the Gen 3 and that this serpent's destruction is connected to the new creation. For a similar understanding see Shepherd, *The Text in the Middle*, 15.

the serpent—the dragon—that Isaiah anticipated God would judge as his greatest enemy at the end of time. This judgment will occur with the coming of the new creation. It is for this reason that Rev 20:2 (cf. 12:9) says that the serpent (ὄφις) of old is a dragon (δράκοντα). It is also the case that within Revelation that God judges the serpent in conjunction with the dawning of the new creation (cf. 20:2, 10–11; 21:1–8).[88]

2.2.2.2.2. *The Serpent in Habakkuk*

Habakkuk 3:13–14 understands that one day the Messiah will defeat the serpent. We will not argue for this reading now because we will first need to consider David's battle against Goliath to understand how Hab 3:13–14 is messianic. For this reason, we will forego our discussion of Hab 3:13–14 until chapter 3 of this book.

2.2.3. The Serpent in the Writings

The serpent motif is less prominent in the Writings, but it does appear. This section will focus on the references made in the Psalms.

2.2.3.1. *The Serpent in Psalms*

The Psalms frequently allude to Gen 3:14–15.[89] Two significant examples are found in Pss 74 and 110.

2.2.3.1.1. *The Serpent in Psalm 74:12–15*

Psalm 74:12–15 refers to the exodus and the serpent motif that we are tracing. Within the psalm, verses 12–15 seem to demonstrate that the Lord has previously defeated those enemies who "revile [his] name forever" (v. 10). The psalmist desires for the Lord to once again destroy his foes (v. 11). The psalmist then proves that the Lord is capable of defeating his enemies because from old, God, who is king (v. 12; cf. Exod 15:18), divided the sea by his might (Ps 74:13a). When this happened, he "broke the heads of the sea monsters on the waters" (שברת ראשי תנינים על־המים; v. 13b) and "crushed

---

88. This study has gleaned most of this section on Isaiah from Shepherd, *The Text in the Middle*, 14–16.

89. See Pss 18:43 (ET v. 42); 44:19; 45:5; 58:5–12 (ET vv. 4–11); 60:14 (ET v. 12); 68:21–22 (ET vv. 20–21); 72:9; 89:11–24 (ET vv. 10–23); 91:11–13; 108:14 (ET v. 13).

the heads of Leviathan" (v. 14a). The text apparently refers to the broken heads of the sea monsters in order to allude to God's victory over Egypt at the exodus. In this way, the psalmist reveals that he understands Egypt as the collective seed of the serpent.

Intriguingly, v. 15a mentions that God "split open springs and brooks" (בקעת מעין ונחל). This is an allusion to Gen 7:11b, which reads, "On that day all the fountains of the great deep burst forth" (נבקעו כל־מעינת). John Goldingay also sees here an allusion to Noah's flood: "Spring likewise recalls Gen. 1–11 (7:11; 8:2), while 'rivers' can be a term for the Red Sea (Ps. 66:6). Once more, then, these parallel cola speak of Yhwh's action in terms that could recall both creation and the Red Sea. On both occasions Yhwh parted waters so dry land would appear."[90] This helps confirm our previous interpretation of the exodus because we saw in it allusions back to Noah's flood. In Ps 74:12–14, God crushes the head of Egypt, the collective seed of the serpent, who is an "enemy" reviling against the Lord and his people (vv. 8–10). Psalm 74 likens the Lord's judgment against Egypt, the collective seed of the serpent, to his judgment against the wicked world during Noah's time, the collective seed of the serpent.

2.2.3.1.2. THE SERPENT IN PSALM 110:1–7

Psalm 110 famously begins by saying, "The LORD says to my Lord: Sit at my right hand, until I make your enemies your footstool" (v. 1). Hamilton comments, "The statement that the enemies will be made a footstool for the feet of the Davidic king (110:1) seems to draw on the connection between the damaged heel and head in Gen 3:15."[91] This connection is strengthened by noticing that God will "set" (שית) the king's "enemies" (איב) as a footstool under the Lord's feet. This recalls how God will "set enmity" (ואיבה אשית; Gen 3:15a) between the serpent and the woman's seed. This king awaiting to trod his enemies underfoot will rule from Zion with a scepter (cf. 49:10; Num 24:17; Ps 2:6, 9).

Psalm 110 ends with an allusion to Gen 3, as well. The ESV translates Ps 110:6 to say, "He will execute judgment among the nations, filling them with corpses; he will shatter chiefs over the wide earth."[92] Hamilton notes that verse 6c "could just as well be translated, 'he will crush . . . the head . . .

---

90. Goldingay, *Psalms: Psalms 42–89*, 432.

91. Hamilton, "The Skull Crushing Seed of the Woman," 37.

92. Oddly, the ESV translates "filling" (מלא) as a participle instead of a finite verb. Translated as a finite verb, the verse contains three short sentences that each describe the king's victory: "He will execute judgment among the nations. He will fill with reference to corpses. He will shatter the chief/head over the wide earth" (AT).

on the broad land.'"[93] Thus, when this king tramples his enemies underfoot, the psalm presents the king's victory as him crushing the head. This alludes to Gen 3:15: "he shall bruise your head." Allusions to Gen 3 frame Ps 110, and this encourages the interpreter to understand the king of Ps 110 to be the promised seed of the woman from Gen 3:15.[94] In Ps 110, as we have argued from Gen 3, every enemy of the royal eschatological deliverer is the seed of the serpent, and the seed of the woman will one day trample them underfoot.

2.2.4. The Serpent in the New Testament

Like the OT, the NT contains a serpent motif. The assessment will divide the NT into the Gospels, Pauline Epistles, General Epistles, and Revelation.[95]

2.2.4.1. The Serpent in the Gospels

The Gospels call both sinners in general (Matt 13:38; 23:15) and the Pharisees in particular (Matt 3:7 // Luke 3:7; 12:34; 23:15, 33) the seed of the serpent. Commenting on Matt 3:7, Grant R. Osborne says, "When the Baptist calls them 'offspring of vipers,' he means they are a spreading poison . . . like the serpent in the garden (Gen 3)."[96] Osborne connects the Pharisees actions to the serpent's actions. John and Jesus both speak as though the Pharisees are the offspring of a serpent. Matthew 12:34 makes this suggestion more certain. There Jesus retorts, "You brood of vipers! How can you speak good (ἀγαθὰ), when you are evil (πονηροὶ)?" Like the first serpent, this brood of vipers is not fit to handle matters of "good and evil." Also, like the first serpent, the gospels present the Pharisees as false teachers who corrupt the word of God. As Genesis promised that God would judge the serpent, Matthew makes it plain that God will judge these false-teaching vipers. These vipers prove to be the serpent's seed because like the first serpent, they oppose the work of God, twist God's word, and are hostile toward the seed of the woman (cf. 9:11; 15:1–2; 16:6; 23:33–34).

---

93. Hamilton, "The Skull Crushing Seed of the Woman," 37.

94. For a couple who understand the king of Psalm 110 to be the Messiah see Longman, *Psalms*, 383–84; deClaissé-Walford, *The Book of Psalms*, 838.

95. Hebrews is not formally part of the General Epistles, and it is not considered here because it has no explicit reference to the serpent. Nevertheless, Heb 2:14–15 may have Gen 3:14–15 in view.

96. Osborne, *Matthew*, 113.

John's gospel shares a similar serpent motif. While Jesus spoke with certain Jews, these Jews claimed to be Abraham's children (John 8:31–33). Jesus agrees that they are physically Abraham's descendants (v. 37), and yet Jesus says that their father is actually the devil (v. 44). T. Desmond Alexander summarizes Jesus's point well: "The point is made that the children of God will resemble him by how they live; the same is true regarding the children of the devil."[97] Jesus explicitly calls these Jews the offspring of the devil. It is no surprise then that they display such animosity against Jesus—the seed of the woman—by trying to kill him (vv. 37, 59). Within John, the children of the devil are the seed of the serpent.

2.2.4.2. The Serpent in the Pauline Epistles

Paul demonstrates this serpent motif in Romans.[98] In his conclusion to the letter he writes, "The God of peace will soon crush Satan under your feet" (Rom 16:20a). Until God crushes Satan under the church's feet, the church at Rome must watch out for those false-teachers who deceive (ἐξζπατῶσιν; 16:18; cf. 2 Cor 11:3; 1 Tim 2:14). Rather than being deceived, they should be wise to what is good (σοφοὺς εἶναι εἰς τὸ ἀγαθόν) and innocent to what is evil (ἀκεραίους δὲ εἰς τὸ κακόν; Rom 16:19). The first man and woman sought to be wise with matters pertaining to both good and evil, and they succumbed to the serpent's deception (Gen 3:6). Paul tells these Christians to only be wise in what is good and to avoid the deception of the false-teachers. In other words, these false teachers are like the serpent. They are the serpent's seed. Douglas J. Moo states, "The promise of victory over Satan, while including victory over the false teachers of vv. 17–19, is much broader, extending to the final eschatological victory of God's people when Satan is thrown into the 'lake of fire.'"[99] The reason Paul can say that God will crush Satan under the church's feet is because Christ is the singular seed (Gal 3:16), and those in him are both God's and Abraham's seed as well (3:29).[100]

---

97. Alexander, *From Eden to the New Jerusalem*, 108.

98. Much of the serpent motif seen in the conclusion of Romans can also be found in 2 Cor 11:1–15. For a comparison of Romans and 2 Corinthians see Barnett, *The Second Epistle to the Corinthians*, 501–02. We will consider 2 Cor 11:1–15 in chapter 7.

99. Moo, *The Epistle to the Romans*, 932–33.

100. DeRouchie and Meyer, "Christ or Family as the 'Seed' of Promise?," 36–43.

2.2.4.3. The Serpent in the General Epistles

Among the General Epistles, 1 John most clearly presents a serpent motif. This motif contained in 1 John is most similar to that briefly discussed in John 8. First John 3:10 says it is evident who "the children of the devil" are. They neither do righteous deeds nor love their brother. In 1 John 3:12–15, Cain serves as an example of someone who was "of the evil one" (ἐκ τοῦ πονηροῦ).[101] First John explains why Cain did not love his brother but rather killed him in verse 12: "Because his own deeds were evil and his brother's righteous" (v 12). Cain murdered his brother because he did not do righteous deeds (v. 12). First John presents Cain (like Genesis did) as the seed of the devil, who John understands to be the serpent. In keeping with what we have argued, 1 John understands enmity, as opposed to love, to be a primary characteristic of the devil's offspring, and Cain is the main example.

2.2.4.4. The Serpent in Revelation

Four times Revelation calls the devil the serpent of old (Rev 12:9, 14, 15; 20:2). We have already seen that Revelation identifies the serpent in the garden as God's greatest enemy because John reads Gen 3 through Isa 27:1. Just as Isaiah coupled the serpent's judgment with a new creation, so too does Revelation. God judges the ancient serpent (Rev 20:2) by throwing it into the lake of fire and sulfur (v. 10). Revelation then mentions the "earth and sky" (ἡ γῆ καὶ ὁ οὐρανὸς) fleeing from God's presence (v. 11). Concerning verse 11, Beale says this, "The first verse of ch. 21 presumably follows on the heels of 20:11, where it is said that 'heaven and earth fled away from the presence [of God], and no place was found for them.'"[102] Then in 21:1 we read, "I saw a new heaven and a new earth, for the first heaven and the first earth had passed away, and the sea was no more." We see that after God judges the serpent (20:10), the old creation disappears (v. 11), and the new creation comes (21:1). Revelation has a serpent motif and it connects the serpent's destruction with the coming of the new creation. Also, throughout Revelation, the serpent and its seed consistently display enmity against the woman's seed (12:4; 19:19).

101. To see how others have understood Cain to be of the devil, see Yarbrough, *1, 2, and 3 John*, 198–99, 201.

102. Beale, *The Book of Revelation*, 1039.

2.3. THEOLOGICAL SUMMARY OF
THE SERPENT IN THE BIBLE

This chapter began by analyzing the serpent in Gen 3 in order to better enable us to detect an allusion to the serpent. In order to accomplish this goal, we considered the serpent's identity (along with the identity of the seed of the serpent and the seed of the woman), the serpent's insurrection, and the Lord's judgment against all involved in the serpent's insurrection. After considering the different interpretations (naturalistic, symbolic, *sensus plenior*, and messianic) of the serpent in Gen 3, we adopted the messianic interpretation. It understood the serpent to be the greatest enemy of God, which later Scripture understands to be the devil or Satan. It also understood the seed of the woman to be the royal eschatological deliverer and the seed of the serpent to be all who act like the serpent by opposing the seed of the woman.

While analyzing the serpent's insurrection we noted that the serpent is one who opposes God or expresses enmity against God by questioning and contradicting God's word, tempting and deceiving God's people, and exercising authority over humanity. While investigating God's judgment against all involved in the serpent's insurrection, we noted numerous key words, images, and concepts that later biblical authors could use to allude back to the serpent from Gen 3. Following Dempster we also came to understand that the point of the Lord's promise of the seed of the woman was not only to defeat the serpent, but also to restore the world and humanity to an Edenic-like state in which none of the serpent's influence or effects appear.

Throughout the second half of the chapter, we considered allusions to the serpent in the Law, Prophets, Writings, and NT. We saw that a serpent motif deriving from Gen 3 runs through the entire Bible. The passages we considered displayed various links back to our findings in Gen 3. While investigating this serpent motif, a couple of patterns emerged. First, both the OT and NT consistently presented those who oppose the Lord's people and royal eschatological deliverer as the seed of the serpent. Second, the OT and NT also routinely linked the destruction of the serpent and his seed to the coming of a new creation. This confirms Dempster's interpretation that the Lord's promise to provide the seed of the woman includes a return back to an Edenic-like state, a new creation.

Our findings raise questions as to whether Samuel contains a serpent motif. It is certainly possible since the motif is prevalent throughout Scripture and every book we considered in the Former Prophets contained this serpent motif. Moreover, if Samuel contains references to the serpent and its seed, does it link this destruction to the coming of the new creation or the seed of the woman? Lastly, if Samuel does contain a serpent motif, can one deduce the significance of that motif and how it relates to the larger message of the book? The remainder of this book will answer these questions.

Excursus: Isaiah and Zechariah as Jesus's Background in John 3:14–15

Rather than trying to make sense of Jesus's use of Num 21:4–9 by connecting this passage back to Gen 3 like Ronning has, it seems more likely that Jesus is reading Num 21:4–9 through Isaiah and Zechariah. The key texts from Isaiah influencing Jesus's comments are Isa 11:10–12, 49:22, 52:13, and 62:10. All of these texts speak of the Lord raising up the Messiah. For this reason, we will see that Jesus interprets these texts to all refer to the same thing (i.e., his crucifixion and glorification).

In Isa 11:10–12 the Lord "raises" (נשׂא) a "battle standard" (נס) with the result that he will draw all people to the battle standard. Scholars understand this "battle standard" to be a reference to the Messiah.[103] Thus, Isa 11:10–12 predicts a day when the Lord will raise up the Messiah and will draw all people to him. In Isa 62:10 a battle standard (נס) is again raised up (רום). It stands as a signal that the Lord's salvation is for the ends of the earth (vv. 10–11; cf. 49:6; Acts 1:8).[104] Likewise, in Isa 49:22 the battle standard (נס) is yet again raised up (רום). As was the case before, when this battle standard is raised, verse 22 details that the nations along with the children of Israel come to the battle standard.

There are three things we must note at this point. First, because of the similarities that Isa 11:10–12 shares with 49:22 and 62:10, it is best to identify the battle standard in all of these texts as the Messiah. Second, in all of these texts the Lord draws people from the ends of the earth to the Messiah once he raises up the Messiah. Third, since these texts speak of the Messiah as a battle standard, they suggest that Isaiah envisions a future battle in which the Messiah will participate. Only those who resort to the messianic battle standard as their rallying point will survive. It is for this reason that 49:24 calls those Israelites who rally to the battle standard the Lord's "spoils" (מלקוח; cf. Mark 3:27).[105]

---

103. Motyer, *The Prophecy of Isaiah*, 125; Oswalt, *Isaiah*, 189.

104. Motyer, *The Prophecy of Isaiah*, 508; Oswalt, *Isaiah*, 656.

105. Within Mark's gospel, Jesus understood Isa 49:22–24 messianically. For Jesus, the spoils of Isa 49:24 refer to those individuals the Messiah saves. See Garland, *A Theology of Mark's Gospel*, 272–73.

In Isa 52:13—53:12 the reader learns what it means for the Lord to raise up the Messiah, the suffering servant.[106] This is so because in Isa 52:13 the Lord once again raises up the Messiah using the same language that occurred in Isa 11:12, 49:22, and 62:10. Isaiah 52:13 reads, "Behold, my servant shall act wisely; he shall be high (רום) and lifted up (נשא), and shall be exalted." Isaiah 52:13 begins the so-called fourth servant song (52:13—53:12).[107] This suggests that it introduces the themes of the remainder of the passage, which includes the servant obediently dying as a sacrifice for the sins of the people (53:10–11) and being rewarded for his obedience (v. 12).[108] Interestingly Isa 52:13—53:12 presents the Lord's rewards to the Messiah as the spoils won from a victory (v. 12). Once the Lord has won the battle, he gives the Messiah many people as a prize, and the messianic servant divides the spoils of victory with this multitude of people (53:12; cf. 49:24).[109]

Thus, as was the case in the texts we considered previously, Isa 52:13—53:12 anticipates the Messiah being raised and lifted up. In addition, the raising of the Messiah once again occurs in the context of a future battle. It is also not a coincidence that after the Messiah is raised up, the nations will be saved (54:1–3), just as the raising up of the messianic battle standard also resulted in the salvation of the nations.[110] Given these similarities, it is reasonable to understand the raising of the Messiah as a battle standard in Isa 11:10–12, 49:22, and 62:10 to refer to the same raising up and exaltation of the Messiah in 52:13, which included the Messiah's sacrificial death and subsequent reward.

We have now laid a sufficient foundation to begin to understand Jesus's statement in John's gospel. That John's gospel has Isaiah's texts about the messianic battle standard in view is evident by noticing that within both Isaiah and John the lifting up/exaltation of the Messiah is the means by which

106. For the messianic identity of the suffering servant of Isa 52:13—53:12 see Kaiser, "The Identity and Mission of the Servant of the Lord," 87–107.

107. Scholars regularly identify Isa 52:13—53:12 as a unit. See Childs, *Isaiah*, 407; Oswalt, *The Book of Isaiah*, 376.

108. For the Messiah being a sacrifice for the sins of his people within Isa 52:13—53:12 see Allen, "Substitutionary Atonement and Cultic Terminology in Isaiah 53," 171–90; Chisholm, "Forgiveness and Salvation in Isaiah 53," 191–212. For the Lord rewarding the Messiah for his obedience even to the point of death see Kaiser, "The Identity and Mission of the Servant of the Lord," 106–07; Gary V. Smith, *Isaiah 40–66*, 463–64.

109. For a defense of this reading of Isa 53:12 see Olley, "'The Many,'" 330–56.

110. For Isa 54:1–3 detailing the salvation of the nations brought about by the messianic servant see Beale, *The Temple and the Church's Mission*, 131; Köstenberger, *Salvation to the Ends of the Earth*, 165; Motyer, *The Prophecy of Isaiah*, 445–46; Oswalt, *The Book of Isaiah*, 415–18.

the Lord draws all people to himself. D. A. Carson makes this point from John's gospel. Noticing that John 3:14 and 12:32 are parallel texts, he writes the following about the lifting up of Jesus in John 3:14: "It is this exaltation that draws people to him."[111] In both Isaiah and John, God draws the world to salvation through the exaltation of the Messiah.

It is also apparent that the raised and exalted (ὑψωθήσεται) Messiah from Isa 52:13 serves as the background for Jesus's statement in John 3:14 about how he will be lifted up (ὑψωθῆναι). Andreas J. Köstenberger makes this point when he notices that both Isa 52:13 and John's gospel understand the lifting up of the Messiah to be (1) a reference to Jesus's being lifted up on the cross and (2) a figurative expression referring to Jesus's exaltation from God as the result of his obedience unto death.[112] Just as is the case in Isaiah with respect to the Messiah, in John's gospel the raising up of Jesus is his sacrificial death and future reward, and it results in the salvation of the nations. That John's usage of the lifting up of Jesus aligns with Isaiah's usage of the lifting up of the Messiah shows that Isaiah is the proper background against which one should understand John 3:14.

The final question to be answered is why does Jesus compare his death on the cross and subsequent reward to Moses lifting up the bronze serpent. The reason Jesus makes this comparison is mainly because of two reasons. First, Jesus compares his lifting up on the cross to the bronze serpent because Jesus and the serpent were lifted up as battle standards (נס). In Num 21:8–9 Moses lifted up the serpent on a "battle standard" (נס) causing the serpent to function as part of the battle standard.[113] Instead of lifting up a flag, Moses lifted a serpent on the battle standard signaling to those under God's judgment that they can find safety by looking to the raised serpent/standard. Likewise, John understood Jesus's sacrificial death upon the cross to fulfill Isaiah's battle standard expectations. Like the serpent, Jesus was raised as a battle standard.

Second, Jesus compares his lifting up on the cross to the lifting up of the bronze serpent because just as those who looked to the bronze serpent in faith would live, so too those who look to the suffering Messiah in faith will live. In Num 21:9, the text reads, "And Moses made a bronze serpent,

111. Carson, *The Gospel According to John*, 201.

112. See Köstenberger, "John," 436. Though he does not connect John 3:14 to Isa 52:13, F. F. Bruce does agree that John carefully chose to use the ὑψόω for Jesus's crucifixion because it signifies "a literal lifting up in space but also exaltation in glory" (see Bruce, *The Gospel of John*, 88).

113. Translations typically say that Moses lifted the bronze serpent up on a pole. See the ESV, NET, NIV, and RSV. The NASB correctly states that Moses raised the serpent up on a battle standard.

and he set it on the battle standard, and it came about if the serpent bit anyone, he would look to (והביט אל) the bronze serpent and live" (AT). In similar fashion, Zech 12:10 speaks of people looking to the Messiah: "And I will pour on the house of David and the inhabitants of Jerusalem a spirit of grace and pleas for mercy, and they will look to me (והביטו אלי), on him whom they have pierced, and they shall mourn for him, as one mourns for an only child, and weep bitterly over him, as one weeps over a firstborn" (AT).[114] In both of these texts, the expression "look to" is best interpreted as an expression of faith.[115]

The reason that Zech 12:10 pertains to our present discussion is because both the book of Zechariah and John's gospel present the pierced one of Zech 12:10 as Isaiah's suffering servant, who is also the raised battle standard. Anthony R. Petterson provides strong evidence that Zechariah intended to link his promised pierced one with Isaiah's suffering servant. The similarities he notes are worth quoting at length:

> Both are represented as humble and gentle (Zech 9:10; 42:2). Both bring blessing to the nations (Zech 9:10; Isa 42:1, 4, 6; 49:6). Both release captives from the pit or dungeon (Zech 9:11–12; Isa 42:7; 61:1). Both gather those who have been scattered from Israel (Zech 9:12; Isa 49:5–6). Significantly, both are struck (Zech 13:7; Isa 53:4) and pierced (Zech 12:10; Isa 53:5). Both are associated with shepherd imagery (Zech 13:7–9; Isa 53:6–7), though, the servant is likened to a sheep rather than a shepherd. Both suffer on account of a scattered flock (Zech 10:2; Isa 53:6). Both are rejected by the people (Zech 12:10; 13:7; Isa 53:3). Both figures are connected with the pouring out of the Spirit upon people (Zech 12:10; Isa 44:3–5). . . . Both are said to suffer by Yahweh's intent (Zech 13:7; Isa 53:6, 10), and their deaths result in forgiveness for the sins of the people (Zech 13:1; Isa 53:5–6). Furthermore, the people later mourn over both figures (Zech 12:10; Isa 53:4–12).[116]

114. For a defense of the messianic reading of Zech 12:10 see Petterson, *Behold Your King*, 224–45.

115. Commenting on Zech 12:10, Mark J. Boda recognizes that the phrase "look to" (הנבט + אל) signals an expression of faith. He writes, "This would then leave the phrase *wᵉhibbîṭû 'ēlay* on its own and make it an expression of faith, as can be the case with *nābaṭ'el* Hiphil (e.g., Isa 51:1–2; Ps. 34:6[5])" (Boda, *The Book of Zechariah*, 712). His comments can likewise apply to Num 21:9 since the same construction (*hiphil* of נבט אל +) occurs there. Dennis R. Cole affirms that Num 21:9 describes an act of faith. He writes, "So looking with hope for salvation and healing upon a form of that which has rendered one in a position of living or dying was a wondrously paradoxical act of faith in a God who controlled all power over life or death" (Cole, *Numbers*, 350).

116. Petterson, *Behold Your King*, 240–41.

Given the abundance of similarities, Pettersons's concluding remark is warranted: "These similarities seem too numerous to be coincidental."[117] Within the OT, Isaiah's suffering servant and raised battle standard is Zechariah's pierced one to whom people should look in faith.

John's gospel also provides evidence that the evangelist understood the pierced one of Zech 12:10 to be Isaiah's suffering servant and raised battle standard. When Jesus dies by crucifixion in John 19:37, the evangelist quotes Zech 12:10 to show that Jesus's death fulfills the prophecy of Zech 12:10.[118] This means that within John, Jesus's death by crucifixion simultaneously fulfills the raising up of Isaiah's messianic servant as a battle standard (John 3:14) and Zechariah's promised pierced one (19:37). Thus, John views these prophecies from Isaiah and Zechariah to both refer to Jesus's crucifixion.

Since Isaiah and Zechariah's prophecies are parallel to each other within both the OT and John's gospel, then what is true of the pierced one of Zech 12:10 is also true of Isaiah's suffering servant. Thus, when Zech 12:10 speaks of people who "look to" the pierced one in faith, the evangelist rightly understands this to mean that the people should "look to" Isaiah's battle standard in faith as the Israelites "looked to" the serpent on the battle standard in faith.

In sum, Isaiah presents the Messiah as both a suffering servant and a battle standard. Isaiah predicted that the Lord would raise up the messianic battle standard as a sacrifice for sins to bring forgiveness and life to the world. Zechariah understood Isaiah's raised battle standard to be the pierced one to whom people should look in faith. As Moses raised up the serpent on the battle standard as a means of life for all who would look to it in faith, so too God raised up the Messiah as a battle standard to be the means of life for all who would look to him in faith for the forgiveness of their sins.

---

117. Petterson, *Behold Your King,* 241.
118. See Köstenberger, "John," 504–06.

3

GOLIATH AS A SERPENT

THIS CHAPTER WILL SEEK to demonstrate that the Samuel narrative presents Goliath as a serpent.[1] It will do this by considering how the Samuel narrative introduces Goliath. Then, it will consider Goliath's death. This chapter will then argue that Hab 3:13–14 poetically describes David's victory over Goliath as a victory over a serpent. Lastly, a summary will conclude the chapter.

3.1. GOLIATH'S DESCRIPTION

Goliath's armor plays a significant role in how the narrative introduces him. Both Fokkelman and Gregory Wong draw attention to the contrast between

---

1. The textual issues in the David and Goliath narrative are complex. A slight majority of scholars favor the OG over the MT. Emmanuel Tov is one of these scholars. He argues that those translating the LXX[B] would not delete material (see Tov, "The Composition of 1 Samuel 16–18 in Light of the Septuagint," 333–62). Auld and Craig Y. S. Ho also prefer the OG. They argue that the MT adds material to contrast with previous material about Saul (Auld and Ho, "The Making of David and Goliath," 19–39). Still, others prefer the MT. Jan-Wim Wesselius prefers the MT because it introduces David similarly to how Genesis–2 Kings introduces major characters (see Wesselius, "A New View on the Relationship Between the Septuagint and Masoretic Text in the Story of David and Goliath," 5–26). Benjamin J. M. Johnson argues that 4QSam[a] agrees with the MT (see Johnson, "Reconsidering 4QSama and the Textual Support for the Long and Short Versions of the David and Goliath Story," 534–49). There is no scholarly consensus as to whether the short or long David and Goliath narrative should be preferred. This chapter will concentrate on the MT and will mention variants when one may affect the argument.

Goliath's armor and David's lack of armor.[2] Fokkelman notes that Goliath's description in 1 Sam 17:4–7 "holds special content: an exceptionally long description of the Philistine, consisting of nine (!) nominal clauses."[3] In these four verses the MT says that Goliath was a champion fighter (איש־הבנים; v. 4a). He was six cubits and a span tall (v. 4b).[4] On his head was a helmet of bronze (כובע נחשת; v. 5a),[5] and he wore "scaly armor" (שריון קשקשים) weighing five thousand shekels of bronze (נחשת; v. 5b).[6] Goliath also had bronze greaves on his legs (מצחת נחשת),[7] and a scimitar of bronze (כידון נחשת).[8] The end of Goliath's spear weighed six hundred shekels of iron. The following three sections will consider Goliath's scale armor, bronze armor, and title as a "champion" (איש־הבנים).

3.1.1. Goliath's Scale Armor

Regarding Goliath's armor, McCarter says, "The particular cuirass in question here is of *plate* or *scale* armor."[9] He goes on to say that the word for "scales" (קשקשת) is used for "scales of fish and other marine life."[10] Excluding 1 Sam 17:5, the OT mentions the word "scale" seven times in six verses, and it refers to marine life without exception.[11] Of these texts, Ezek 29:1–6 is worth considering in detail due to its lexical similarities with 1 Sam 17.

In Ezek 29:1–6, the Lord tells Ezekiel to prophesy against Egypt (v. 2). Ezekiel then describes Pharaoh as a great sea monster (התנים הגדול) in the Nile (v. 3; cf. 32:2). As a sea monster, Pharaoh has "scaly" (קשקשת) skin, and God will punish the scaly Pharaoh. After putting hooks in Pharaoh's jaws and drawing him and his "fish" (i.e., subjects) out of his waters (v. 4), God

2. See Fokkelman, *The Crossing Fates*, 177; Wong, "A Farewell to Arms," 43–55.

3. Fokkelman, *The Crossing Fates*, 147.

4. The LXX[BL], 4QSam[a], and Josephus (*Ant.* 6.171) say that Goliath is four cubits and a span tall. For a discussion on Goliath's height see the following: Hays, "Reconsidering the Height of Goliath," 701–14; Billington, "Goliath and the Exodus Giants," 489–508; Hays, "The Height of Goliath," 509–16.

5. Both the MT and LXX[L] say that Goliath's helmet was "bronze." The LXX[B] lacks the word "bronze."

6. All of the various OG manuscripts say "shekels of bronze and iron."

7. The MT mentions a singular "greave" (וּמִצְחַת). As will be discussed later, this should be repointed as a defectively written feminine plural construct to "greaves" (וּמִצְחֹת), as the LXX[B] and Syriac read.

8. Molin, "What Is a Kidon," 334–37.

9. McCarter, *I Samuel*, 292, (emphasis his).

10. McCarter, *I Samuel*, 292.

11. See Lev 11:9, 10, 12; Deut 14:9, 10; Ezek 29:4.

will leave him in an open field. There the beasts of the earth and the birds of the heavens will devour Pharaoh and all his subjects (v. 5). Once this is finished the text says, "Then all those living in Egypt will know that I am the LORD" (v. 6).

Much of this language is reminiscent of David's dealings with Goliath. As noted already, Goliath has "scaly" armor, and Ezekiel presents Pharaoh as a scaly sea monster. Though Ezekiel presents Pharaoh as a sea monster (תנין) and this section is suggesting that Samuel presents Goliath as a serpent (נחש), this is not a significant problem because these words can function as synonyms and can refer to the same entity (cf. Isa 27:1).

It is common place for the Bible to associate Pharaoh with a serpent. Ronning notes—as did the previous chapter following his lead—that the Bible links Pharaoh's defeat as a sea monster with language reminiscent of God's promise to bruise the head of the serpent from Gen 3:15 (cf. Ps 74:13–14).[12] Also, God crushed Egypt's head as though it were a sea creature at the exodus (Isa 51:9–10).[13] In the previous chapter we saw that Isa 27:1 predicts the demise of the serpent from Gen 3:15 to be during the time of the new creation. Within Isaiah, then, Egypt's defeat as a sea dragon (תנין) foreshadows the serpent's later demise. Once again, Egypt—and implicitly Pharaoh, Egypt's leader—is linked with the serpent. It is also important to note that Pharaoh (Ezek 29:4) and Goliath (1 Sam 17:5) are the only two individuals who are said to be "scaly" within the Bible. If Ezek 29:1–6 is alluding to 1 Sam 17, then it is likely that Ezekiel understood the text of Samuel to present Goliath in a serpentine fashion.

Both passages use similar language regarding the fate of God's defeated adversary. In 1 Sam 17:46a David pronounces judgment on Goliath and the Philistines, saying, "I will give the dead bodies of the host of the Philistines this day to the birds of the air and to the wild beasts of the earth" (לעוף השמים ולחית הארץ). Only Ezek 29:5 and 1 Sam 17:46 contain the exact phrase "to the wild beasts of the earth" (לחית הארץ). Furthermore, only nine texts in the OT contain the exact phrase "to the birds of the air" (לעוף השמים) found in these same two verses.[14]

In addition, the result of God's victory in both passages is comparable. Ezekiel 29:6a says, "And all the inhabitants of Egypt will know that I am the LORD" (וידעו כל־ישבי מצרים כי אני יהוה). In 1 Sam 17:46b it says, "All the earth may know that there is a God in Israel" (וידעו כל־הארץ כי יש אלהים

---

12. Ronning, "The Curse on the Serpent," 232.

13. Ronning, "The Curse on the Serpent," 220–23.

14. Those nine verses are Gen 2:20; 1 Sam 17:44, 46; Ps 79:2; Jer 7:33; 16:4; 19:7; 34:20; Ezek 29:5. The same verses also contain similar but not identical language to the phrase "to the wild beasts of the earth" previously mentioned.

לישׂראל‎). After the victories in both Ezekiel and Samuel, those outside of Israel will recognize Israel's God for his actions.

Both passages are the only passages in the Bible in which God judges and defeats a scaly individual who represents his nation. In both passages it says that after God is victorious, the birds of the air and the beasts of the field will devour the defeated scaly foe. Lastly, in both passages the result of God's victory will be that others will know who the true God is.[15]

Ezekiel apparently links Pharaoh's aquatic defeat to Goliath's defeat. The most likely explanation for these links between Pharaoh, the defeated sea monster, and Goliath is that Ezekiel saw in Goliath's defeat God's victory over a serpentine adversary.

3.1.2. Goliath's Bronze Equipment

Besides the iron pointed spear, Goliath's other items were bronze (נחשׁת‎). These items are his helmet, scale armor, greaves, and scimitar. Responding to the different bronze items Fokkelman writes, "With this continual harping on bronze we might initially think that we are face to face with a warrior from the Late Bronze Age, but the quadruple [bronze references] terminates in the glittering spearhead of iron so that it is the Iron Age that has duly started."[16] David Toshio Tsumura suggests that the reason Goliath only had one iron item was because iron was newly available and costly.[17]

Tsumura's assessment of the historical background may well be correct, but this is difficult to know for certain. Either way, it is worth asking if there is a possible literary purpose for why the text repeats four times that Goliath's equipment was made of bronze. The author could have certainly communicated that all of Goliath's equipment was bronze without repeating

---

15. The wider context of Ezekiel and Samuel might provide an additional link between Ezek 29:1–6 and 1 Sam 17. In both books an individual identified as "David" emerges as a royal figure who shepherds the flock of God after God defeats the scaly enemy. Within Samuel, David refers to the historical king whom God raised up to replace Saul and shepherd the flock of Israel (2 Sam 7:8). After defeating Goliath, he became heir apparent to the throne in the eyes of Israel. Within Ezekiel, David refers to a future messianic figure, the son of David (Ezek 34:23–24). For a defense of this reading of Ezekiel see Block, *The Book of Ezekiel*, 296–97, n. 137; Duguid, *Ezekiel*, 395–96. Though the distance between Pharaoh's defeat in Ezek 29:1–6 and the emergence of the son of David in 34:23–24 may seem too great, it is interesting that God reintroduces Egypt's serpentine defeat again in chapter 32 and that Ezekiel lists Egypt's defeat last in his nations corpus making it the final foreign nation defeated before the son of David emerges in chapter 34.

16. Fokkelman, *The Crossing Fates*, 148–49.

17. Tsumura, *The First Book of Samuel*, 444.

the word over and over again. In the words of Fokkelman, the text does demonstrate a "continual harping on bronze."[18] Is there a literary explanation to satisfy why the author harps on something as seemingly insignificant as the word "bronze"?

Ronning suspects that the text emphasizes Goliath's "bronze" (נחשת) materials in order to subtly associate him with a serpent (נחש).[19] In Hebrew these words are very close, and the Bible has even previously made use of this play on words in Num 21:9, which speaks of a "bronze serpent" (נחש נחשת).[20] Since we have already seen evidence that the narrative attaches serpentine connotations to Goliath through his scale armor, Ronning's suggestion is all the more possible and fits within the context. This is especially true since the scale armor is bronze. Also, the present author is not aware of another proposed interpretation that seeks to explain on a literary level why the text focuses so intently on Goliath's bronze armor and weaponry. On a literary level, the repetition of the word "bronze" subtly yet effectively increases Goliath's serpentine associations.

3.1.3. Goliath as the In-Betweens-Man

In 1 Sam 17:4 the narrative literally calls Goliath the "in-betweens-man" (איש־הבנים).[21] Within Scripture, Goliath alone receives this unusual description, and so scholars have sought to explain its significance. Fokkelman points out that verse 3 says that the Philistines and Israelites were separated by a valley between them (ביניהם).[22] It was in this unoccupied space that Goliath stood. Van Wijk-Bos notes that "in a literal sense, the champion, Goliath from Gath, stands in the space between the armies where the duel would be fought."[23] According to this view, Goliath is the "in-betweens-man" because of his physical location. He is the only person standing between the two armies.

Differing from Fokkelman and van Wijk-Bos, Ronning understands Goliath's title as the "in-betweens-man" to be an allusion to Gen 3:15 because

---

18. Fokkelman, *The Crossing Fates*, 148–49.

19. Ronning, "The Curse on the Serpent," 296.

20. While discussing Nahash, king of the sons of Ammon, Auld shows sensitivity to the lexical similarity between "serpent" and "bronze" when he writes that Nahash's name is best understood to mean "snake" even though his Hebrew name "could also suggest 'bronze.'" See Auld, *I & II Samuel*, 122, n. 12.

21. The LXX[B] has "powerful man" (ἀνὴρ δυνατὸς) instead of "in-betweens-man."

22. Fokkelman, *The Crossing Fates*, 147.

23. See van Wijk-Bos, *Reading Samuel*, 95.

the word "between" (בֵּין) occurs four times in Gen 3:15.[24] Ronning does not suggest that Goliath's title by itself is enough for one to conclude that an allusion to Gen 3:15 is present. His case is a cumulative one, and he understands Goliath's unusual title to allude to Gen 3:15 along with other contextual factors such as Goliath's scaly armor, the four-fold use of the word "bronze," and how 1 Sam 17 fits within larger biblical-theological themes. Concerning these themes, Ronning writes that David qualifies as being of the woman's seed in a spiritual sense and that "this episode of individual combat could be considered another example of the role of an individual champion being the agent of victory for the rest of the promised seed, and of the leader of the forces of wickedness as being the particular object of the curse."[25]

Having seen the interpretations, we may now weigh them. When weighing these two interpretations, it is important to note that they are not mutually exclusive. Fokkelman and van Wijk-Bos's interpretation that Goliath is called the "in-betweens-man" because he stands in the physical space that lies between Israel and the Philistines is certain. The close proximity between the pertinent words in 1 Sam 17:3–4a make this clear: "And the Philistines were standing on the mountain on the one side, and Israel was standing on the mountain on the other side, and a valley was between them (בֵּינֵיהֶם). And the in-betweens-man (אִישׁ־הַבֵּנַיִם) came out from the camps of the Philistines" (AT). Goliath is the "in-betweens-man" because he stands between the armies of the Philistines and the Israelites.

Though Fokkelman and van Wijk-Bos's interpretation is valid, Ronning's claim that Goliath's unusual title alludes to Gen 3:15 is possible though uncertain. Admittedly, simply noting that the text connects the word "between" (בֵּין) to Goliath should not compel one to see an allusion to Gen 3:15 since this word is so common. Despite this, there are two lines of evidence that make Ronning's interpretation possible.

The first line of evidence is that Goliath's title as the "in-betweens-man" probably connotes more than merely standing between two groups of people. This is the case because standing between two groups of people is not unique within the Bible and as far as the present author is aware, it is only in the case of Goliath that performing this action receives a unique title. For example, in Num 17:13 (ET 16:48) Aaron "stands between the dead and the living" (וַיַּעֲמֹד בֵּין הַמֵּתִים וּבֵין הַחַיִּים). In Deut 5:5 Moses recalls when the LORD made a covenant with Israel at Mount Horeb, and when he "stood between the LORD and [the Israelites]" (עֹמֵד בֵּין יְהוָה וּבֵינֵיכֶם). Even within Samuel, military groups surround Joab. When this happened, he "saw that

---

24. Ronning, "The Curse on the Serpent," 296–97.
25. Ronning, "The Curse on the Serpent," 297.

the battle was set against him both in front and in the rear" (2 Sam 10:9a). Though this text does not use the words "between" (בין) or "stand" (עמד), conceptually it is similar to what Goliath did. Both Joab and Goliath stood between various armies.

In none of these instances does the person standing between the others receive a special title. Since a special title is not normally given to someone who stands between others, this suggests that the text intends to signal more than Goliath's physical location by calling him the "in-betweens-man." What then might Goliath's title suggest if it probably connotes more than just his physical location? Given the other serpentine links within the passage, it is possible that it alludes to Gen 3:15.

The second line of evidence suggesting that Goliath's title as the "in-betweens-man" might allude to Gen 3:15 derives from noting how the context of 1 Sam 17 conceptually matches elements from Gen 3:15. In Gen 3:15 God said that he would set enmity between the seed of the woman and the seed of the serpent. If in 1 Sam 17 we can find the seed of the woman, the seed of the serpent, and hostility between the two, then an allusion to Gen 3:15 becomes more likely.

The previous chapter has shown that the biblical text presents Israel as a foreshadowing or type of the coming seed of the woman, and the nations represent the seed of the serpent. This would make the Philistines the serpent's seed. Also, if Ronning is correct that Goliath's title alludes to Gen 3:15, then Goliath, being the in-betweens-man, would be the personification of "enmity," which God said he would set between the two opposing seeds. It follows then that Ronning's view becomes more plausible inasmuch as Goliath represents the enmity between Israel and the Philistines. Within 1 Sam 17, Goliath clearly displays hostility toward Israel by trying to bring reproach on Israel.[26] Though the word "enmity" (איבה) does not appear in 1 Sam 17,[27] Abigail connects Goliath's defeat with the defeat of all of David's enemies (איב) in 25:29.[28] By standing between the Philistines and the Israelites Goliath effectively represents the hostility between the two nations. Though it is difficult to know for certain, Goliath's title, the "in-betweens-man," may allude to Gen 3:15 by highlighting the enmity that exists between the seed of the serpent and the seed of the woman.[29]

26. The nominal form of "reproach" (חרפה) occurs in verse 26. The verbal form (חרף) occurs in verses 10, 25, 26, 36, 45. The references in verses 25, 26 are not present in LXX[B] since it lacks verses 12–31.

27. For being in a passage as prominent as Gen 3:15, it is surprising that the word "enmity" (איבה) only occurs four other times: Num 35:21, 22; Ezek 25:15; 35:5.

28. Bergen, 1, 2 Samuel, 250.

29. Goliath's pride is another possible connection with the serpent. Goliath is "tall"

3.2. GOLIATH'S DEATH

This section will argue that the Samuel narrative casts Goliath as a serpent in his death. It will do this by overviewing the various arguments regarding how David defeated Goliath. Did David's stone strike Goliath in the head or in a greave covering his leg? If David struck Goliath in the head, then scholars such as Ronning, Hamilton, and Leithart have clear warrant for understanding Goliath's defeat as an allusion to the serpent's bruised head in Gen 3:15.[30] This section will present the different arguments scholars have given for both positions and then evaluate the interpretations.

3.2.1. Striking Goliath's Head?

The majority of scholars affirm that the text of Samuel says that David struck Goliath's forehead (מצח) with a stone. We know from 1 Sam 17:49 that David's stone caused Goliath to fall face down. Noting this, Tsumura argues that hitting Goliath on the shin "probably would not have knocked a giant down, and certainly would not have left him helpless when David came and took his sword."[31] Robert D. Bergen provides an additional argument for the majority position. He says that David striking Goliath in the shin "is not supported by any ancient translations, nor has it been followed by modern versions."[32] He continues by adding another argument: "Furthermore, it seems illogical to assume that David's primary offensive efforts would have been directed against an armored portion of Goliath. The traditional

(גבה), and within Samuel "height" (גבה) is a dominant theme that represents prideful rebellion against God (see Polzin, *Samuel and the Deuteronomist*, 34; Dempster, *Dominion and Dynasty*, 136, 139). Also, Fokkelman notes how Goliath pridefully uses the first person singular (*The Crossing Fates*, 150). His height and language show that he represents pride and rebellion against God. His scale armor and bronze armor suggest that he is serpentine, and his title, the in-betweens-man, may also suggest as much. Goliath's pride is another possible link with the serpent because of Job 41:26 (ET v. 34). This verse states that Leviathan "sees everything that is high (גבה); he is king over all the sons of pride." We have already seen in the previous chapter that texts like Isa 27:1 link Leviathan with the serpent from Gen 3:15. Also, Pharaoh, who speaks as a sea monster in Ezek 29:3, pridefully uses the first person singular as Goliath does. Leviathan, Pharaoh as a sea monster, and Goliath all represent pride. For an extended argument regarding the satanic identity of Leviathan within the book of Job see Fyall, *Now My Eyes Have Seen You*, 157–174.

30. See Ronning, "The Curse on the Serpent," 296–97; Hamilton, "The Skull Crushing Seed of the Woman," 35; Leithart, *A Son to Me*, 100.

31. Tsumura, *The First Book of Samuel*, 465.

32. Bergen, *1, 2 Samuel*, 197, n. 61.

translation is clearly preferable."[33] In sum, Tsumura and Bergen present four reasons that David struck Goliath in the head: (1) Goliath fell down, (2) Goliath would not helplessly surrender his sword if he were hit in the lower leg, (3) ancient translations unanimously render the disputed word in verse 49 as "head," and (4) David would not attack Goliath's legs because they were armored.

3.2.2. Striking Goliath's Shin?

Ariella Deem first argued that David's stone sunk into Goliath's greave and not his forehead.[34] She suggests that the greave covering each of Goliath's legs must have provided no covering over Goliath's knees so that Goliath would be able to bend his knees. It is into this exposed spot that David's stone sunk. Deem argues that Goliath's singular "greave" (וּמִצְחַת) in 1 Sam 17:5 should be repointed as a defectively written feminine plural construct (וּמִצְחֹת). This repointing is likely because it is doubtful that Goliath would proceed into battle with only one greave,[35] and it agrees with the other an- cient translations that all use a plural form. She also notes that the only time "forehead" appears in the plural, it has a feminine plural construct ending (מִצְחוֹת; Ezek 9:4).[36] Thus, according to Deem and contrary to *HALOT*, it is possible that the word in question in 1 Sam 17:49 is actually "greave," and that "greave" is a homonym of "forehead" having the same spelling and pointing as forehead in its singular (מֵצַח) and plural (מִצְחֹת) forms.[37]

Fokkelman has advanced Deem's argument. He suggests that if the stone would have hit Goliath in the forehead, Goliath would have fallen backward.[38] Furthermore, Fokkelman argues that the narrative carries an ironic punch if David struck Goliath's greave; a boy with a stone conquered Goliath's armor, which initially looked so impressive.[39]

Gregory T. K. Wong has advanced the argument even farther. He first argued that because of the similarities between the Testament of Judah and

---

33. Bergen, *1, 2 Samuel*, 197, n. 61.

34. Deem, "And the Stone Sank into His Forehead," 349–51.

35. Jack M. Sasson does suggest that the singular "foot" (רגליו) is a euphemism for Goliath's genitalia. See Sasson, "Reflections on an Unusual Practice Reported in ARM X:4," 409–10. Other scholars have not followed Sasson's interpretation.

36. Not including 1 Sam 17:49, "forehead" (מצח) occurs in Ex 28:38; 2 Chr 26:19, 20; Isa 48:4; Jer 3:3; Ezek 3:7, 8, 9; 9:4.

37. See Köhler et al., *HALOT*, 2:623.

38. Fokkelman, *The Crossing Fates*, 186.

39. Fokkelman, *The Crossing Fates*, 186.

David's life, the Testament of Judah understood David to have struck Goliath's greave (cf. T. Jud. 3:1).[40] Wong then published again arguing that there are rhetorical reasons supporting the interpretation of David striking Goliath's greave.[41] His argument is that after initially describing Goliath's armor and weaponry (1 Sam 17:5–7), the author again mentions all of these items to show that God does not need them to secure victory. Wong is correct that the author of Samuel does repeat all of Goliath's armor and weaponry from Goliath's initial description.[42] The only possible exceptions to this are Goliath's greaves. If Wong is correct that the author is repeating all of Goliath's armor to show that God can achieve victory without such means, then this is evidence that the מצח in verse 49 is Goliath's greave from verse 6 and not his forehead.

Extending Wong's first argument, it is possible that the Testament of Judah is neither the only nor the earliest ancient source alluding to David striking Goliath's foot. The book of Daniel suggests that David's stone struck Goliath's shin or foot. In Daniel 2, Nebuchadnezzar dreams of an image representing four kingdoms that God destroys by striking in the foot (רגל) with a stone (Dan 2:34). Concerning the stone striking the statue Dempster states, "The gigantic stature of the image that is destroyed by a small stone cannot help but bring to mind also the confrontation of Goliath with David and the resultant defeat of the former with a small stone from the brook."[43] Alexander Rofé concurs when he writes, "Is there not some resemblance between the stone which felled the Philistine and the stone in Daniel 2 which, cut without hands, smashed a mighty and terrible image?"[44] Though neither of these authors argue that David struck Goliath in the lower leg region, their observation that Dan 2 alludes to David defeating Goliath suggests that the author of Daniel understood David to have struck Goliath in the lower leg region.

Within Daniel, there is further evidence that one should link Goliath's defeat with the image from Dan 2. Scholars agree that Daniel chapters 2 and 7 parallel each other.[45] When these chapters are read together, particular

40. Wong, "Goliath's Death and the Testament of Judah," 425–32.

41. Wong, "A Farewell to Arms," 46–53.

42. Wong is correct that Goliath's equipment in 1 Sam 17:5–7 reappears throughout the remaining narrative. The helmet of bronze and armor in verse 5 reappear again in verse 38. Goliath's scimitar from verse 6 reappears in verse 45, and Goliath's spear from verse 7 is mentioned in verses 45 and 47.

43. Dempster, *Dominion and Dynasty*, 214.

44. Rofé, "The Battle of David and Goliath," 139.

45. See Shepherd, *Daniel in the Context of the Hebrew Bible*, 75; Lucas, *Daniel*, 68–69; Dempster, *Dominion and Dynasty*, 215.

details remind the reader of Goliath. The statue/image of four kingdoms in Dan 2 is exceedingly large (v. 31), and it contains iron and bronze (v. 35). God also destroys this statue with a stone (v. 34), and then establishes his kingdom (v. 44). Two of the four beasts in Dan 7 are a lion and a bear (vv. 4-5). The fourth beast also utters great boasts against God (vv. 8, 25).

Furthermore, Dempster shows multiple links between Daniel's description of the image/beasts and Genesis's creation account. From these allusions he deduces that the image/beasts represent pride, are a parody of the divine creation, and that the fourth beast's boasting alludes to the serpent's dialogue in Gen 3.[46] After God judges these kingdoms, he will establish his kingdom, and the "one like a son of man," who some rightly understand to be the ultimate Davidic king, will reign forever (vv. 11-14).[47]

These descriptions remind one of Goliath. We have already seen that the Samuel narrative casts Goliath as a serpentine creature, which could encourage the reader to associate Goliath with the serpent from Gen 3. Goliath was exceptionally large, and he used bronze and iron for his fight (1 Sam 17:4-7). He also uttered monstrous boasts against God (v. 43), and David said that he would destroy Goliath as he had destroyed a lion and a bear (vv. 34-37).[48] God judged Goliath when David struck him with a stone (v. 49). After Goliath's death, God promised that he would establish the coming messianic kingdom through David's seed (2 Sam 7:11b-17).[49]

In sum, Daniel presents evidence that David struck Goliath in the lower leg region with a stone. On account of the links between Goliath and the image/beasts, Daniel suggests that Goliath represents pride and is associated with the serpent's anti-God ways.

46. Dempster, *Dominion and Dynasty*, 214-15.

47. For a defense of interpreting the "son of man" as a messianic individual see Shepherd, "Daniel 7:13 and the New Testament Son of Man," 99-111. For a brief explanation for why some understand the son of man to be the ultimate Davidic king see Dempster, *Dominion and Dynasty*, 216-17. The book of Revelation further supports much of this reading by associating aspects of Daniel's beasts with the serpent (cf. Rev 12:9—13:7).

48. Fokkelman notices the comparison between David defeating Goliath just as he defeated a lion and bear. Concerning this he writes, "[Goliath] is represented as a wild animal which will suffer the same fate as the other wild animals which attack the shepherd." See Fokkelman, *The Crossing Fates*, 171.

49. Chapter 6 of this book will argue for a messianic reading of 2 Sam 7. Also, John Joseph Collins argues that the kingdom in Dan 2:44 comes from the Davidic kingdom announced in 2 Sam 7 (see Collins, *Daniel*, 170-71).

3.2.3. David Struck Goliath's Shin

Deciding between the two competing interpretations is difficult. Both sides have arguments in favor of their position. By way of reminder, the four reasons certain scholars have argued that David struck Goliath's head are that (1) striking Goliath in the foot/shin would not knock Goliath down, (2) striking Goliath in the shin would not cause him to helplessly surrender his sword, (3) the ancient translations unanimously render מצח as "forehead," and (4) David would not attack Goliath's legs because they were armored.

Understanding מצח as "greave" can answer each of these objections relatively well. If Deem's suggestion that Goliath's knees were exposed so that he could bend his legs is correct, then a stone to the knee could have knocked him down. Also, Goliath's heavy armor could cause him to fall more easily if the blow from the stone made him lose his balance. This heavy armor could have prevented Goliath from quickly rising, as well. Admittedly, it is difficult to understand how David could have taken Goliath's sword from him if he were conscious, but perhaps Goliath's inability to rise gave David sufficient time to snatch the sword from Goliath's control. Though ancient translations did render מצח as "head," Wong has argued that the Testament of Judah understood מצח to be a "greave," and this chapter has argued that the book of Daniel presents evidence that David struck Goliath's lower leg region. Lastly, it does not work to say that David would not attack Goliath's leg because if Goliath's knees were exposed, then this could have been Goliath's one small weakness.

Interpreting מצח to be "greave" in 1 Sam 17:49 also has arguments in its own favor. Fokkelman is probably right when he says that it is more likely that Goliath would fall face down from a blow to the leg rather than a blow to the head.[50] The irony of Goliath's strong armor becoming his greatest weakness by not allowing him to rise up after having his knee crushed is also appealing.[51] Also, Wong's insight that the author of Samuel repeats Goliath's equipment from verses 5–7 throughout the remainder of the narrative to demonstrate that God does not need this equipment to secure victory finds support from the narrative itself when in verse 45 David says, "You are coming to me with a sword and with a spear and with a scimitar, but I am coming to you in the name of the LORD of hosts" (AT), and again in verse 47 when David says that the Lord will defeat Goliath so that "all this assembly may know that the LORD saves not with sword and spear."[52]

50. Fokkelman, *The Crossing Fates*, 186.

51. Fokkelman, *The Crossing Fates*, 186.

52. Wong, "A Farewell to Arms," 46–53.

This suggests that מצח in verse 49 is a "greave" because if one translates it as "forehead" then it would be the only piece of Goliath's equipment from verses 5–7 that is not repeated. The similarities between the Testament of Judah and David's life along with the book of Daniel's allusion to David defeating Goliath suggest that ancient interpreters understood David to have struck Goliath in the lower leg region, as well.[53]

On balance, it is more likely that מצח in verse 49 is Goliath's "greave" and not his forehead. Surely if the מצח in verse 49 is Goliath's forehead, then it is not difficult to see in Goliath a serpent who suffers defeat from a bruised head like the serpent from Gen 3:15. With that said, the present author attempts to offer a mediating position. Given that we have already seen the author's desire to ascribe serpentine characteristics to Goliath, it is entirely possible that he intentionally chose the word "greave" because it is a homonym with "forehead." Thus, when David's stone sank into Goliath's מצח, the author forces the reader to decide if it actually sank into Goliath's greave or his forehead. In this way, the author is intentionally muddying the waters—hence the present debate—because he wants the reader to consider if David did crush Goliath's forehead in order to foster associations with God's promised judgment through the seed of the woman against the serpent in Gen 3:15.

3.2.4. Goliath's Fall and Decapitation

Scholars routinely link Goliath's death to Dagon's destruction.[54] God caused Dagon to fall facedown to the ground (1 Sam 5:3). After the Philistines set their god aright, God caused Dagon to fall again. This time, the Lord decapitated Dagon. Similarly, after falling facedown to the ground in 17:49, David decapitated Goliath (v. 51). Goliath's death certainly echoes Dagon's. Surely one reason the narrative says that Goliath fell facedown was to create a link with Dagon's demise. The Lord defeated the Philistines' champion just as he previously defeated their god.

Yet, Goliath may have fallen for another reason. When Goliath fell facedown, this may allude to the serpent eating the dust of the earth (Gen 3:14). Both Rabbah Leviticus and Rabbah Song of Songs state that Goliath fell facedown so that his "mouth that taunted and blasphemed be put in the dust, as it is written, 'Hide them in the dust together, bind their faces in the hidden place' (Job XL, 13)."[55] Though both of these midrashim connect

---

53. Wong, "Goliath's Death and the Testament of Judah," 425–32.

54. See Auld, *I & II Samuel*, 212; Leithart, *A Son to Me*, 108–09.

55. See Israelstam and Slotki, *Midrash Rabbah: Leviticus*, 131; Simon, *Midrash*

Goliath's fall to eating dust, they do not cite Gen 3:14 but rather Job 40:13.[56] Still, previous interpreters have linked Goliath falling facedown to God putting his adversaries face in the dust.

Not only did David cause Goliath to fall down, but he also decapitated Goliath. David killed Goliath not with the stone but by removing his head (1 Sam 17:46, 51; ראש). Leithart captures the significance of this: "Goliath was dressed like a serpent with his scale armor, and he died like a serpent, with a head wound, just as the Philistine god Dagon had his head crushed."[57] As God promised that the serpent would eat the dust (Gen 3:14) and have his head bruised (v. 15), so too David made Goliath fall facedown (i.e., eat the dust; 1 Sam 17:49), and then he delivered a mortal blow to Goliath's head (v. 51).

3.3. HABAKKUK 3:13–14 AS AN INTERPRETATION OF DAVID VERSUS GOLIATH

In this section we will look outside of the Samuel narrative to find evidence that Goliath is serpentine. Habakkuk 3:13–14 is a poetic description of David's victory over Goliath. Habakkuk 3:13–14 falls within God's third response to Habakkuk, and it contains numerous textual difficulties.[58] Besides the textual issues, scholars also question if Habakkuk's theophany looks back to the past or forward to the future.[59]

Rabbah: Esther & Song of Songs, 190. These two midrashim provide three other reasons that Goliath may have fallen facedown. These reasons are (1) so that David should not be troubled to walk extra distance, (2) because Dagon was Goliath's god (cf. Lev 26:30), and (3) because Deut 33:29 says that Israel will tread upon their enemies' high places.

56. That the midrashim connect Goliath's fall to those who eat dust in Job 40:13 might be additional evidence that some have understood Goliath to be serpentine. The ones who are in the dust in Job 40:13 are the prideful ones (גאה) from verses 11–12, and then God calls Leviathan the "king over all the sons of pride" in 41:26 (ET v. 34). In context, the prideful ones who deserve to be in the dust from 40:13 are apparently the sons of Leviathan, the king of pride. If Leviathan's subjects deserve to be in the dust, then how much more does Leviathan? Given that we have already seen Scripture present Leviathan as God's greatest enemy (i.e., Satan), it is possible that Job presents Leviathan as the serpent who will one day be judged in the dust along with his offspring. As previously mentioned, for an argument about the satanic identity of Leviathan within the book of Job see Fyall, *Now My Eyes Have Seen You*, 157–174.

57. Leithart, *A Son to Me*, 108–09.

58. For two discussions of these difficulties see Roberts, *Nahum, Habakkuk, and Zephaniah*, 130–48; Ronning, "The Curse on the Serpent," 297–306.

59. After raising the question as to whether the Hab 3 theophany looks forward or backward, Waylon Bailey remains agnostic on the issue (see Barker and Bailey, *Micah, Nahum, Habakkuk, Zephaniah*, 359).

Most commentators agree that Habakkuk's theophany is filled with exodus, Sinai, and conquest language.[60] One thing scholars do not agree on is the details of verses 13–14. Ought one understand את in verse 13 as "with" or as the direct object marker? Who is the anointed one, and who is the head of the house of the wicked? What does it mean to be laid bare from foundation to neck? Though these questions are difficult, understanding Hab 3:13–14 as a poetic description of the David and Goliath story alleviates these problems.

If one accepts O. Palmer Robertson's understanding of את as the preposition "with,"[61] then Hab 3:13 reads, "You [i.e., God] went out for the salvation (לישע) of your people, for salvation (לישע) with your anointed one (משיחך)[62] you crushed (מחצת) the head (ראש) of the house of the wicked, laying him bare from foundation to neck" (AT). We will argue from the translation above that Hab 3:13 is a poetic portrayal of the David and Goliath narrative. After this, we will attempt to show that verse 14 refers to the same narrative.

Samuel teaches that God conquered Goliath with David for the salvation of his people. If Hab 3:13 is poetically describing the David and Goliath narrative, then David would be God's "anointed one" who saves God's people. Samuel the prophet anointed (משח) David as king in 1 Sam 16:13. David is the anointed one through whom God won salvation for his people.[63]

If our present understanding of Hab 3:13–14 is correct, then Goliath would be the "head of the house of the wicked." Seeing Goliath as the "head" has strong explanatory power because this reading could unite two distinct interpretations. Some scholars—like J. J. M. Roberts—understand the "head of the house of the wicked" to be a sea dragon because of similarities with various ANE literature.[64] Others—like O. Palmer Robertson—understand

---

60. O'Neal, *Interpreting Habakkuk as Scripture*, 115, 117.

61. Robertson, *The Books of Nahum, Habakkuk, and Zephaniah*, 237.

62. Roberts notes that "the LXX and Barb have a plural [instead of the singular 'anointed one'], but the other Greek translations . . . all have the singular." He argues that the word "head" is a corruption, but since the various translations contain the word "head," his argument is unlikely (see Roberts, *Nahum, Habakkuk, and Zephaniah*, 142).

63. People disagree about the identity of the "anointed one" (משיח) in this verse. Bailey understands the משיח to be different people throughout history (see Barker and Bailey, *Micah, Nahum, Habakkuk, Zephaniah*, 369). Ralph L. Smith understands the משיח to probably be the Davidic king in Jerusalem (*Micah–Malachi*, 116). Robertson believes that the משיח is primarily Cyrus, though this does not have to exclude the son of David (see Robertson, *The Books of Nahum, Habakkuk, and Zephaniah*, 237–38).

64. Roberts, *Nahum, Habakkuk, and Zephaniah*, 156. Smith (*Micah–Malachi*, 116) and Albright ("The Psalm of Habakkuk," 17) also see the head of the house of wicked as an enemy that has been cast as a dragon.

the "head of the house of the wicked" as an authoritative individual similar to how a husband would be the head of a household.[65] Interestingly, when one understands Samuel to present Goliath as a serpentine figure wearing sea-scale armor, then there is harmony to both Roberts and Robertson's positions because in Scripture serpents (נחש) can also be sea dragons (cf. Isa 27:1).[66] Goliath is a serpent, and he is also an authoritative individual functioning as the "head of the house of the wicked," since he functioned as the Philistines' leader.[67]

Furthermore, verse 13 states that God and the anointed one laid bare the head of the house of wicked from thigh to neck. This reference to "laying bare" also corresponds to the David and Goliath narrative. One can infer that David stripped Goliath's armor off his body because the narrator knew the armor's weight (1 Sam 17:5–7) and because the birds of the air and the beasts of the field would eat his body (v. 46).[68] Moreover, the Habakkuk text states that God stripped the head of the house of wicked from "thigh to neck" (יסוד עד-צואר). The phrase "thigh to neck" could refer to God undercutting all of the enemy's supportive strength,[69] but others understand the "thigh" to refer to a dragon's tail or lower extremities.[70] That the phrase in question may refer to stripping a dragon from his lower extremities to his neck nicely corresponds with Goliath. What is most important to notice is that the text does not say that God's enemy was stripped from head to toe, as one might expect. Rather, God stripped this enemy from his lower extremities to the neck. Likewise, Goliath was only stripped from his lower extremities to his neck because David had already decapitated Goliath's head.

65. Robertson, *The Books of Nahum, Habakkuk, and Zephaniah*, 239.

66. It is interesting that both Ezekiel and Habakkuk seem to understand Goliath not merely as a serpent, but as a sea serpent. This makes sense from an Israelite's perspective because Goliath is from Philistia, the direction of the sea. He comes from the sea as a serpent. He is a sea serpent. For a few passages that link the Philistines' geographical proximity to the sea, see Exod 23:31; Isa 11:14; Zeph 2:5–7.

67. It is not difficult to see Goliath as the "father" of the wicked since he was a "titanic symbol of evil" (Dempster, *Dominion and Dynasty*, 147).

68. Ronning first made this argument. See "The Curse on the Serpent," 306–07.

69. See Robertson, *The Books of Nahum, Habakkuk, and Zephaniah*, 240; Barker and Bailey, *Micah, Nahum, Habakkuk, Zephaniah*, 370.

70. Albright has translated יסוד, which the ESV above translated as "thigh," as either "tail-end, fundament, [or] thigh." Concerning this phrase from Hab 3:13 he writes, "Here again there is no need of emendation: we have a vivid sketch of the prostrate body of a dragon" (Albright, "The Psalm of Habakkuk," 17). Others who have followed Albright in understanding that יסוד refers to a part of a dragon's tail or lower extremities are Smith (*Micah–Malachi*, 113, 116) and Hamilton ("The Skull Crushing Seed of the Woman," 50, n. 61).

Habakkuk 3:14 also has similarities with the David and Goliath narrative.[71] The Hebrew reads, "You [i.e., God] pierced with his staves (בְמַטָּיו) the head of his warriors.[72] They came to scatter me,[73] exulting as one who eats the afflicted (עָנִי) in secret." On this verse Robertson states, "The fiendishness of the enemy is seen in their gloating. . . . What sort of savage would take delight in victimizing the helpless? As a wild animal lurks and then drags and devours its prey in secret, so this ruthless oppressor assaults his victims."[74]

From this verse and Robertson's interpretation a few points should be made. First, we see that God defeated the "head of the house of the wicked" with his own weapon and that this leader had warriors. God did defeat Goliath with his own weapon and by so doing defeated the Philistine warriors accompanying Goliath.

Second, verse 14 says that God's enemies seek to devour those who are afflicted (עָנִי). In 2 Sam 22:28 David says that God saves (תּוֹשִׁיעַ) a humble (עָנִי) people, and he brings down those who are raised up (רָמִים; i.e., are prideful). Within Samuel, these verses are most reminiscent of the David and Goliath story. God saved his humble, afflicted people in conjunction with bringing down Goliath and his pride. On account of this, God saving the afflicted in Hab 3:14 is similar to when he saved his afflicted ones from the prideful Goliath.

Third, Robertson's interpretation compares the gloating warriors to a savage animal seeking to devour (אכל) its afflicted prey. We have already seen that the David and Goliath narrative compares Goliath to a lion or a bear from whose mouth David had to deliver his father's sheep (1 Sam 17:34–35). Thus, as Fokkelman points out, Israel is cast as a flock of sheep and Goliath as a wild animal gloating as he seeks to devour Israel.[75] Once again, Hab 3:14 appears to be a poetic description of the David and Goliath narrative.

71. Roberts calls the Hebrew in verse 14 "quite obscure" (see Roberts, *Nahum, Habakkuk, and Zephaniah*, 157). Bailey says it is "extremely difficult textually" (see Barker and Bailey, *Micah, Nahum, Habakkuh, Zephaniah*, 371). Ronning suggests that one should be willing to allow "for the possibility of textual corruption in verses 13–14" (see Ronning, "The Curse on the Serpent," 306). The New English Translation of the Septuagint provides two different translations of Hab 3 because of the textual difficulties (Howard, "The Twelve Prophets," 809–10).

72. The meaning of פרז in verse 14 is uncertain. The context suggests that it means something comparable to "warrior." For two translations that understand פרז to mean "warrior" see the ESV and NET.

73. Robertson understands the "me" to be the prophet Habakkuk envisioning the coming assault. He speaks in the first person because of how caught up he is in the theophany. See Robertson, *The Books of Nahum, Habakkuk, and Zephaniah*, 241.

74. Robertson, *The Books of Nahum, Habakkuk, and Zephaniah*, 241.

75. Fokkelman, *The Crossing Fates*, 171.

Habakkuk 3 even contains intertextual links with Samuel. Habakkuk 3:19b–c quotes 2 Sam 22:34.[76] Habakkuk 3:19a is possibly derived from 2 Sam 22:33a.[77] Lastly, Hab 3:18 bears a close resemblance to 1 Sam 2:1.[78] Habakkuk did not arbitrarily reference 1 Sam 2:1 and 2 Sam 22:34. Within Samuel, both of these verses come from parallel poems within Samuel that end by discussing the coming "anointed one" (cf. 1 Sam 2:10; 22:51).[79] Habakkuk's references to these poems fits within the larger context because of his previous mention of the "anointed one" in Hab 3:13. Since Hab 3:18–19 cites "anointed one" poems from within Samuel, this helps confirm our argument that one should understand the "anointed one" of Hab 3:13 as David, the anointed king from Samuel. Since Habakkuk's theophany ends with language from Samuel's parallel "anointed one" poems, this greatly increases the likelihood that the material about the anointed one in Hab 3:13–14 also derives from Samuel.

Putting it all together, Hab 3:13–14 is a poetic description of the David and Goliath narrative. These verses recall a time when the Lord saved his people through his anointed one from the head of the house of the wicked, a dragon like leader who was stripped from his lower extremities to his neck upon his defeat. The Lord defeated this wicked leader and those warriors with him by using their own weapons against them, and the Lord's victory was like the victory one has over a wild animal. Corresponding to this is the David and Goliath narrative from Samuel. The Lord saved his people by sending out his anointed king, David. By using Goliath's own sword against him, David defeated Goliath, the representative of the wicked Philistines who was acting as their leader. Upon defeat, Goliath was stripped from foot to neck, and the Lord defeated the warriors aligned with Goliath. The

76. Habakkuk 3:19b–c reads, "He makes my feet like the deer's; he makes me tread on my high places" (וישם רגלי כאילות ועל במותי ידרכני). Second Samuel 22:34 reads, "He made my feet like the feet of a deer and set me secure on the heights" (משוה רגליו [רגלי] כאילות ועל במותי יעמדני).

77. Habakkuk 3:19a reads, "GOD, the Lord, is my strength" (יהוה אדני חילי), and 2 Sam 22:33a reads, "God is my strong refuge" (AT; האל מעוזי חיל).

78. Habakkuk 3:18 reads, "Yet I will rejoice in the LORD; I will take joy in the God of my salvation" (ואני ביהוה אעלוזה אגילה באלהי ישעי), and 1 Sam 2:1 reads, "My heart exults in the LORD ... because I rejoice in your salvation" (עלץ לבי ביהוה . . . . כי שמחתי בישועתך). Also, it is worth noting that since Hab 3:18 alludes to 1 Sam 2:1, it is more likely that Habakkuk's allusions are to Samuel and not Psalms even though 2 Sam 22:34 parallels Ps 18:34 (ET v. 33) and 2 Sam 22:33a parallels Ps 18:33 (ET v. 32).

79. Polzin, *Samuel and the Deuteronomist*, 34; Fokkelman, *Throne and City*, 354. For more on the poems of 1 Sam 2:1–10 and 2 Sam 22:1–51 being parallel poems about the coming "anointed one" see section 7.1. below.

Samuel narrative compares this victory to David's previous victories over savage animals such as the lion and the bear.

The reason that it is significant that Hab 3:13–14 describes David's victory over Goliath is found in Goliath's description as the "head of the house of the wicked." Through the anointed one, God "crushes" (מחץ) this "head" (ראש). As we saw in the previous chapter when considering Ps 110, the Lord defeating his enemies by "crushing" (מחץ) the "head" (ראש) is an allusion to the promised victory over the serpent in Gen 3:15. Hamilton concurs that Hab 3:13 alludes to the serpent's defeat: "Just as Yahweh promises a crushed head to the serpent in Gen 3:15, Yahweh is described crushing the head of the wicked in Hab 3:13."[80] Habakkuk 3:13–14 alludes to Gen 3:15 by placing Goliath in the place of the serpent and David in the place of the seed of the woman.

Previously we asked if Habakkuk's theophany looks back to the past or forward to the future. The present author agrees with Robertson's assessment when he says, "Habakkuk colors the reality of the expectation of God's future manifestation by recalling the many concrete instances of his intervening in the history of the past."[81] In the case of Hab 3:13–14, the concrete instance that Habakkuk recalls is David's victory over Goliath, and the future expectation is when the Lord will send a future anointed one to defeat the serpent and all of its hosts.

3.4. SUMMARY

This chapter sought to demonstrate that the Samuel narrative presents Goliath as a serpent. This chapter provided multiple reasons for this interpretation under three different headings: (1) Goliath's description, (2) Goliath's death, and (3) Hab 3:13–14 as an interpretation of David defeating Goliath.

Under the first heading, Goliath's description, we made several observations suggesting that he is serpentine. First, while discussing how the David and Goliath narrative introduced Goliath, we noted that Goliath wore scale armor, and that this word for "scale" (קשקשים) elsewhere always applies to aquatic animal life. We also noted that the only other person in the OT who is scaly is Pharaoh (Ezek 29:1–6) and that this passage contained additional links with the David and Goliath narrative. We concluded that the best explanation for why Ezekiel would pattern Pharaoh's serpentine demise after Goliath's was because Ezekiel saw in David's victory over Goliath the defeat of a serpent.

80. Hamilton, "The Skull Crushing Seed of the Woman," 37.
81. Robertson, *The Books of Nahum, Habakkuk, and Zephaniah*, 219–20.

Second, while describing Goliath's appearance, the narrative stated four times that Goliath's equipment was made of bronze. We argued that the most likely literary explanation for the text's odd fixation upon Goliath's bronze equipment is that the author mentions Goliath's "bronze" (נחשת) equipment to associate him with the serpent (נחש) through a play on words.

Third, we considered if Ronning was correct in asserting that Goliath's title, the "in-betweens-man" (איש־הבנים), alludes to the hostility "between" (בין) the seed of the woman and the seed of the serpent as mentioned in Gen 3:15. We concluded with Fokkelman and van Wijk-Bos that the odd title certainly signaled Goliath's geographical location since he was the only man standing between the Philistines and the Israelites. In addition to Goliath's title denoting his geographical location, we argued that it was possible but by no means certain that Ronning's proposal is correct. We allowed for this possibility because individuals who stood between others in the Bible (e.g., Moses and Aaron) do not normally receive a unique title for standing in that particular location. This suggested Goliath's unusual title might signal something besides his geographical location. We also noticed thematic similarities between 1 Sam 17 and Gen 3:15 that supported Ronning's position. Given the passage's tendency to cast Goliath as a serpent, Ronning is possibly correct in suggesting that Goliath's unique title is meant to allude to the enmity mentioned in Gen 3:15, but we were not certain of this.

In the next portion we considered if 1 Sam 17 presented Goliath as a serpent in his death. Against Leithart, Hamilton, and Ronning who all understand Goliath's crushed forehead to be an allusion to the serpent's defeat in Gen 3:15, we concluded that it is more likely that David did not strike Goliath's head (מצח) with the stone but rather his greave (מצח). Multiple reasons were offered in support of this interpretation. We concluded this section by offering a mediating position. We suggested that since "greave" (מצח) and "forehead" (מצח) are homonyms, the author intentionally wrote ambiguously when he said that David's stone sunk into Goliath's מצח. Though he provides enough clues within the narrative for the reader to decide that the stone actually struck Goliath's greave, his use of a homonym encourages the reader to entertain the idea that David's stone actually sank into Goliath's forehead. Through this ambiguity he fosters another link between Goliath and the serpent.

We then considered the possible significance of Goliath falling facedown when the stone struck him and his subsequent decapitation. After recognizing the links between Dagon and Goliath's demise, we also noticed that Goliath's facedown posture was conceptually similar to the serpent's judgment from Gen 3:14. God's judgment against both of them resulted in their belly being on the ground and their mouth being on the dust of the earth. Concerning Goliath's decapitation, we saw that Goliath did not die until David removed his head with his sword. Just as the serpent's final defeat will come from a blow to the head, so too Goliath's demise ultimately came from a blow to his head.

Lastly, we argued that Hab 3:13–14 is a poetic interpretation of David defeating Goliath. We substantiated this interpretation by providing multiple observations such as David being the "anointed one" and Goliath being the "head of the house of the wicked" from verse 13. This is significant because Habakkuk poetically describes Goliath's defeat in language reminiscent of the serpent's judgment from Gen 3:15. Habakkuk saw in Goliath's defeat a foreshadowing of when God's final anointed one would defeat the serpent once and for all.

4

NAHASH AS A SERPENT

THIS CHAPTER WILL SEEK to demonstrate that Samuel presents certain characters associated with the name "Nahash" as serpentine. Unto that end, it will consider each passage in which the proper noun Nahash appears.[1] We will consider these passages in three separate sections: (1) 1 Sam 11–12; (2) 2 Sam 10; and (3) 2 Sam 17. In so doing we will be able to demonstrate the first half of our thesis: Samuel does contain a serpent literary motif.

4.1. NAHASH IN 1 SAMUEL 11–12

Nahash first appears in 1 Sam 11. First Samuel also mentions him briefly in 12:12. We will give more attention to Nahash in 1 Sam 11 because it is here that the narrative introduces him and because he figures more prominently in chapter 11 than chapter 12.

1. The MT mentions Nahash by name in 1 Sam 11:1–2; 12:12; 2 Sam 10:2; 17:25, 27. The OG also mentions Nahash in 1 Sam 11:10 by explicitly stating to whom the men of Jabesh spoke. Also, 4QSam[a] mentions Nahash's name two times in a possible introduction to the Nahash narrative between 1 Sam 10:27—11:1. Scholars dispute the authenticity of 4QSam[a]'s introduction. Long (*The Reign and Rejection of King Saul*, 219, n. 115), Eves ("One Ammonite Invasion or Two," 308–26), and McCarter (*I Samuel*, 199) believe the passage to be original. Others—such as Fokkelman and Tsumura— think it is secondary (see Fokkelman, *Vow and Desire*, 461; Tsumura, *The First Book of Samuel*, 303). The present author affirms the superiority of the MT because nothing within it could have readily caused the supposed haplography argued by some to occur. Still, a decision is difficult. With that said, whether or not one sees 4QSam[a] as original does not impact this chapter's argument.

4.1.1. Nahash in 1 Samuel 11

In order to understand Nahash's role in 1 Sam 11, we will first overview that chapter's purpose and structure. Then, we will take an extended look at the relationship between Judg 19–21 and 1 Sam 1:1—2:11. Here we will argue that Samuel continues to anticipate the king Israel needed in Judg 17–21 if they are ever to do what is right in the Lord's eyes.[2] We will see that the compositional unity between Judges and Samuel encourages the reader to identify the anticipated king at Judges's conclusion with the Messiah in Samuel. This is the case because Samuel associates language from Judg 19–21 with the coming Messiah and Saul. On account of the messianism within Judges's conclusion and the links connecting Saul with Judges, we will consider the relationship between Saul and the Messiah. This section concludes by asserting that Samuel casts Saul as though he were the Messiah in his victory over Nahash in order to echo the seed of the woman's eschatological victory over the serpent from Gen 3:14–15.

4.1.1.1. The Function and Structure of 1 Samuel 11

First Samuel 11's function within the overall narrative is rather transparent. First Samuel 10 begins with Samuel privately anointing Saul as king over Israel (10:1). The chapter then details how God chose Saul as king through lots because Israel had previously asked for a king (8:5; 10:24). Chapter 10 concludes with individuals rejecting Saul's kingship (v. 27). First Samuel 11 ends by Israel publicly declaring Saul as their king (11:15). Thus, within the narrative's flow, the Nahash account is the means by which the nation recognizes Saul as its king. McCarter expresses this well: "Clearly the purpose of this arrangement is to show that Saul, who was already king *de jure*, has now become king *de facto* . . . and earned the loyalty of all Israel."[3] Tsumura agrees when he writes, "The present chapter marks the transition from Samuel's judgeship to Saul's kingship. Here Saul is formally established as king."[4]

Despite the rather clear function of 1 Sam 11 within the narrative, scholars organize the passage differently. Brueggemann divides the Nahash narrative into three different sections. These sections are (1) the problem: there seems to be no one to save Jabesh-Gilead (vv. 1–4); (2) the intervention:

2. Thus, the present author agrees with a pro-monarchic view of Judges's conclusion. This section later contains references supporting this view, and it offers a pro-monarchic argument on account of the compositional unity regarding Judges's conclusion and Samuel's introduction.

3. McCarter, *I Samuel*, 205, (emphasis his).

4. Tsumura, *The First Book of Samuel*, 301.

deliverance is promised (vv. 5–11); and (3) the resolution: the LORD accomplishes salvation (vv. 12–15).[5] Fokkelman also sees a three part structure, which he simply calls the beginning, middle, and end, yet he divides the text differently (vv. 1–3, 4–9, 10–11).[6] He also argues for a chiastic structure emphasizing the Spirit coming on Saul.[7] Tsumura differs from Brueggemann and Fokkelman by suggesting a five part structure that stretches through verse 15 (vv. 1–3, 4–9a, 9b–10, 11–13, 14–15).[8] Fortunately, the narrative's presentation of Nahash as a serpent does not depend on one particular outline.

4.1.1.2. The Similarities and Relationship between 1 Samuel 11 and Judges 19–21

Much in 1 Sam 11 sounds like the book of Judges. Albrecht Alt states,

> Saul's charismatic leadership, the military service of the tribes, the overwhelming success; up to this point one would think oneself simply confronted with a story from the book of Judges, except perhaps that the circle of people who were borne along by the enthusiasm of the leader is wider here than elsewhere. But in the final terse sentences comes the unexpected twist: the victorious tribes bring Saul to their sanctuary and by their act of homage make him what no charismatic leader ever was before: the king of Israel.[9]

Beyond these general correspondences, multiple scholars have noted numerous similarities between 1 Sam 11 and Judg 19–21. Polzin points out that both stories concentrate on the towns of Jabesh-Gilead and Gibeah (Judg 19:12–16; 21:8–10; 1 Sam 11:1, 4, 9).[10] They also both feature "right" (ימין) and "eye" (עין) language (Judg 19:14; 21:2; 1 Sam 11:2, 10).[11] Both

---

5. Walter Brueggemann, *First and Second Samuel*, 82–83. Because of the awkward phraseology of Brueggemann's section headings, I have slightly altered their wording without changing his meaning.

6. Fokkelman, *Vow and Desire*, 455. Fokkelman also argues that 11:12–13 are separate from verses 1–11 since they form a frame around these verses with 10:26–27 (Fokkelman, *Vow and Desire*, 454) and that chapter 12 should begin after 1 Sam 11:13 (see Fokkelman, *Vow and Desire*, 482–83). Regardless of where one believes that chapter 12 should start, what matters is that the reader understands that chapters 11 and 12 are connected. The present author understands Samuel's speech in 12:1–25 as occurring at Gilgal (11:14–15) and in response to Israel making Saul king (11:15).

7. Fokkelman, *Vow and Desire*, 456.

8. Tsumura, *The First Book of Samuel*, 303–14.

9. Alt, *Essays on Old Testament History and Religion*, 194.

10. Polzin, *Samuel and the Deuteronomist*, 112.

11. Polzin, *Samuel and the Deuteronomist*, 113.

stories also contain the otherwise unparalleled request of people saying, "Bring the men that we may put them to death" (Judg 20:13; 1 Sam 11:12).[12]

Fokkelman notices additional similarities. Both texts contain a man chopping up someone or something in order to rally Israel to enter battle (Judg 19:29; 1 Sam 11:7).[13] Once Israel gathers for battle, both texts say that they gather "as one man" (Judg 20:1, 8, 11; 1 Sam 11:7).[14] Furthermore, both texts contain "sons of worthlessness" who act wickedly (Judg 19:22; 20:13; 1 Sam 10:27; cf. 11:12).[15] To these similarities, Tsumura recognizes that after both texts record the cutting of the concubine and oxen, the pieces are sent "throughout all the territory of Israel" (בכל־גבול ישראל) (Judg 19:29; 1 Sam 11:3, 7).

Clearly these two texts have much in common. With Polzin one is forced to say, "It is as if the chaotic situation described at the end of the book of Judges—when there was no human deliverer, whether judge or king, to set Israel on the right path—deliberately looks forward to a sequel here in 1 Samuel 11."[16]

What then is the relationship between these two passages? Polzin understands 1 Sam 11's allusions to Judg 19–21 to mean that Saul is the ultimate judge and one should not view him as a king. For Polzin, 1 Sam 11 teaches that Israel learned they do not need a king. They should have retained the judge model of leadership.[17]

Polzin argues this because of two reasons. First, he understands the similarities between Judg 19–21 and 1 Sam 11 as comparisons and not contrasts. This is why he sees Saul as a judge and not a king. Second, he leans heavily upon his reading of 1 Sam 11:12. Occurring after Saul's victory, that verse reads, "Then the people said to Samuel, 'Who is it that said, "Shall Saul reign over us?" Bring the men, that we may put them to death.'" Polzin understands that verse to mean that the people of Israel desire to kill those who wanted Saul as king. Thus, Polzin argues that 1 Sam 11 teaches that the judge model of Israelite leadership is preferable to the kingly model.

Polzin's arguments fail to convince because he misreads 1 Sam 11:12. This verse communicates the opposite of Polzin's interpretation. He fails to see verse 12 as a reference back to 1 Sam 10:27a, which reads, "But

12. Polzin, *Samuel and the Deuteronomist*, 112.

13. Fokkelman, *Vow and Desire*, 470.

14. Fokkelman, *Vow and Desire*, 470.

15. Fokkelman, *Vow and Desire*, 471.

16. Polzin, *Samuel and the Deuteronomist*, 112.

17. Polzin states, "After all . . . the story in chapter 11 is . . . about Israel's missed opportunity to reverse a monarchic path leading ultimately to exile" (*Samuel and the Deuteronomist*, 115).

some worthless fellows said, 'How can this man save us?'" The worthless men were rejecting Saul's kingship because they doubted Saul could "save" (יְשִׁעֵנוּ) Israel. After Saul delivers (תְּשׁוּעָה; 11:9) Israel, Israel demands to kill those who opposed Saul's kingship (v. 12). Contrary to Polzin's view, 1 Sam 11:12 teaches that Israel desired Saul to be king.[18]

Unlike Polzin, Fokkelman sees the similarities between Judg 19–21 and 1 Sam 11 as contrasting these two narratives. Fokkelman notes many points of discontinuity. In Judges, Israel attacks Jabesh-Gilead, but in 1 Samuel a foreign army attacks Jabesh-Gilead. In Judges the man cuts up his concubine after being responsible in some measure for her sexual abuse, but in Samuel, there is no sexual abuse, and Saul cuts up a yoke of oxen. Surely, there is a difference between cutting up a human and oxen. Lastly—and most importantly—the point of the abhorrent behavior in Judg 17–21 is to demonstrate that Israel needs a king but does not have one (cf. Judg 17:6; 18:1; 19:1; 21:25).[19] In 1 Sam 10, Samuel had already anointed Saul as king over Israel, and chapter 11 ends by Israel publicly recognizing Saul as their king. The point of Judges's conclusion is the opposite of 1 Sam 11.[20] Fokkelman is correct to say that the relationship between Judges 19–21 and 1 Sam 11 "is indeed that of an opposition."[21]

4.1.1.3. The Relationship between Saul and Judges 19–21

Since multiple elements within Judges's conclusion appear in 1 Sam 11, and Judges's conclusion focuses on Israel's lack of a king, it is worth asking what the relationship is between Saul and Judges's kingless conclusion. In order to best answer this question (and thereby understand how Samuel suggests Nahash is a serpent), we will analyze Judges's conclusion and Samuel's introduction.

Regarding Judg 17–21, scholars disagree as to whether the book ends approving a future monarchy or not.[22] The present author agrees with the

---

18. Tsumura argues against Polzin's reading by noting that "Polzin's intertextual approach ignores the more immediate context in which the present episode is placed. In fact, chapter 10 already anointed Saul as a king *designate*." See Tsumura, *The First Book of Samuel*, 308–09, (emphasis his).

19. Scholars recognize that statements regarding Israel's lack of a king signal significant narrative movement within Judg 17–21 and frame these same chapters. See Polzin, *Samuel and the Deuteronomist*, 112; Younger, *Judges/Ruth*, 334; Block, *Judges, Ruth*, 475. As we will see, scholars disagree as to whether these statements are pro-monarchic or not.

20. Fokkelman, *Vow and Desire*, 470–71.

21. Fokkelman, *Vow and Desire*, 471.

22. Numerous scholars support both positions. Susan Niditch understands the

pro-monarchic view. Judges 17–21 longs for a king who will come with the result that Israel will no longer sin. This section will seek to argue for this pro-monarchic view by understanding the compositional strategy uniting Judges and Samuel.

Before we consider the compositional strategy between Judges and Samuel, the remainder of this paragraph briefly details the argument for Nahash as serpent in 1 Sam 11 lest one lose sight of the forest for the trees. This section will argue that Samuel's introduction and Judges's conclusion work together to communicate that the Messiah will be the king that Judges's conclusion expects will prevent "everyone from doing right in his own eyes." In other words, whoever finalized Samuel as we now have it understood the Messiah to be the expectant king from Judges's conclusion. Hence, when the Samuel narrative introduces Saul's emerging kingship with language from Judg 19–21 as he defeats Nahash in 1 Sam 11, he appears to be the king Judg 17–21 anticipated. Since we have already seen that Gen 3:15 anticipates that the royal eschatological deliverer will defeat the serpent, when Saul is cast as the longed-for king from Judges, whom Samuel identifies as the Messiah, this suggests that his victory over Nahash foreshadows the royal eschatological king's victory over the serpent.

Naturally, Judg 17–21 concludes Judges. Two sections (chs. 17–18, 19–21) constitute this concluding unit.[23] Scholars frequently point out that these narratives share similar language about Israel's lack of a king, but they often fail to identify the similar introductions for chapters 17 and 19.

Before we comment on the shared language introducing each of Judges's two concluding sections, first notice the references to Israel's lack of a king. Both Judg 17:6 and 18:1 read, "In those days there was no king in Israel." Twice the author expands this phrase by adding the words, "and

---

statements about Israel's lack of a king to not be "an indictment of early chaos, but an accepting commentary on a romantic, battle-ridden foundation period in the history of the nation" (Niditch, *Judges*, 180). William J. Dumbrell also sees Judg 21:25 as not endorsing the monarchy. He understands Judges to be addressed to exiled Israel in order to help them see that the Lord alone has preserved Israel; see Dumbrell, "'In Those Days There Was No King in Israel, Every Man Did What Was Right in His Own Eyes,'" 23–33. Block sees Judg 21:25 as simply asserting that Israel consistently rebelled against the Lord before they had a king. In Block's view, the text does not suggest that a king would remedy Israel's problems. Rather than fixing Israel's problems, Block points out that Israel's kings were marked by unfaithfulness to the covenant (Block, *Judges, Ruth*, 475–76). Others support the traditional, pro-monarchic view. Younger understands Israel's sin to be the result of their lack of a king (Younger, *Judges/Ruth*, 334). Also, using narrative criticism, Philip E. Satterthwaite concludes that Judges uniformly presents the coming monarchy positively. See Satterthwaite, "'No King in Israel,'" 75–88. The remainder of this section agrees with the pro-monarchic view.

23. See O'Connell, *The Rhetoric of the Book of Judges*, 297, 299; Niditch, *Judges*, 180.

everyone did what was right in his own eyes" (17:6; 21:25). In Judg 17–18, this "kingless" refrain signals a transition in the narrative, while the refrain frames chapters 19–21.[24] The two expanded refrains work together to bracket Judges's conclusion (17:6; 21:25). These sections—and thus the whole of Judges—look forward to the day when Israel will have a king who will cause Israel to do what is right in the Lord's eyes.[25]

Beyond a common refrain, these two sections have similar introductions. Both Judg 17:1 and 19:1 begin their respective section by mentioning that there "was a man" (ויהי־איש) in "the hill country of Ephraim (הר־אפרים)."[26] This shared introduction has the literary effect of communicating that Judg 19:1 continues the message of Judg 17–18. Both stories begin the same way because they are making the same basic point about Israel's need for a king. Thus, Judg 19–21 continues to hope for a king who will cause Israel to do what is right in the Lord's eyes. In sum, Judg 19–21 begins by mentioning a man sojourning in the hill country of Ephraim, and it concludes by looking forward to Israel's future king—a king who will cause Israel to do right in God's eyes.

Like Judg 17:1 and 19:1, we know that 1 Sam 1:1a also begins a new section since it begins the book of Samuel. This verse reads, "And there was a man from Ramathaim-zophim of the hill country of Ephraim and his name was Elkanah" (1:1a; [AT]).[27] As we saw in Judg 17:1 and 19:1, 1 Sam 1:1

24. Amit, *The Book of Judges*, 345.

25. With Block and Lawson, it is best to see the refrain "everyone did what was right in his own eyes (בעיניו)" (Judg 17:6, 21:25) as an equivalent to the refrain, "the people of Israel did what was evil in the sight (בעיני) of the LORD" (3:7, 12; 4:1; 6:1; 10:6; 13:1). See Block, *Judges, Ruth*, 476; Younger, *Judges/Ruth*, 334–35.

26. Judges 17:1 reads, "There was a man of the hill country of Ephraim whose name was Micah" (ויהי־איש מהר־אפרים ושמו מיכיהו). Judges 19:1a says, "In those days, when there was no king in Israel, a certain Levite was sojourning in the remote parts of the hill county of Ephraim" (ויהי בימים ההם ומלך אין בישראל ויהי איש לוי גר בירכתי הר־אפרים).

27. In the MT, 1 Sam 1:1a reads, "ויהי איש אחד מן־הרמתים צופים מהר אפרים ושמו אלקנה." The OG differs slightly from the MT in three ways. It reads, "ἄνθρωπος ἦν ἐξ Αρμαθαιμ Σιφα ἐξ ὄρους Εφραιμ καὶ ὄνομα αὐτῷ Ελκανα." First, it lacks the MT's initial conjunction. Second, it follows a noun + verb ordering instead of the MT's verb + noun order. Third, the OG lacks the word "one" (εἷς) for the MT's "אחד." McCarter proposes that the MT is adapting to Judg 13:2, which introduces Samson's birth narrative (see McCarter, *I Samuel*, 51). On account of this, he concludes that neither the word והיה nor אחד are original. By discounting the originality of והיה, McCarter argues that 1 Samuel begins a fresh narrative, and it does not depend on Judges. McCarter overlooks the similarities between Judges 17:1, 19:1, and 1 Sam 1:1 in his analysis, though. These are the only three texts that contain the phrases "hill country of Ephraim" (הר אפרים) as well as "and there was a man" (ויהי איש). Each of these three texts also begins three successive new sections. If beginning each of these three successive sections is an intentional compositional strategy, then those elements in common with 1 Sam 1:1 and Judg 17:1 and 19:1 are likely original. Intriguingly,

introduces a story that begins with "a man" (ויהי איש) in "the hill country of Ephraim (הר אפרימ)." Judges 17:1, 19:1, and 1 Sam 1:1 are the only three verses in which the subject, a man in the hill country of Ephraim, is governed by the verb "and it was" (ויהי). This suggests that the narrator of Samuel wanted readers to view 1 Sam 1:1 as continuing the narrative of Judges.[28]

Furthermore, one should understand this shared introduction in 1 Sam 1:1a to signal that the Samuel narrative is still anticipating this king from Judg chapters 17–21, since this same introduction in Judg 19:1 signaled that the narrative was continuing to anticipate a coming king from chapters 17–18.[29] Moreover, since Judg 17:1 and 19:1 both introduced sections anticipating a coming king, then it is likely that 1 Sam 1:1 is not so much introducing the whole book of Samuel as it is introducing the first section within Samuel that continues to anticipate this coming king.

Tsumura rightly affirms that Samuel's first section stretches from 1:1 to 2:11.[30] Like Judg 19–21, 1 Sam 1:1—2:11 ends with a kingly focus. First

_____

with the OG of 1 Sam 1:1, neither Judg 17:1 nor 19:1 use the word "certain" (אחד; εἷς) to modify "man" (איש; ἄνθρωπος) as 13:2 does. Since it appears that the MT of 1 Sam 1:1 is likely part of a compositional strategy uniting Judges and Samuel, then this suggests that the word "certain" (אחד) in the MT is not original. Also, since 1 Sam 1:1 clearly begins a new book, a scribe would more likely remove an initial conjunction rather than add one. The initial conjunction in the MT of 1 Sam 1:1 is the harder reading since it is odd to begin a literary work with the word "and." In sum, it seems that 1 Sam 1:1 is continuing the story from Judg 17–21. Judges 17:1, 19:1, and 1 Sam 1:1 all begin a new section by introducing a story that begins with a man in the hill country of Ephraim.

28. As previously mentioned, this book follows the *BHS*'s ordering of the Tanak. In this ordering, Ruth follows Proverbs rather than Judges.

29. Contrary to McCarter, who said that 1 Sam 1:1 begins a fresh literary unit, with Fokkelman the present author agrees that Samuel's literary background is Judges. See Fokkelman, *Vow and Desire*, 1.

30. Tsumura, *The First Book of Samuel*, 104. Though Tsumura subdivides 1:1—2:11 differently, the present author understands 1 Sam 1:1—2:11 to be the following parallel:
A. Narrative's introduction with a husband and barren wife (1 Sam 1:1-6)
 B. Main character of section thus far (Hannah) petitions for a child, and Eli promises a coming child (vv. 7–18)
  C. Group of people worship (v. 19a)
   D. Mention of people going home (v.19b)
    Transition-Conception, birth, and praising God (vv. 19c–20)
 B1-Promised child present and a conversation with Eli (vv. 21–28a)
  C1- Two people (Eli & Hannah) worship (vv. 28b–2:10)
   D1- Mention of someone going home and someone staying where they are (v. 11).
Intriguingly, Luke has copied this same parallel, which suggests he too saw 1 Sam 1:1—2:11 as a section:
A. Narrative's introduction with a husband and a barren wife (Luke 1:5-7)
 B. Main character of section thus far (Zechariah) makes a petition, and Gabriel promises a coming child (vv. 8–20)

Samuel 2:10c–e reads, "The LORD will judge the ends of the earth, and he will give strength to his king, and he will exalt the horn of his anointed" (AT). Notice the similarity between Judg 19–21 and 1 Sam 1:1—2:11's introduction and conclusion.

Fig. 4.1. Compositional Unity between Judges and 1 Samuel

	Judg 19–21	1 Sam 1:1—2:11
Section Introduction	And it was in those days, and there was no king in Israel, and there was a man, a Levite, sojourning in the remote regions of the hill country of Ephraim (17:1a; AT).	And there was a man from of Ramathaim-zophim of the hill country of Ephraim (1:1a).[31]
Section Conclusion	In those days, there was no king in Israel. Everyone did what was right in his own eyes (21:25).	The LORD will judge the ends of the earth, and he will give strength to his king, and he will exalt the horn of his anointed. And Elkanah went to Ramah in his house, and the boy was serving the LORD before Eli the priest (2:10c–11; AT).

Since the shared introduction of 1 Sam 1:1a signaled that the Samuel narrative continues to anticipate a king whose absence concluded Judg 19–21, then the sole mention of a king toward the conclusion of 1 Sam 1:1—2:11

C. Group of people "worship" (ἐθαύμαζον—a word normally used in Luke as a worshipful response to a miracle of God; cf. 9:43) (1:21–22)
   D. Mention of someone going home (v. 23)
      Transition: Conception and praising God (vv. 24–25)
B1- Child is promised from Gabriel (vv. 26–38)
  C1- Two people (Elizabeth and Mary) worship (vv. 39–55)
   D1- Mention of someone going home and staying (v. 56).
After 1 Sam 2:11, the narrative then gives three different stories showing how Samuel is superior to Eli's sons (2:12–21, 22–26, 27—3:19). Each of these sections ends by mentioning Samuel "growing/becoming great" (גדל). Likewise, after Luke 1:56, the narrative contains three different stories showing how Jesus is superior to John the Baptist through step parallelism (1:57–80; 2:1–40, 41–52). (For a treatment of Luke's step parallelism see Kuhn, "The Point of the Step-Parallelism in Luke 1–2," 38–49). Each of these sections ends by mentioning that John or Jesus "grew/increased." These observations further confirm that Luke 1:5–56 copies 1 Sam 1:1—2:11, and they thereby demonstrate that Luke understood 1 Sam 1:1—2:11 as a section.

  31. This translation incorporates my previous text critical decisions.

suggests that Samuel's final author understood the king, the anointed one, in 1 Sam 2:10 to be the same king Judges anticipated.

If we are correct in understanding the king in 1 Sam 2:10 to be the expected king from Judg 17–21, then identifying the king in 1 Sam 2:10 would also provide the identity of the king Judges anticipated. Clues aid the interpreter in identifying the king of 1 Sam 2:10. First, within the narrative flow of Samuel, Hannah anticipates this king before Saul reigns as Israel's first king. This suggests that Israel's kingship is not the impetus for Hannah's hope, and it discourages the reader from identifying a historical king from the OT as the king of 1 Sam 2:10.[32] Second, scholars routinely point out that 1 Sam 2:10 parallels 2 Sam 22:51.[33] Since the "anointed one" in 2 Sam 22:51 anticipates David's coming "seed" (זרע), this increases the probability that 1 Sam 2:10 has the son of David, the Messiah, in view.[34] Third, 1 Sam 2:10 connects the anointed king with the Lord judging the "ends of the earth" (אפסי־ארץ).[35] This exact phrase, "ends of the earth" (אפסי־ארץ), occurs twelve times within the OT. Of these twelve occurrences eight—not including 1 Sam 2:10—are in messianically charged passages.[36] Fourth, Isa 2:4 says that the Lord will judge the nations, and yet 11:1–4 teaches that the messianic shoot of David will judge all peoples. Isaiah connects the Lord judging all the nations to the Davidic offspring similarly to how 1 Sam 2:10 connects the Lord judging the ends of the earth with the anointed king.

---

32. Concerning Hannah expecting a king before Israel had a king, Sailhamer says, "At the close of her hymn, Hannah moves to another theme: the prophetic hope of the coming of God's messianic king (1 Sam 2:10). She does this by means of an echo of the poems in the Pentateuch. . . . Hannah's 'anointed one' and 'king' allude to the 'messianic king' in the poetry of the Pentateuch (Num 24:7)" (see Sailhamer, *The Meaning of the Pentateuch*, 16).

33. See Polzin, *Samuel and the Deuteronomist*, 34; Fokkelman, *Throne and City*, 354.

34. Concerning the interplay between 1 Sam 2:10 and 2 Sam 22:51, Dempster explains that Hannah's "song's antiphonal response is David's song of thanksgiving. . . . Hannah's song looks to the future for the overthrow of a tyrannical dominion that will be replaced by a just king, a Messiah, who will bring justice beyond Israel to the ends of the earth (1 Sam. 2:10). . . . [In David's song] God will magnify his salvation to his king and extend covenant loyalty to his Messiah (22:51)" (Dempster, *Dominion and Dynasty*, 134).

35. Notice how the two clauses immediately following "the LORD will judge the ends of the earth" both begin with *waw*. In this way 1 Sam 2:10 connects the anointed king to the Lord's judgment of the ends of the earth.

36. See Deut 33:17; 1 Sam 2:10; Pss 2:8; 22:28 (ET v. 27); 67:8 (ET v. 7); 72:8; 98:3; Prov 30:4; Isa 45:22; 52:10; Mic 5:3 (ET v. 4); Zec 9:10. Those eight occurrences in messianically charged passages are Pss 2:8; 22:28 (ET v. 27); 72:8; Prov 30:4 (cf. John 3:13); Isa 45:22 (cf. Phil 2:10); 52:10; Mic 5:3 (ET v. 4); Zech 9:10.

Though many commentators speak of the king in 1 Sam 2:10 in general terms, and they do not attempt to identify him,[37] good reasons exist for identifying him with the Messiah. Shepherd understands the king in 1 Sam 2:10 to be "a messianic figure." For Shepherd this "messianic figure" is the "individual seed of the Davidic covenant."[38] Though Hamilton does not explicitly identify the king of 1 Sam 2:10 with the Messiah, he does say, "This reference to the military might of Israel under the anointed king explains the idea that 'Yahweh will judge the ends of the earth,' which is itself elaborating on the idea that the adversaries of Yahweh will be shattered. This shattering has overtones of broken heads (Gen. 3:15)."[39] Both Hamilton and the present author understand Gen 3:15 to be a messianic prediction. First Samuel 1:1–2:11 presents the Messiah to be the anticipated king from Judg 17–21 under whose reign Israel will no longer do what is right in their own eyes. Samuel teaches that the Messiah will undo the problems within Judg 17–21.

4.1.1.4. The Relationship between Saul and the Messiah

As seen before, the Nahash narrative in 1 Sam 11 contrasts material from Judg 19–21. In Judges, after sexual abuse occurred, disseminating human body parts throughout the tribes caused Israel to assemble as one man to battle against one of its own tribes because Israel had no king. In Samuel, Saul disseminates oxen parts throughout Israel to rally Israel as one man in order to battle against a foreign people because Israel did have a king (1 Sam 10:24). First Samuel 11 uses Saul's rise to kingship to present Saul as the king who remedies the problems in Judg 19–21. Since 1 Sam 1:1—2:11 presents the Messiah as the one who will reverse the problems of Judg 17–21, Saul comes off as though he were the Messiah in 1 Sam 11 when he appears to be the expected king from Judges's conclusion.[40]

---

37. See Auld, *I & II Samuel*, 39; Fokkelman, *Vow and Desire*, 99–100; McCarter, *I Samuel*, 75; van Wijk-Bos, *Reading Samuel*, 34.

38. Shepherd, *Daniel in the Context of the Hebrew Bible*, 29.

39. Hamilton, *God's Glory in Salvation through Judgment*, 161.

40. Amit, O'Connell, and Brettler, rightly affirm that 1 Sam 8–10 presents Saul in a negative light by associating him with sinful aspects from Judg 19–21 through his connection to Benjamin (Judg 20:17–20; 1 Sam 9:1) and Gibeah (cf. Judg 20:10; 1 Sam 10:26) (see Amit, *The Book of Judges*, 346–51; O'Connell, *The Rhetoric of the Book of Judges*, 303; Brettler, *The Book of Judges*, 88–89). Though these associations of Saul do not bode well for his fate, they do not nullify the text's positive portrayal of Saul in 1 Sam 11. It is surely difficult to read 1 Sam 11 as a negative portrayal of Saul. We see then that Samuel presents Saul in a mixed fashion. His clan and place of birth cause one to question his moral fiber, but his actions in saving Jabesh-Gilead from Nahash suggest that he might be the promised king who will cause Israel to cease from doing what is

It is on account of Saul's messianic presentation that 1 Sam 11 encourages the reader to interpret Nahash as a character within Samuel's serpent motif. We have seen in chapter 2 of this book that Gen 3:14–15 anticipates that the seed of the woman, the royal eschatological deliverer, will defeat the royal serpent (נחש) that reigns as king over this world. Building on Judg 19–21 and 1 Sam 1:1—2:11, the Nahash narrative casts Saul as if he was the promised Messiah from 1 Sam 2:10, whom Samuel presents as the royal eschatological deliverer from the Pentateuch.[41] Seen in this messianic light, one would expect Saul to defeat the serpent and thereby secure his royal kingship. This is exactly what one finds in 1 Sam 11. By conquering Nahash (נחש), the serpent-king, Saul, the "Messiah," delivers Israel and secures his kingship.[42]

4.1.2. Nahash in 1 Samuel 12

Nahash appears once again in 1 Sam 12:12. Before this section considers Nahash's role in chapter 12, it will first provide a brief overview of the chapter's context, function, and various outlines.

---

right in their own eyes. The reader must be patient to see who the real Saul is.

Eventually the reader discovers that the real Saul is a "fool" (1 Sam 26:21). Saul's initial messianic overtones make his later folly all the more emphatic. A similar phenomenon sometimes occurs in movies and novels when the creator initially portrays the villain with positive characteristics in order to make that same villain appear all the more heinous at the conclusion. Thus, even though Samuel's initial messianic portrayal of Saul suggested he might overcome his sinful pedigree, within the narrative as a whole this only highlights the discrepancy of who Saul should be (i.e., Messiah-like) and who Saul turns out to be.

In addition, since Amit, O'Connell, and Brettler each recognize that Samuel uses Judg 19–21 to color the reader's view of Saul, this increases the likelihood that one should see 1 Sam 1:1 as a compositional bridge connecting Judges to Samuel with the effect that 1 Sam 1:1—2:11 continues to look for a king to remedy Israel's waywardness.

41. The sixth and seventh chapters of this book will demonstrate that Samuel's Messiah is the Pentateuch's royal eschatological deliverer. For now, see above for Sailhamer's comment that the king Hannah expects in 1 Sam 2:10 is the Pentateuch's promised eschatological deliverer.

42. Concerning the Nahash narrative Auld writes, "We may wonder whether the grant of their plea was part of the chivalry of the time, or whether it simply confirms that Snake (nāḥāš) has his sights on all Israel and not simply on a single outlying city" (see Auld, *I & II Samuel*, 122).

4.1.2.1. Overview of 1 Samuel 12

First Samuel 12 immediately follows Saul's victory over Nahash. After this victory, Israel renews the kingdom[43] in Gilgal by establishing Saul's reign (11:14–15).[44] After renewing the kingdom, Samuel declares the Lord's testimony (12:5–6) against Israel's wicked request for a king.[45] Scholars divide Samuel's address differently with some seeing three sections and others four.[46] Either way, the chapter's function within the literary flow is to show God's negative opinion of Israel selecting a king, and how Israel must live before God under their new king.[47]

43. Scholars debate the meaning of the phrase "renew the kingdom there" (ונחדש שם המלוכה) in 1 Sam 11:14. J. Robert Vannoy understands the phrase to mean that Israel renewed the Lord as king (see Vannoy, *Covenant Renewal at Gilgal*, 68). Tsumura has followed Vannoy and also believes that the kingdom in 10:16, 25 is a political kingdom and that Israel renews the kingdom as a spiritual kingdom because in 11:15 they renew the kingdom "before the LORD" (see Tsumura, *The First Book of Samuel*, 312–13). Long disagrees with Vannoy. Slightly modifying Baruch Halpern's view, Long argues that a kingdom emerges in three stages: (1) the king is anointed, (2) the king has a victory, and (3) the nation confirms the king's leadership (see Long, *The Reign and Rejection of King Saul*, 225–28; Baruch Halpern, "The Constitution of the Monarchy in Israel," 95, 125, 173–74). Following this scheme, Samuel anoints Saul as king in chapter 10, Saul defeats Nahash in 11:1–11, and Saul begins his reign (i.e., Israel renews the kingdom) in verses 12–15. Fokkelman notes that in verse 14 both Israel and Samuel "renew the kingdom." He concludes that "to renew the kingdom" means something different for Samuel than it does for Israel, and that the narrator understands "renewing the kingdom" similarly to Samuel, though not identically (see Fokkelman, *Vow and Desire*, 487–90). Concerning the phrase, McCarter simply states, "Since Saul has already been proclaimed king at Mizpah, his office need not be granted again. Thus the kingship is simply 'renewed' at Gilgal" (*I Samuel*, 205). The present author finds Long's argument the most persuasive. After inaugurating the kingdom in chapter 10 (cf. vv. 16, 25), Israel and Samuel further establish Saul's reign in 11:14–15 and thereby renew the kingdom.

44. Lyle M. Eslinger notes that some like Veijola argue that the events in chapter 12 did not occur in Gilgal (see Veijola, *Das Königtum in der Beurteilung der Deuteronomistischen Historiographie: eine Redaktionsgeschichtliche Untersuchung*, 83). Still, Eslinger appropriately states, "Considered from a literary perspective, 12.1 does not seem to introduce a new scene; in fact, continuity predominates" (Eslinger, *Kingship of God in Crisis*, 383).

45. Scholars debate why the Lord considered Israel's request for a king to be evil (cf. 8:6–7, 20). Jason S. DeRouchie convincingly argues that Israel sinned by choosing a king for themselves rather than having the Lord choose his own king (cf. 8:6; 12:13, 17; Deut 17:14–15). See DeRouchie, "The Heart of YHWH and His Chosen One in 1 Samuel 13:14," 482–84.

46. Both Fokkelman (*Vow and Desire*, 493), and Wijk-Bos (*Reading Samuel*, 70) see three sections (vv. 1–5, 6–19, 20–25). Auld (*I & II Samuel*, 126–37) and Tsumura (*The First Book of Samuel*, 316–26) each see four sections. These different outlines do not impact one's interpretation of Nahash in this passage.

47. Tsumura differs from the chapter's function stated above. He says that the

4.1.2.2. Nahash's Role in 1 Samuel 12

Samuel references Nahash after recounting how the Lord repeatedly saved Israel by doing righteous acts in 1 Sam 12:7–11. He first recalls how God responded to Israel's cries for help because of Pharaoh's oppression by sending Moses and Aaron to bring Israel to the land of Canaan (v. 8; cf. Exod 2:23; 3:7). During the time of the judges, Israel frequently forgot the Lord (1 Sam 12:9). Still when Israel cried out to the Lord, he would send judges to save them (vv. 10–11; cf. Judg 3:9, 15; 10:10—11:1). Despite the Lord's past faithfulness, when Israel saw Nahash come against them, they did not cry out to the Lord for salvation, but rather they desired a king to save them (v. 12).

We may observe two things about Nahash from this passage. First, the passage shows that Israel asked for a king because their enemy, Nahash, was opposing them. Israel desired a king because they feared Nahash. They did not trust in the Lord. Israel asked for a king because of Nahash's encroachment.[48] Fokkelman writes, "Instead of repenting under Ammonite pressure

---

purpose of 1 Sam 12 is to "convey Samuel's new role and his relationship with the people rather than God's covenantal relationship with the people" (Tsumura, *The First Book of Samuel*, 315). Tsumura's statement fails to take into account verses 20–25. Others disagree with Tsumura by arguing that chapter 12 does contain a covenant renewal. Eslinger summarizes chapter 12 by saying, "Samuel leads Israel in a covenant renewal that incorporates the monarchy" (Eslinger, *Kingship of God in Crisis*, 427). Based on similarities with Joshua's speech in Josh 24, J. Muilenburg claims that 1 Sam 12 is a covenant renewal (Muilenburg, "The Form and Structure of Covenantal Formulations," 361–64). Vannoy agrees saying that one should understand the chapter as "the record of the covenant renewal ceremony held for the dual purpose of providing for covenant continuity at a time of transition in leadership in covenant restoration after abrogation" (Vannoy, *Covenant Renewal at Gilgal*, 178). Tsumura, van Wijk-Bos, and Brent F. Knutson each think otherwise due to the concentration of legal language (see Tsumura, *The First Book of Samuel*, 315; van Wijk-Bos, *Reading Samuel*, 71; Knutson, "Literary Genres in PRU IV," 2:173). Certainly legal language appears in Samuel the prophet's indicting pronouncement. Furthermore, though Israel admits doing wrong (12:19), they never recommit themselves to serving the Lord as they did during Joshua's farewell address (cf. Josh 24:16–18, 21, 24). This makes a covenant renewal in 1 Sam 12 unlikely.

48. Scholars suggest different solutions to the chronological difficulty between 1 Sam 12:12 and chapters 8–11. Vannoy notes that there is a tension and yet concludes that there is nothing necessarily contradictory between chapters 8–11 and 12:12 (Vannoy, *Covenant Renewal at Gilgal*, 39). Tsumura says that perhaps chapter 8 does not mention Nahash's role in prompting Israel's desire for a king even though he was threatening Israel (*The First Book of Samuel*, 323). Eves agrees with Tsumura's historical reading and suggests that Nahash's threat against Israel in chapter 8 provides evidence that the material between 10:27—11:1 in 4QSam[a] is original (see Eves, "One Ammonite Invasion or Two," 319). Fokkelman, van Wijk-Bos, and Auld each suggest that the prophet Samuel's words in 12:12 rewrite history (see Fokkelman, *Vow and Desire*, 514; Auld, *I & II Samuel*, 133; van Wijk-Bos, *Reading Samuel*, 71). The present author affirms that 1 Sam 12:12 is historically true. Nahash was threatening Israel in chapter 8,

and instead of calling upon God for help, the people ask for a king. . . . Samuel's rhetoric arranges these historical data so that the request for a king signifies negative things: not learning the lesson of history, not coming to repentance, and ignoring God."[49]

Second, the speech of Samuel the prophet in 1 Sam 12:7–12 suggests that the Lord would have defeated Nahash just like he defeated Egypt and the nations who enslaved Israel in Judges. Hence, Samuel compares the oppression of the foreign enemies within Judges and Nahash to the Egyptians' oppression. Eslinger notes this saying, "As in the exodus (v. 8), Yahweh sent various individuals throughout Israel's premonarchic period to rescue Israel."[50] This comparison speaks of the foreign nations within Judges and Nahash as though they were a continuation of Egypt's oppression.[51]

We have previously seen that the biblical narratives present Egypt as a corporate representation of the serpent's seed. One could read God defeating the foreign nations within Judges and Nahash as additional examples

---

and this caused Israel to desire a king. What then is the literary purpose of waiting until chapter 12 to reveal that Israel requested a king because of Nahash's looming presence? First Samuel 12:12 suggests that Israel desired a king because they feared Nahash and doubted the Lord's saving ability. This suggests that Israel chose Saul as their king out of desperation. Thus, it was primarily Israel—not the Lord—who chose Saul as their king. Samuel the prophet proceeds to make this exact point in verse 13. Choosing Saul out of a necessity caused by a lack of faith in the Lord further suggests that Saul's kingship originates from sin. We have already noted that Saul is a Benjaminite from Gibeah—which according to Judg 19–21 is a dubious place to come from. Now we see that Israel desired a king because it sinfully doubted the Lord instead of crying out to him in faith as their fathers did in Exod 3 and Judges. Also, by waiting till chapter 12 to inform the reader that Saul probably knew that Nahash was already lurking before Israel chose him as king, the narrative allows the reader to initially read Saul's defeat over Nahash positively (i.e., messianically). Then, when the reader learns that Nahash was exhibiting threatening behavior before Saul defeated him and yet Saul did nothing until it was almost too late, Saul appears less impressive. The author creates a literary tension between 1 Sam 8–11 and 12:12 to exacerbate the grievous nature of Israel's sin, to show that Saul's kingly origins derive from Israel's sin, and to down play Saul's previous messianic portrayal.

49. Fokkelman, *Vow and Desire*, 515. Hans Wilhelm Hertzberg concurs. He writes, "The people's desire for a king . . . is a new form of the constantly renewed apostasy. . . . When a new adversary, Nahash, appears, there follows not the usual, well tested cry to Yahweh, but the demand for a king" (Hertzberg, *I and II Samuel*, 99).

50. Eslinger, *Kingship of God in Crisis a Close Reading*, 398.

51. The account of biblical history in Neh 9 also compares the Lord's victories over Egypt with his victories over the foreign nations within Judges. The Lord heard Israel's cry (זעקה) at the Red Sea, and he delivered Israel. After Israel had entered the land, grew fat (v. 25), and did evil (v. 26), the Lord would enslave Israel to foreign nations (v. 27a, 28a), and then Israel would cry (צעק) to the Lord, and he would deliver them (v. 27b, 28b).

of the serpent's defeat, but this is not demonstrable. For one to make this argument, they would need to demonstrate that the book of Samuel itself presents Egypt as the seed of the serpent. Only then would there be warrant for connecting Nahash's defeat with the serpent's defeat in 1 Sam 12:12. One should not see in 1 Sam 12:12 evidence for or against the thesis that Samuel contains a serpent motif. The point of 1 Sam 12:12 is that God would have defeated Nahash without a king if Israel would have trusted in him.

4.2. NAHASH IN 2 SAMUEL 10

This section will first consider the context of 2 Sam 10, noting how it relates to what precedes and follows it. In this same section we will consider the passage's structure, and we will briefly overview the chapter's introduction since the introduction to chapter 10 is most relevant to the argument of this book. After this, we will consider if the Samuel narrative presents Nahash as a serpent and his son, Hanun, as the seed of a serpent.

4.2.1. Context, Outline, and Overview of 2 Samuel 10

Second Samuel 10 relates to chapter 9 because both chapters detail David showing "kindness" (חסד; cf. 9:1; 10:2) to another. Van Wijk-Bos explains: "Chapters 9 and 10 portray David intent on showing 'loyalty' (Hebrew *hesed*), in both cases to a son on account of a perceived debt to the father, one on a personal level and one on the larger political scene."[52] Second Samuel 10 also connects to what follows.[53] Some like McCarter believe that chapters 10–12 are a theological introduction to chapters 13–20.[54]

Scholars employing literary criticism generally divide the section into three sub-sections. Gnana Robinson sees verses 1–5, 6–14, and 15–19 to be these sub-sections.[55] Fokkelman also divides the text similarly because he sees verses 6–14, 15–19, and 11:1 + 12:26–31 as three successive stages of David's war against the sons of Ammon.[56] He rightly

52. van Wijk-Bos, *Reading Samuel*, 185. Peter R. Ackroyd also notices this link. He writes, "The theme of loyalty provides a neat link with chapter 9" (Ackroyd, *The Second Book of Samuel*, 96).

53. Since the next chapter in this book considers how 2 Sam 10 relates to the narratives that follow, this section will be intentionally brief.

54. McCarter, *II Samuel*, 276.

55. Robinson, *Let Us Be Like the Nations*, 201–03.

56. Fokkelman, *King David*, 41. Van Wijk-Bos also notes that 11:1 and 12:26–31 frame the David and Bathsheba narrative. See van Wijk-Bos, *Reading Samuel*, 188.

suggests that the final stage of battle, 11:1 + 12:26–31, frames the David and Bathsheba narratives.[57]

For our purposes, the passage's introduction, 10:1–5, is the most important. In 2 Sam 10:1–2, the narrative notes that Nahash, the king of the sons of Ammon, has died. Hanun, his son reigns in his place. Because of Nahash's death and the transition of power to Hanun, David sends servants to show "kindness" (חסד) to Hanun (v. 2). On account of his princes' advice, Hanun thinks David is spying out his kingdom (v. 3). In response, Hanun humiliates each of David's servants by shaving off half of their respective beards and by sending them back to Jerusalem partially naked (v. 4). Upon meeting his shamed servants, David tells them to remain in Jericho until their beards regrow (v. 5). Because of Hanun's actions, war ensues between Israel and the sons of Ammon along with those reinforcing Hanun's efforts (vv. 6–19; 11:1 + 12:26–31).

4.2.2. Hanun as the Serpent's Seed in 2 Samuel 10

Though this narrative says little about Nahash and Hanun, Hanun does have serpentine associations. The first thing to notice is that Hanun is Nahash's son. Second Samuel 10:1–3 stresses that Hanun is Nahash's son by mentioning his descendancy three times. In verse 1, Hanun is the son who reigns in Nahash's place. In verse 2, David sends servants to show kindness (הסד) to Hanun concerning his father. In verse 3, Hanun's princes say to Hanun, "Do you think, because David has sent comforters to you, that he is honoring your father?" The narrative identifies Hanun as Nahash's son these three times. Intriguingly, the narrative refers to Hanun as king only once (v. 1). Within these verses the narrative shows more interest in Hanun descending from Nahash than Hanun becoming a king.

Fokkelman has noticed that the narrative continually insists that Hanun is Nahash's son. He writes, "It is conspicuous that in 2c as well as in 2d Nahash is present as 'ābīw, i.e., he is seen merely as a relation to his son; cf. v. 3b 'ābīkā."[58] Though the narrative's focus on Hanun's descendancy from Nahash is "conspicuous," Fokkelman does not provide an explanation for why the author deems this important.

On the other hand, if this book is successfully able to argue that Samuel presents Nahash as a serpent within a larger serpent motif that is significant

57. See also Morrison, 2 Samuel, 126. A. A. Anderson also divides chapter 10 like Robinson, Fokkelman, and Morrison do, except he sees verse 19 as the chapter's conclusion. See Anderson, 2 Samuel, 146.

58. Fokkelman, King David, 43.

to the book's message, then emphasizing Hanun's parentage would be expected since Gen 3:15 speaks of both the serpent and its seed. Though not making this argument, Auld hints in this direction by writing the following about David sending comforters to Hanun in verse 2: "We are given no opportunity to find out the real purpose behind David's embassy, for Snake's son is persuaded by his advisers that David's solicitous concern for his Ammonite neighbor is far from genuine."[59] Hanun being the serpent's seed best explains the narrative's conspicuous emphasis on Hanun's sonship.

Two more pieces of evidence from the immediate context suggest that Hanun is the serpent's seed, both of which are conceptual.[60] The first is Hanun's hostility against Israel. We have already seen that Samuel has presented Goliath and Nahash as serpents. Both Goliath and Nahash expressed hostility and opposition against Israel. The text accentuates Hanun's hostility by mentioning that he responded aggressively not against a declaration of war but against David's act of kindness. Though David sent his servants to comfort Hanun in order to show "kindness" (חסד) because of the loss of Hanun's father, Hanun harshly responds in such a way that basically guarantees war. The narrative uses David's kind gesture in order to make Hanun's actions against Israel look all the more unnecessary and hostile.

The relationship between 2 Sam 9 and 10 also accentuates David's kindness and Hanun's unwarranted hostile behavior. As noted, in chapter 9 David shows "kindness" (חסד) to Mephibosheth, even though he is a descendant of Saul (9:1, 3). David showed genuine kindness to the descendant of his enemy. Since 10:2 informs the reader that Nahash was David's ally,[61]

59. Auld, *I & II Samuel*, 444.

60. In the following chapter we will consider how the various serpent passages work together in order to determine what is the significance of Samuel's serpent motif. To accomplish this, we will place each serpent passage within its larger narrative context. Upon doing this, we will see additional evidence from the larger context that suggests that Samuel presents Hanun as a serpent.

61. Scholars agree that Nahash was likely David's ally because David opposed Saul like Nahash did. Craig E. Morrison writes, "How had King Nahash expressed his loyalty (*ḥesed*) to King David? Nahash had been defeated by Saul after he threatened the people of Jabesh-Gilead, who remained ever loyal to Saul, their liberator, even after his death, secretly removing his corpse from the walls of Beth-shan (1 Sam 31:11–12)" (Morrison, *2 Samuel*, 128). Morrison's view is superior to McCarter's, who argues that "it seems probable" that Nahash's act of kindness to David was sending his son, Shobi, with provision for David's escape from Jerusalem in 2 Sam 17:27–29 (see McCarter, *II Samuel*, 270). There is no compelling reason to think that the events in chapter 10 occur historically after the events in 17:27–29. Certainly, the narrative has not been arranged to encourage McCarter's reading.

One may object that Hanun cannot be serpentine since David was an ally with his father and sought to continue that alliance with Hanun. Viewed in isolation these elements would be a significant challenge to this book's argument. With that said, pointing

Hanun's rejection of David's kindness is all the more baffling. Since David offered sincere kindness to his enemy's descendant, surely, he would offer sincere kindness to his ally's son. The contrasting responses to David's kindness in chapters 9 and 10 are intended to highlight Hanun's unwarranted hostility toward Israel. Though chapter 10 does not use the words "hostility" or "enmity," the narrative communicates that Hanun opposed Israel for no rational reason. The larger context is structured in such a way so as to emphasize Hanun's unnecessary aggression toward David and Israel. This expresses the seed of the serpent's enmity against the seed of the woman.

The second concept linking Hanun with serpentine characteristics is shameful nakedness. Hanun's opposition to Israel resulted in David's servants feeling shame in no small measure because of their forced nakedness. Instead of welcoming David's kindness, Hanun shaved portions of David's servants' beards, and he "cut off their garments in the middle, at their hips, and sent them away" (v. 4). By cutting off the garments of David's servants "in the middle at their hips," Hanun exposed their nakedness. Naturally, David's servants were "greatly ashamed" (נכלמים מאד). Anderson writes, "The cutting of the garments may well have had a similar significance, plus the additional humiliation: enforced indecent exposure!"[62]

Similar to the serpent in the garden, Hanun's opposition against God's people resulted in the shameful nakedness of David's servants. Though the man and woman were originally "naked and were not ashamed" (ולא יתבששו; Gen 2:25), after the serpent's deception their innocent nakedness was gone. Upon seeing their nakedness in this new light, they experienced shame. Noting these similarities, Ronning writes the following about the nations who oppose Israel in Samuel: "An indication of their identification as offspring of the serpent is accomplished by a word-play in 2 Samuel 10, where Hanun son of Nahash ('Snake') the Ammonite humiliates the servants of David by cutting off their garments, uncovering their nakedness like Ham and like the serpent of Genesis 3."[63] Like the serpent, Hanun expresses his opposition against God's people by shaming them with their

---

out that David tried to show kindness to Hanun does not derail this book's argument because it does not pay sufficient attention to the larger context. As this book is attempting to do, one must demonstrate how David's attempted kindness with Hanun functions within the larger context. Within 2 Sam 10 as a whole, David's attempted act of kindness toward Hanun reveals Hanun's irrational hostility against Israel. The author mentions David's previous alliance with Nahash for the purpose of demonstrating Hanun's serpentine characteristics.

62. Anderson, 2 Samuel, 147. Other commentators agree with Anderson's reading. See van Wijk-Bos, Reading Samuel, 188; Morrison, 2 Samuel, 129. McCarter even thinks that Hanun may have castrated David's servants (see McCarter, II Samuel, 270).

63. Ronning, "The Curse on the Serpent," 310.

nakedness. Hanun is the serpent's seed, and David's victory over this serpent and those aligned with him presents David in a messianic light.

4.3. NAHASH IN 2 SAMUEL 17

The final two times the narrative references individuals named Nahash is in 2 Sam 17:25, 27. In order to best understand why the narrative mentions individuals named Nahash in these verses we will consider (1) the story line up to and context of 17:25–27, (2) why the narrator mentions Nahash in verse 25, and (3) why the narrator mentions Nahash in verse 27.

4.3.1. The Story Line up to and Context of 2 Samuel 17:25–27

Immediately after David's victory over Hanun (ch. 10), David's troubles begin. The only thing the narrative presents as awful as David taking Bathsheba (11:1–5) is how he murders Uriah (vv. 6–27).[64] God disapproves of David's actions, and he promises that the "sword shall never depart from [David's] house" (12:10a). The Lord makes good on his promise, and his sword (i.e., judgment) on David's house begins. About this coming "sword," Morrison writes, "The rebellions of Absalom (2 Sam 15–19) and of Sheba son of Bichri (2 Sam 20) jump to mind."[65]

The narrative does prominently feature Absalom's rebellion. Second Samuel 15:1–6 shows how Absalom "stole the hearts of the men of Israel." In other words, Absalom deceived—like the serpent—Israel, and he opposed David.[66] Shortly thereafter, he caused David to flee from Jerusalem

---

64. On the significance of David "taking" (לקח) Uriah's wife see Janzen, "The Condemnation of David's 'Taking' in 2 Samuel 12:1–14," 209–20. Some think that when David took Bathsheba he raped her (see Garland and Garland, "Bathsheba's Story: Surviving Abuse and Loss," 25; Davidson, "Did King David Rape Bathsheba?," 81–95). Others argue that Bathsheba willingly seduced David (see Hertzberg, *I and II Samuel*, 310; Nicol, "The Alleged Rape of Bathsheba," 43–54). Finally, some think that Bathsheba did not intend to seduce David and that David did not rape Bathsheba, though he did have an affair with Bathsheba (see Abasili, "Was It Rape?," 1–15). The present author finds Abasili's proposal most convincing. This is the case because the text does not find fault with Bathsheba like one would expect if she was actively trying to commit adultery, and it presents David's interaction with Bathsheba very differently than it presents Amnon's rape of Tamar (cf. 2 Sam 11:1–4; 13:1–22).

65. Morrison, *2 Samuel*, 156.

66. Concerning the expression, "stole the hearts of the men of Israel," Morrison notes that the "NRSV renders the expression with 'to deceive,' a translation that may be closer to the meaning here, namely, that Absalom duped the people of Israel into trusting him" (Morrison, *2 Samuel*, 198). See also Ronning, "The Curse on the Serpent," 314.

(vv. 13–14). Though David was on the run, God's providence caused Absalom to heed Hushai's advice and not Ahithophel's—which bought David valuable time (17:5–15). Through secret communication, David heard that Ahithophel had advised that Absalom pursue David immediately (vv. 16–21). Then, David and his men crossed the Jordan (v. 22). The text (vv. 24–26) then gives four general statements: (1) David arrived at Mahanaim, (2) Absalom crossed the Jordan, (3) Absalom appointed Amasa as his general, and (4) Absalom's forces camped at Gilead. The narrative then provides background information about David's arrival at Mahanaim (vv. 27–29).[67] Samuel mentions the name "Nahash" one time in both the general verses (vv. 24–26) and the background verses (vv. 27–29).

4.3.2. Nahash in 2 Samuel 17:25

In order to best understand why the text mentions Nahash in 2 Sam 17:25, we must first consider a potential textual problem. We will then consider the various solutions offered. Lastly, we will explain the literary significance of Nahash being Amasa's grandfather.

4.3.2.1. The Textual Problem of Nahash in 2 Samuel 17:25

According to 2 Sam 17:25, Amasa's father was named Ithra,[68] and his mother was named Abigail.[69] Nahash was Abigail's father and thus Amasa's grandfather. This Nahash was certainly different than Hanun's father. This poses problems to the interpreter because 1 Chr 2:12–17 shows that Abigail is David's sister—which suggests that Abigail's father is actually Jesse. McCarter succinctly summarizes this problem and the textual data: "There is an apparent error, but there is no reliable textual witness to contradict it. As Zeruiah's sister, Abigail was Jesse's daughter (cf. 1 Chron 2:16). A number of Greek MSS, including LXX^LMN, actually read *iessai*, 'Jesse,' in place of *naas*,

---

67. For a similar way of understanding verses 24–29 see Fokkelman, *King David*, 233.

68. The MT reads that Amasa's father was named "Ithra the Israelite" (יתרא הישראלי). The MT of 1 Chr 2:17 differs. It understands Amasa's father to be "Jether the Ishmaelite" (יתר הישמעאלי). One's opinion on this text critical issue does not influence this section's argument.

69. Abigail, Amasa's mother, is probably not the Abigail of 1 Sam 25. McCarter explains, "It is unlikely that Ithra can be identified with Nabal, and this lessens the probability that the two Abigails were identical, though it remains possible" (McCarter, *II Samuel*, 394).

'Nahash,' here; but this is a result of secondary correction."[70] According to S. R. Driver, "It is uncertain how the two statements are to be reconciled."[71]

4.3.2.2. Proposed Solutions for the Textual Problem of Nahash in 2 Samuel 17:25

Scholars suggest three main solutions explaining why the text says "Nahash" was Abigail's father. Julius Wellhausen initially argued that a scribe accidentally inserted the name "Nahash" from 2 Sam 17:27 into verse 25.[72] In Wellhausen's view, Nahash is not Abigail's father or Amasa's grandfather. This view struggles because there is little reason why a scribe would insert a word from verse 27 back into verse 25.

Ronning proposes that Nahash is possibly Nahshon, David's ancestor (cf. Ruth 4:20; 1 Chr 2:10–11). He reasons that Nahshon was part of the exodus generation that opposed Moses's leadership. Now Nahshon's descendant is once again opposing the Lord's chosen leader (i.e., David) by joining Absalom's rebellion. Ronning also suggests that by linking Amasa to Nahash, the author suggests that Amasa and all who oppose David are the serpent's seed.[73] Though the next section will seek to demonstrate that the Samuel narrative casts Amasa as the serpent's seed, Ronning fails to convince that the name "Nahash" is supposed call to mind Nahshon because the name Nahshon never appears in Samuel.

The majority view of scholars is that Nahash was an earlier husband of Jesse's wife,[74] though some maintain the possibility that Nahash could be a female's name.[75] If one reads Nahash as a female, she would be Jesse's sec-

---

70. McCarter, *II Samuel*, 392.

71. Driver, *Notes on the Hebrew Text of the Books of Samuel*, 326.

72. Wellhausen, *Der Text der Bücher Samuelis Untersucht*, 201. Driver notes that Wellhausen later changed his view because Wellhausen thought that "greater weight should be attached to [2 Sam 17:25] than to [1 Chronicles]" (Driver, *Notes on the Hebrew Text of the Books of Samuel*, 326).

73. Ronning does not adequately explain if he thinks Nahash (נחש) is a corrupted form of Nahshon (נחשׁון) or if he thinks the name "Nahash" is supposed to cause the reader to consider Nahshon and thereby have a double meaning. Ronning also leaves open the possibility that Nahash is Jesse's wife's first husband. For this discussion see Ronning, "The Curse on the Serpent," 314–15.

74. For a couple scholars who believe that Nahash might be Jesse's wife's former husband, see McCarter, *II Samuel*, 394; Hertzberg, *I and II Samuel*, 357.

75. For one scholar who leaves open the possibility that Nahash is a woman's name, see Driver, *Notes on the Hebrew Text of the Books of Samuel*, 326. Against this, Wellhausen states that Nahash is not a woman's name (Wellhausen, *Der Text Der Bücher Samuelis Untersucht*, 201).

ond wife. If one reads Nahash as the husband of Jesse's first wife, this would explain how Abigail's father is Nahash and David's father is Jesse.

4.3.2.3. *The Literary Purpose of Nahash in 2 Samuel 17:25*

Though the majority view is superior to the others, harmonizing 1 Chr 2:13–17 and 2 Sam 17:25 does not explain why the narrator provided Amasa's lineage. Fokkelman suggests that the narrator lists Amasa's genealogy in order to show that Joab and Amasa are cousins. Pairing these two together anticipates their rivalry and Amasa's later death (20:10).[76] Fokkelman is correct, but 17:25 could have shown that Amasa and Joab are cousins and paired them against each other without mentioning Abigail's father, Nahash. Apparently, the text desires to do more than show that Amasa and Joab are cousins paired against each other. The text desires to associate Amasa with Nahash.

The most likely explanation for why the narrative strangely introduces an otherwise unknown individual named Nahash is to present Amasa as a seed of a serpent. We already noted that 17:25 pairs Amasa and Joab together because it anticipates Joab murdering Amasa in 20:10–12. Given Amasa's serpentine descendancy, it is no surprise that the narrative also casts Amasa as a serpent in his death.

In 20:10–12 Joab murders Amasa by striking Amasa's stomach (חמש). Amasa's entrails then fall on the ground. While the soldiers follow Joab to kill Sheba, the son of Bichri (v. 11), they could not help but stop to watch Amasa rolling (מתגלל) in his blood on the ground (v. 12). A few things about this scene deserve further consideration.

Within Samuel, four passages contain a man striking (נכה) another man in the belly (חמש) with the result that he dies.[77] Of these four instances, the deaths of Asahel, Abner, and Amasa have significant similarities and may be viewed as parallel with each other.

These three narratives likely parallel each other because one of the sons of Zeruiah—Abishai, Joab, and Asahel—appear in each of these instances (2:23; 3:27; 20:10). As mentioned, in each of these instances the text explicitly states that the person was struck (נכה) in the stomach (חמש). Also, in every passage the one who was struck "died" (וימת). Even though Fokkelman and van Wijk-Bos only see Joab murdering Abner as a parallel with Joab murdering Amasa, there is a link between Abner striking Asahel and

76. Fokkelman, *King David*, 234.
77. See 2 Sam 2:23; 3:27; 4:6; 20:10.

Joab striking Amasa that is not present when Joab kills Abner.[78] All who came to where Asahel had died "stood still" (ויעמדו; 2:23), just as the people who saw Amasa's body "stopped" (ועמד) after Joab killed him (20:12).

It is on account of these similarities that the deaths of Asahel, Abner, and Amasa parallel each other, and it is on account of these parallels that two features in Amasa's death stand out. First, only in Amasa's death account does it mention that his internal organs (מעיו) fall to the ground (20:10). Since Joab struck Amasa's belly, we know that these organs are his belly parts. Amasa died with his belly parts on the ground. Second, only Amasa's death account describes Amasa's actions immediately after the killer delivers the fatal blow. When Joab struck Amasa, the text mentions that he rolled around in his blood on the ground (20:12). Contrasting with Amasa's vivid and gory death, when Abner struck Asahel, the narrative simply says that he fell and died (2:23). Likewise, when Joab struck Abner, the text simply states that "he died" (3:27).

Since these three texts parallel one another, it is worth asking why Amasa's death narrative contains the extra details of his belly parts falling to the ground and him rolling around on the ground while he dies. Are these differences between Amasa and the others' death merely stylistic, or is there a literary purpose for including them, and if so, what is that literary purpose?

We have already seen evidence that Samuel presents those who are associated with the name "Nahash" as serpentine, and we have also seen that Amasa descends from one named "Nahash." Could Amasa's serpentine parentage explain these additional details that are absent in parallel passages? If Amasa's death contains serpentine allusions, then this would further suggest that the author of Samuel uses the name Nahash to foster serpentine associations and that Amasa is a seed of a serpent.

It is possible to see serpentine elements in Amasa's death in 2 Sam 20:10–12. God judged the serpent by making it move about with its "belly" (גהון) being on the dusty ground. Furthermore, the serpent's defeat would come with its belly being on the ground (Gen 3:14–15). It is to associate Amasa with the serpent that the text mentions that his belly parts spilled to the ground. Amasa's defeat coincides with his belly being on the ground. This additional detail not found in the parallel passages connects Amasa's death to the serpent's judgment.

Identifying Amasa as a seed of the serpent also explains why the author felt the need to inform the reader that Amasa died rolling in his blood. One who has delivered a fatal blow to a serpent knows how they roll around

---

78. Fokkelman, *King David*, 327–28; van Wijk-Bos, *Reading Samuel*, 233.

on the ground immediately before they die. Harry W. Greene, a professor of ecology and evolutionary biology at Cornell University and a herpetologist, writes in his book that dying snakes are normally "twisted in death throes or jumbled in a heap."[79] Amasa's death imitates how snakes die.[80]

The most plausible explanation for why the narrative portrays Amasa as a serpent is because he aligned with Absalom instead of David. We have already briefly noted that Absalom is serpent-like because he "stole the hearts of the people" by deceiving them. We have also seen within Samuel that those who actively oppose Israel's well-being are cast as serpents (e.g., Nahash, Goliath, Hanun). Amasa opposed David and Israel by following the serpentine deceiver. Amasa's union with Absalom explains why after Joab strikes Amasa's belly, he immediately says, "Whoever favors Joab, and whoever is for David, let him follow Joab" (20:11). Thus, Amasa's death scene brings together both Amasa's serpentine characteristics and his disloyalty to David. For these reasons the narrative mentions that Amasa's grandfather's name is Nahash and that Amasa died with his belly on the ground rolling around like a fatally wounded snake. Amasa is the serpent's seed, and one can infer based on Amasa's connection with Absalom, that Samuel also understands Absalom to be serpentine.

4.3.3. Nahash in 2 Samuel 17:27

Immediately after the text finishes detailing the general information about Amasa (v. 25) and Absalom's encampment (v. 26), Shobi, the son of Nahash, appears (v. 27). Instead of opposing Israel's best interests like his father and brother previously did,[81] Shobi supports David as he flees from Absalom. Shobi is the opposite of his two serpent relatives. One must not identify Shobi with the serpent because he lacks the unifying feature among the serpent and all its seed—hostility against the woman's seed (cf. Gen 3:15). This, of course, is highly ironic because Shobi is a descendant from Nahash.

79. Greene, *Snakes: The Evolution of Mystery in Nature*, 275.

80. It is also noteworthy that this study has not been able to demonstrate textual serpentine links with either Abner and Asahel. Concerning Abner, Asahel, and Amasa's parallel deaths, it is no coincidence that Samuel only connects Amasa with an individual named Nahash and that only Amasa's death is presented as the death of a serpent.

81. Concerning Shobi, Driver writes, "[He is the] son of Nahash, and consequently brother of Hanun (10, 1), whom David, after his capture of Rabbah (12, 29–31), had presumably made governor over the Ammonites" (Driver, *Notes on the Hebrew Text of the Books of Samuel*, 326).

To what effect is this irony? According to Jeremy Camery-Hoggart, one of irony's functions is that it "forces the reader to decision."[82] In this instance, the irony of Shobi supporting David while Amasa opposes David forces the reader to decide which descendant of Nahash is the true serpent. We have seen that Amasa is the serpent.

Thus, this text makes an important point about the serpent's seed. One is fundamentally a seed of the serpent not because of their ethnicity or parentage, but because of their actions. Shobi is not the serpent's seed because he supports David and Israel's well-being. Amasa is of the serpent's seed because he opposes Israel and the main protagonist within the flow of Samuel, who in this case is David. The irony of Shobi supporting David forces the reader to view Amasa's rebellion against David as all the more egregious.

4.4. SUMMARY OF NAHASH IN SAMUEL

This chapter considered each time the Samuel narrative mentions the name Nahash. We have concluded that Samuel routinely presents those named Nahash and those associated with Nahash as the serpent or the serpent's seed. In 1 Sam 11, the narrative suggested that Nahash was serpentine because of how Samuel and Judges work together to cast Saul in a messianic light. Casting Saul in a messianic light increased the likelihood that Nahash is serpentine because we have already seen that Gen 3:14–15 anticipates the seed of the woman will conquer the serpent.

The prophet Samuel then told Israel that they should not have chosen a king because they feared Nahash (12:12). The prophet suggested that God would have defeated Nahash as he defeated Egypt and the foreign nations within Judges. We concluded that 1 Sam 12:12 does not provide evidence for or against this book's claim that Samuel contains a serpent motif. The point of 1 Sam 12:12 was simply that God would have defeated Nahash without a king if Israel would have trusted in him.

In 2 Sam 10, Hanun, the son of Nahash, needlessly opposes Israel. We noted that the text focuses more on Hanun being Nahash's son and less on Hanun being the new king over the sons of Ammon. We understood this unlikely focus to indicate that Hanun is the serpent's offspring. Hanun's pointless aggression against Israel further demonstrated that Hanun exhibits the hostility that the seed of the serpent shows toward God's anointed one and Israel. Lastly, Hanun's opposition expressed itself by shaming David's

---

82. Camery-Hoggatt, *Irony in Mark's Gospel*, 4. In his context, Camery-Hoggatt is talking about irony's effect on a sociological group, but his point still pertains to this book. Irony forces the reader to make a decision.

servants by exposing their nakedness. This echoed how when the serpent opposed God by deceiving the first man and woman, they felt shame over their nakedness.

Samuel last mentions individuals named Nahash in 2 Sam 17:25, 27. In these two verses the narrative ironically portrays Amasa as a serpent and not Shobi, even though he is the son of Nahash, the previous king of the sons of Ammon. The narrator mentions that Amasa's grandfather's name is Nahash in order to foster serpentine associations with Amasa. The text then confirmed these associations by presenting Amasa as a serpent when Joab murdered him. The narrative did this by mentioning how Amasa's inward belly parts fell to the ground after Joab struck his belly in order to remind the reader that God said the serpent would suffer defeat while its belly would be on the ground. After Joab struck Amasa, Amasa then rolled around on the ground like fatally wounded snakes do. We concluded that Samuel's author decided to portray Amasa as the serpent's seed because he—unlike Shobi—opposed David by aligning with Absalom. We inferred that the author also understood Absalom to be a serpent based on his connection to Amasa. Supporting this inference was Absalom's practice of deceiving the hearts of the men of Israel similar to how the serpent deceived Eve.

5

THE SERPENT WITHIN SAMUEL

THUS FAR, WE HAVE established the first half of this book's thesis by demonstrating that a serpent motif is present within Samuel. Nahash, Goliath, Hanun, Amasa, Absalom and those aligned with these figures are all serpentine. Having established the presence of this motif, we are now able to begin to determine what the significance of this motif might be within Samuel and thereby accomplish the second half of this book's thesis.

To accomplish this, we must determine how the various serpent stories relate. By considering each serpent story within its larger context, we will argue that what unifies these serpent stories is that they all demonstrate that neither Saul nor David is the Messiah. Samuel primarily does this by raising messianic expectations whenever Saul or David defeats a serpent. Then after one of these kings slays a serpent, one of two things happen. Either the narrative immediately presents that king negatively to show that he is not the Messiah, or the narrative immediately presents that king positively suggesting to the reader that perhaps the king is the Messiah. We will see that the narrative presents Saul and David far worse after they defeat Nahash (1 Sam 11) and Hanun (2 Sam 10), and that the narrative presents David positively after he defeats Goliath (1 Sam 17). At the chapter's conclusion, it will be apparent that Samuel's serpent-slayers are not the longed-for seed of the woman from Gen 3:15 who will decisively defeat the serpent.

We will seek to demonstrate that each serpent story that we have identified contributes to the book's messianism under three headings: (1) the

Hanun story, (2) the Nahash, Goliath, Absalom, and Amasa stories, and (3) a summary of Samuel's serpent motif.

5.1. THE LITERARY FUNCTION OF THE HANUN STORY

As mentioned, this chapter will seek to relate the various serpent stories to one another in order to demonstrate that they are part of a coherent literary strategy. In order to best accomplish this, we will first consider the chapters immediately following David's victory over Hanun in 2 Sam 10 noting similarities between Samuel and Genesis along the way. After this, we will consider the significance of David's fall in light of the similarities between Samuel and Genesis.[1]

5.1.1. The Details of David's Fall after Defeating Hanun

Scholars uniformly agree that the narrative begins to portray David far more negatively starting in 2 Sam 11. Meir Steinberg writes,

> Note the location of chapter 11. On the one hand, it is preceded by a consistently favorable presentation of David as a God-fearing, successful king. On the other hand, it is followed by a long chain of mishaps and disasters: the aftermath of the Bathsheba affair, Tamar's rape and Amnon's murder, Absalom's usurpation of the throne, the Sheba ben Bichri rebellion, the three-year famine, and the census followed by the plague.[2]

Clearly, the narrative presents David negatively after he defeats Hanun. In order to be able to determine why this is the case, it is important to understand how the narrative depicts David's fall.

David's fall transparently begins in 2 Sam 11 with the David and Bathsheba account. A few scholars have noted that language within this story alludes to the first woman's sin in the garden. Phillip G. Camp observes that just as Eve "saw" (ראה) that the fruit was "good" (טוב) for food, that it was a delight to the eyes, and that she "took" it (לקח; Gen 3:6), so too David "saw" (ראה) that Bathsheba was "beautiful" (2 Sam 11:2; טוב). Then, David

---

1. Multiple scholars besides those we will briefly mention have observed significant correspondence between Samuel and Genesis. See Sean M. McDonough, "'And David Was Old, Advanced in Years,'" 128–31; Biddle, "Ancestral Motifs in 1 Samuel 25," 617–38; Rudman, "The Patriarchal Narratives in the Books of Samuel," 239–49.

2. Sternberg, *The Poetics of Biblical Narrative*, 528–29, n. 30.

"took" (לקח) her through the messengers that he sent (v. 4).[3] Also, we have already seen these same terms—"see," "good/beautiful," and "take"—appear in Josh 7:21. In that text Howard noted that the narrative likens Achan's sin to Eve's sin.

Brueggemann also sees Gen 3 as the background for 2 Sam 11:1–6. He notes four similarities between David's sin and the sin of Gen 3: David along with the first man and woman are all (1) attracted to what is forbidden, (2) aware that they have done wrong immediately after the sin, (3) recipients of God pronouncing judgment on their house, and (4) partially helped in the midst of their despair by the birth of a son (i.e., Solomon and Seth).[4]

Camp mentions other similarities between these texts. Both texts show that the sinner has a conversation immediately before they sin. Eve spoke with the serpent to see if it was wrong to eat of the fruit (Gen 3:1–5), and David asked his messengers to whom Bathsheba was married (2 Sam 11:3). Both texts show that the sinners attempted to cover up their sin, as well (Gen 3:7–10; 2 Sam 11:6–27). In both instances, God reveals the sin (Gen 3:11–13; 2 Sam 12:9).[5]

Bill T. Arnold also recognizes in the account of David and Bathsheba a progression similar to that of Eve's sin. He writes that David's sins "illustrate and complement the origin and progression of temptation and sin (from perception and deception to covetousness, transgression, and death) as we learn from Gen 3:1–7."[6] Noting only some of the shared language and similar concepts between Gen 3 and 2 Sam 11, Brueggemann writes, "The linguistic parallels are strong enough to suggest more than coincidental similarity."[7] By using the first woman's sin as the background for David's sin, Samuel associates David with Eve. David has repeated Eve's sin in the garden.

As Sternberg pointed out, David's problems do not stop after the David, Uriah, and Bathsheba narrative. Immediately following that narrative—which covers chapters 11–12—Amnon rapes Tamar (13:14). Though Samuel only explicitly mentions Amnon raping Tamar in one verse (v. 14), this atrocity dominates chapters 13–14. After planning and carrying out the rape (13:1–14), Tamar mourns as a desolate woman (vv. 15–20), and David is angry (v. 21). Because of Amnon's actions, Tamar's brother, Absalom, plots and carries out Amnon's murder (vv. 22–29). David then hears about

---

3. Camp, "David's Fall," 153–54. For a similar argument see Robinson, *Let Us Be Like the Nations*, 205–06.

4. Brueggemann, *David and His Theologian*, 6–10.

5. Camp, "David's Fall," 153–57.

6. Arnold, *1 & 2 Samuel*, 539.

7. Brueggemann, *David and His Theologian*, 8, n. 32.

Absalom murdering Amnon (vv. 30–33), and Absalom flees (vv. 34–39). In chapter 14, Joab sends the wise woman from Tekoa to speak to David about Absalom murdering Amnon. The woman describes Absalom murdering Amnon as though they were her sons. She says, "Your servant had two sons, and they quarreled with one another in the field. There was no one to separate them, and one struck the other and killed him" (v. 6).

Scholars notice that by mentioning one brother murdering another brother in a field the wise woman from Tekoa compares Absalom murdering Amnon to Cain murdering Abel (cf. Gen 4:8).[8] Brueggemann writes, "In the Amnon-Absalom story, the primary point of contact with the Cain-Abel story is in 2 Sam 14:6."[9] Brueggemann notes three main similarities between the Cain-Abel and Amnon-Absalom stories besides the link of one brother killing another brother in a field. These three similarities are (1) there is fear for the life of the guilty one (2 Sam 14:11; Gen 4:14), (2) the guilty brother is guaranteed his life by the judge of the case (2 Sam 14:11b; Gen 4:15), and (3) the murderous brother experiences an exile (2 Sam 14:24; Gen 4:16).[10]

Other scholars agree that Samuel links Absalom murdering Amnon to Cain murdering Abel. Though Larry L. Lyke notes that 2 Sam 14:6 has closer vocabulary to Deut 25:11, he still states, "Thematically and in terms of imagery, the closest analogue in the Hebrew Bible to 2 Sam 14.6 is the Cain and Abel episode."[11] J. Blenkinsopp states that there is "close parallelism between the historical narrative . . . of Gen. iv 1–16" and the wise woman of Tekoa's account of Absalom murdering Amnon.[12] In this way the

8. Rolf August Carlson suggests that 2 Sam 10–12 corresponds to Deut 22:22 more so than Gen 3. He also argues that Deut 22:28–29 serves as the primary background for 2 Sam 13–14 and not the Cain and Abel story. Even if Carlson is correct, that does not nullify the links between 2 Sam 11 and Gen 3, nor does it nullify the links we will see between 2 Sam 13–14 and Gen 4. Despite Carlson seeing Deuteronomy as the organizing schema for 2 Sam 10–20, he still states, "The 'fratricide' described by the wise woman of Tekoa on the command of Joab (2 Sam. 14: 5 ff.) refers expressly to the story of Cain, and his murder of Abel in the 'field' (שדה), v. 6, cf. Gen 4: 8" (see Carlson, "David, the Chosen King," 166, 181).

9. Brueggemann, *David and His Theologian*, 10. Besides seeing the Bathsheba narrative allude to the man and the woman's first sin and also the Amnon-Absalom story allude to the Cain-Abel story, Brueggemann understands the Absalom-David stories to allude to Noah's flood and the Solomon-David narrative in 1 Kgs 1–2 to allude to the Tower of Babel (Brueggemann, *David and His Theologian*, 13–20). The present author finds the latter two suggested links uncompelling.

10. Brueggemann, *David and His Theologian*, 12–13.

11. Lyke, *King David with the Wise Woman of Tekoa*, 88–89.

12. Blenkinsopp, "2 Sam. XI and the Yahwist Corpus," 51.

narrative casts Absalom murdering Amnon as a repeat of Cain murdering Abel.[13]

Immediately after David defeats Hanun, David takes Bathsheba, and he arranges Uriah's death. This story covered 2 Sam 11–12. Immediately after the Bathsheba account, Amnon rapes Tamar. Then Absalom murdered Amnon. This Tamar, Amnon, Absalom account covered chapters 13–14. Two things are evident from chapters 11–14. First, David is a sinner, and his house is under God's judgment. Second, the narrative in 2 Sam 11–12 patterns David's sin after the first woman's sin from Gen 3, and 2 Sam 13–14 patterns Absalom's murder of Amnon after Cain's murder of Abel from Gen 4. In the next section we will consider the significance of why the narrative links the sins of David and his house to the sins from Gen 3–4.

5.1.2. The Messianic Significance of David's Fall after Defeating Hanun

Along with other scholars, we have noted that immediately following David's victory over Hanun, the narrative presents him negatively.[14] In order to determine why the narrative begins to present David negatively, Sternberg's advice is worth following. While specifically attempting to explain why 2 Sam 11 and the following chapters begin to present David negatively, he writes, "Amidst unsettling retrospection and suspenseful prospection, the interpreter must yet go back again and again to the turning point in an attempt to uncover some principle that will make sense of all these incongruous developments."[15] Despite this helpful advice, Sternberg fails to point out such a principle at the "turning point" (i.e., 2 Sam 10–11) that explains why the narrative begins to present David negatively.

As we attempt to find something at the narrative's turning point that will explain why the narrative begins to present David as a sinner, we must first establish the context. Fokkelman notes that David's war against the sons of Ammon frames the David and Bathsheba account (11:2—12:25) because

13. As noted in chapter 2 of this book, Genesis presents Cain as the seed of the serpent. Since Absalom murders Amnon like Cain murdered Abel, this further increases the likelihood that the Samuel narrative understands Absalom to be serpentine. That Amnon parallels Abel reveals that things are worse in David's house than they were in the first man and woman's.

14. Brettler also concurs that the Samuel narrative begins to present David in a decisively negative way starting in 2 Sam 11. See Brettler, *The Creation of History in Ancient Israel*, 97.

15. Sternberg, *The Poetics of Biblical Narrative*, 357.

the war begins in 2 Sam 10 and ends in 12:26–31.[16] This suggests that one should not consider David's fall in chapter 11 without remembering the war against Hanun and the sons of Ammon in chapter 10. Thus, one is warranted to ask how does David's victory over Hanun in chapter 10 relates to his fall in chapter 11.

Oddly enough, even commentators practicing literary criticism—Fokkelman excluded—do not ask how chapters 10 and 11 relate. For example, Garsiel writes, "Chapter 11 is only half of the story. It tells of David's sin, with a focus upon the stages of his degeneration. . . . The second stage of the story, 2 Samuel 12, describes Nathan's rebuke and David's contrition and submission to God."[17] Other scholars considering the text's redaction history fail to ask this question because they believe that 11:2—12:25 was originally an independent document.[18]

How then does chapter 10 relate to chapters 11–12? Fokkelman suggests that the reason the war against the sons of Ammon frames the David-Uriah-Bathsheba narrative is to show that David's palace has become a "war episode." He writes, "The cruelty, the atrocities, and killing, again and again the main features of the theatre of war, have here 'found their way inside' and taken over David's court."[19] For Fokkelman, the connection between chapter 10 and chapters 11–12 demonstrate that just as David's troops are at war against the sons of Ammon, so too David is waging a war within his own kingdom.

Fokkelman's assessment is not the whole story. We have already seen that Hanun, being the son of Nahash, is serpentine. Thus, when David defeats Hanun, he comes off as though he might be the prophesied royal, eschatological serpent-slaying seed of the woman from Gen 3:14–15. This is especially the case since David has already defeated another serpent, Goliath. Immediately after defeating Hanun, the offspring of a serpent, one

16. Fokkelman, *King David*, 41.

17. Garsiel, "The Story of David and Bathsheba," 246.

18. Fokkelman writes, "What is special is that the account of war with its third stage (11:1 + 12:26–31) is positioned about the famous story of David's private life, the notorious triangle of David-Bathsheba-Uriah. We must think through all the consequences of this composition. Most commentaries, however, shirk this duty with the diachronic explanation that 11:2—12:25 was originally independent" (Fokkelman, *King David*, 41). Brueggemann shows the division interpreters see between chapters 10 and 11 when he writes, "It is conventional to treat 2 Samuel 9–10 as the beginning of the Succession Narrative, but these two chapters are commonly regarded as preliminary, not very crucial to the narrative, and not very interesting. The real action, according to most interpreters, begins in 2 Sam 11 with Uriah and Bathsheba" (Brueggemann, *David's Truth*, 42).

19. Fokkelman, *King David*, 94.

should wonder if David is the fulfillment of Gen 3:15. To address this suspicion, the narrative intentionally presents David negatively to show that he is neither the Messiah that the book of Samuel anticipates nor the seed of the woman from Genesis.

Within Samuel one can determine that David's fall in 2 Sam 11 demonstrates that he is not the Messiah because 1 Sam 2:35 anticipates that the Messiah would be upright and one who faithfully honors the Lord. Most translations obscure this point though. The ESV translates the verse to read, "And I will raise up for myself a faithful priest, who shall do according to what is in my heart and in my mind. And I will build him a sure house, and he shall go in and out before my anointed forever (בניתי לו בית נאמן והתהלך לפני־משיחי כל־הימים)."

Karl Deenick has challenged this translation by arguing that the preposition "before" (לִפְנֵי) should be slightly repointed to have the 1 singular pronominal suffix—"before me" (לְפָנַי).[20] This repointing produces the following translation of verse 35b: "And I will build him a sure house, and my anointed shall go in and out before me forever." In Deenick's article, he demonstrates that this translation is grammatically possible and contextually probable.[21]

Deenick's translation has the effect of making the anointed one the same person as the faithful priest whom God will raise up. Since we have

20. Deenick, "Priest and King or Priest-King in 1 Samuel 2:35," 325–39.

21. Walter C. Kaiser Jr. translates 1 Sam 2:35b to say, "And I will build him a sure house, and it shall go in and out before my anointed one forever" (see Kaiser, *The Messiah in the Old Testament*, 76). Deenick's translation is preferable to Kaiser's because Deenick notes that the לפני in verse 30 has the pronominal suffix and is almost certainly parallel to the לפני in verse 35 (see Deenick, "Priest and King or Priest-king in 1 Samuel 2:35," 330). Normal Hebrew word order (verb + subject + object + modifiers) seems to initially favor Kaiser's reading over Deenick's. However, Deenick's defense is worth quoting at length: "According to the grammars it is not at all unusual that a suffixed preposition should occur immediately after the verb and before the subject; in fact, it appears to be the norm. Joüon writes, 'There is a marked tendency for a suffixed preposition to occupy the position immediately after the verb, even before the subject. . . . Despite occasional deviations, the pattern seems well established, so much so that departure from it could suggest some emphasis.' Similarly van der Merwe et al. note, 'Constituents that are expressed by means of a preposition + pronominal suffix . . . stand as close to the verb as possible.' In other words, according to the grammars the reason that לפני occurs before משיחי is not necessarily because the two are in construct relationship, but may simply be because the suffixed preposition prefers the position immediately following the verb. Thus, even though the expression והתהלך משיחי לפני may have avoided the ambiguity, nevertheless, according to the grammars, it would have been extremely unusual" (Deenick, "Priest and King or Priest-king in 1 Samuel 2:35," 326). Nevertheless, even if Kaiser's reading is correct, the argument below is not significantly affected because both Kaiser and Deenick's translations of 1 Sam 2:35 understand the anointed one to be the same individual as the faithful priest.

already seen in chapter 4 of this book that the anointed one in 1 Sam 2:10 is the Messiah, it is likely that the anointed one in verse 35 is also the Messiah. Deenick argues that this messianic reading of verse 35 makes the most sense within the whole of Samuel. The following seeks to demonstrate the difficulties in identifying the faithful priest with Zadok, Samuel, a priestly line, or David.

Most scholars incorrectly believe that the narrative understands Zadok to be the priest in 1 Sam 2:35 because of a misreading of 1 Kgs 2:26–35.[22] First Samuel 2:27–36 predicts that Eli and his father's house will cease serving as priests, and it also anticipates that a priest will arise who is not from either Eli or Eli's father's house. After Solomon expels Abiathar from the priesthood in 1 Kgs 2:26, the following verse (v. 27) plainly cites the prophecy we are currently examining from 1 Sam 2, and it says that this expulsion fulfills the prophecy that Eli's house would cease functioning as priests. What is critical to note is that when Zadok replaces Abiathar in 1 Kgs 2:35, the Kings passage does not say that Zadok is the priest of 1 Sam 2:35. First Kings 2:26–35 explicitly presents Abiathar leaving the priesthood as a fulfillment of the man of God's prophecy against Eli and his house, but it does not explicitly state that Zadok is the faithful priest from 1 Sam 2:35–36.

Indeed, Deenick lists many reasons Zadok cannot be the fulfillment of 1 Sam 2:35–36,[23] not the least of which is that God says he will cut off the house of Eli and the house of Eli's father from serving as priests. In context, Eli's father is almost certainly Aaron. Some think he is Moses,[24] but Eli descended from Aaron and not Moses.[25] First Samuel 2:27 says that God revealed himself to Eli's father's house while this father's house was in Egyptian slavery (v. 27). Since Aaron lived during the time of Israel's slavery under Egypt, he fits this criterion nicely. First Samuel 12:8 corroborates this, saying, "When Jacob went into Egypt, and the Egyptians oppressed them, then your fathers cried out to the LORD and the LORD sent Moses and Aaron, who brought your fathers out of Egypt and made them dwell in this place."

22. See Tsumura, *The First Book of Samuel*, 170; McCarter, *I Samuel*, 92–93; Brueggemann, *First and Second Samuel*, 23–24.

23. Deenick, "Priest and King or Priest-king in 1 Samuel 2:35," 327–28.

24. See McCarter, *I Samuel*, 89, 93; Brueggemann, *First and Second Samuel*, 23.

25. Deenick ("Priest and King or Priest-king in 1 Samuel 2:35," 329) following Gordon J. Keddie (*Dawn of a Kingdom*, 48, n. 8) demonstrates that Eli descended from Aaron and not from Moses: "Ahimelech was 'a descendant of Ithamar' (1 Chronicles 24:3). Ahimelech's father was Ahitub, the son of Phinehas, who was, of course, the son of Eli (1 Samuel 22:9; 14:3)." That Eli descends from Aaron and not from Moses makes it incredibly unlikely that the "father" mentioned in 1 Sam 2:27–31 is Moses.

First Samuel 2:28 also says that God chose Eli's father out of all the tribes of Israel to be his priest. As such, this father would go up to God's altar, burn incense, wear an ephod, and his house was supposed to present offerings to God on behalf of the people of Israel forever (vv. 28, 30). Deenick notices that the passage contains a transparent "reference . . . to the promise of perpetual priesthood given to Aaron (Exod 29:9) and to Aaron's appointment to wear an ephod (cf. Exod 28:1–35; Lev 8:7)."[26] Within 1 Sam 2:27–36, Eli's father is Aaron, and God promises to eventually remove the priesthood from Eli and Aaron's house because Eli has "honored" (כבד) his sons more than the Lord (vv. 29, 31).

It is through Eli's failure to properly honor the Lord with respect to his sons that the author alludes to Lev 10:1–3 and thereby connects the priestly failure of Eli's house with the priestly failure of Aaron's house. The Lord promising to kill Eli's two priestly sons on the same day for Eli's failure to "honor" (כבד) him reminds the reader of Lev 10. In that chapter the Lord kills Aaron's two priestly sons on the same day for failing to "honor" (כבד) him (Lev 10:1–3). From its inception, the Aaronic priesthood has failed to honor the Lord, and Eli's house has perpetuated this problem. By alluding to the Aaronic priesthood's failure, Lev 10:1–3 serves as the background for 1 Sam 2:27–36. These connections further confirm that Aaron is Eli's father within this passage. According to 1 Sam 2:27–36, God will raise up a new priest to replace Eli and Aaron's priestly houses. Therefore, this priest will not come from Aaron's line. As opposed to Aaron's house and Eli's house, this priest and his house will honor God. Since Zadok descends from Aaron, he cannot be the faithful priest of 1 Sam 2:35–36.

Others argue that Samuel, the prophet, is the faithful priest.[27] This is not possible though because God will give the faithful priest of verse 35 a faithful/enduring house (i.e., faithful/enduring descendants).[28] Samuel's de-

26. Deenick, "Priest and King or Priest-king in 1 Samuel 2:35," 328–29.

27. See Polzin, *Samuel and the Deuteronomist*, 42–44; Eslinger, *Kingship of God in Crisis a Close Reading*, 138–40.

28. Translations normally understand God's promise of a "faithful house" (בית נאמן) in 1 Sam 2:35 to merely be a promise to give the faithful priest a family of descendants lasting for many generations (cf. NLT, ESV, NIV, CSB, NASB, and NET). In context, it is better to understand the word "נאמן" to mean not just endurance but to also have moral overtones. The reason God promised that Eli and his house would cease to endure as priests (vv. 31–34) is because they had previously failed to glorify him (vv. 29–30). Glorifying God leads to an enduring house. This means that spiritually faithful houses endure while spiritually faithless houses cease. Thus, Eli and his house's root problem is not that God destined them to perish from the priesthood. Rather, their root problem is that they failed to honor the Lord, and the fruit of this problem is the downfall of Eli's house. Since Eli and his house's root problem is that they failed to honor the Lord (i.e., live faithfully), therefore it follows that the solution to this problem is a new, faithful

scendants were not faithful. His two sons were so wicked that Israel did not want them to be their judges (8:1–5).[29] Samuel having two rebellious sons is meant to remind the reader of Eli and his two rebellious sons. It was on account of Eli and his two wicked sons that God promised in the first place to raise up a faithful priest who would have a faithful house. Since Samuel's two sons fair no better than Eli's two sons, this suggests that the need for the faithful priest and his faithful house has not yet been fulfilled. In addition, the narrative calls Samuel a "faithful/established prophet" and not a faithful priest (3:20).

C. F. Keil and F. Delitzch understand the faithful priest of 1 Sam 2:35 to be all of the priests starting from Samuel and culminating in the Messiah.[30] This view struggles to convince though because "few of the particular promises in 2:35 are specifically connected with either Samuel or Zadok."[31] Also, those priests prior to the coming of the Messiah were of Aaronic lineage, and so they would fail to be the faithful priest for the same reason that Zadok did. Moreover, many of the priests prior to the Messiah were not faithful (cf. Hos 5:1–2; Mal 2:1–9).

Lastly, Daniel S. Diffey has argued that David is the faithful priest of 1 Sam 2:35.[32] Diffey argues this because the narrative presents David as a "faithful" man (1 Sam 22:14) who is after God's own heart (13:14) much like the promised priest will be faithful and do according to what is in God's heart and soul (2:35).[33] Diffey also notes that David acts as a priest (21:6; 2 Sam 6:14) and is promised a faithful/enduring house (1 Sam 25:28; 2 Sam 7:16).

Though initially compelling, Diffey's observations falter for multiple reasons. It is true that 1 Sam 22:14 calls David faithful and that he is initially a righteous man, but we have already seen that David ceases to act faithfully in 2 Sam 11 when he commits adultery with Bathsheba. When David sinned in 2 Sam 11, the "thing that David had done displeased the LORD" (v. 27). First Kings 15:5 agrees: "David did what was right in the eyes of the Lord and did not turn aside from anything that he commanded him all the days of his life, except in the matter of Uriah the Hittite." There is no indication in 1 Sam 2:30–35 that the faithful priest will ever fail to do "according to

high priest—unlike Eli—who has a house that will live faithfully—unlike Hophni and Phinehas—before the Lord. So long as this new house lives faithfully, it will endure.

29. See Fokkelman, *Vow and Desire,* 148–49.

30. Keil and Delitzsch, *Biblical Commentary on the Books of Samuel,* 40–47.

31. Deenick, "Priest and King or Priest-king in 1 Samuel 2:35," 328.

32. Diffey, "David and the Fulfilment of 1 Samuel 2:35," 99–104.

33. For an extensive discussion on the phrase "a man after [the Lord's] own heart" see DeRouchie, "The Heart of YHWH and His Chosen One in 1 Samuel 13," 467–89.

what is in [the Lord's] heart and in the [Lord's] mind." There is certainly no indication that this faithful priest will sin as egregiously as David did.[34]

It is also true that David acts as a priest in 21:6 and 2 Sam 6:14, but 1 Sam 2:35 anticipates a priest who will serve God "forever" (כל-הימים). The narrative makes it plain that David will not live forever (2 Sam 7:12; 23:1). We have also seen that the faithful priest of 1 Sam 2:35 will have a house (i.e., descendants) who will replace the Aaronic priesthood. This means that the faithful priest will be a high priest in a new priesthood and that his descendants will continue this new priestly line just as Eli continued Aaron's old priestly line. Though 2 Sam 8:18 does say that David's descendants are priests, these priests do not replace the Aaronic priesthood but temporarily operate alongside it.[35]

Lastly, while Diffey is correct to note that 1 Sam 25:28 and 2 Sam 7:16 state that David will have a faithful/enduring house, when read within Samuel's larger context, neither of these texts encourage the reader to identify David as the faithful priest. This is primarily the case because within Samuel David's household is not faithful. Like Eli and Samuel before him, David has two wicked sons, Amnon and Absalom. We have already seen within the narrative of Samuel that Eli and Samuel each having two rebellious sons demonstrated the unfulfilled promise of God raising up the faithful priest along with his faithful house. It is best to understand David's two wicked sons in this same manner. David's two wicked sons demonstrate the continued need for God to fulfill his promise to raise up the faithful priest and his faithful house.

Since David's house is not faithful, how then does this align with the Lord's promise of making for David a faithful house in 1 Sam 25:28 and 2 Sam 7:16? In 1 Sam 25:28 Abigail says, "For the LORD will certainly make my lord a sure house (בית נאמן), because my lord is fighting the battles of the LORD, and evil shall not be found in you so long as you live." Notice that Abigail is confident that the Lord will make for David a sure/faithful house because of two reasons: (1) David is fighting the Lord's battles, and (2) no evil will be found within him for all of his days. Thus, the Lord making for David a faithful house is conditioned upon David's conduct. David's house

---

34. By David not doing what is "right in the LORD's eyes" this further demonstrates that he is not the messianic king who will cause Israel to no longer do what is right in each of their own eyes from Judg 21:25. In the case of Uriah, David did what was right in his own eyes. He "saw" that Bathsheba was "good/beautiful," and so he "took" her (2 Sam 11:2–4). Though there is no need to believe that 1 Kgs 15:5 is specifically alluding to Judg 21:25, one can still infer that David cannot be the expected Messiah from Judg 21:25 because he himself does what is right in his own eyes.

35. For an explanation of David's sons functioning as priests and the various views see Bergen, *1, 2 Samuel*, 352–53.

will be faithful so long as it remains true that he fights the Lord's battles and no evil is found within him all of his days.

In similar fashion, Bergen recognizes that Abigail asserts that the Lord making David a faithful house is conditioned upon David continuing to live faithfully to the Lord: "The Lord would 'certainly make a lasting dynasty' for him. However, the Lord reserved this destiny only for one who 'fights the LORD's battles': if David were to squander his resources by redressing petty wrongs, then 'wrongdoing' (lit., 'evil'; Hb. rā'â) would be accounted to him 'as long as you live.'"[36] To paraphrase Bergen's assessment, God will make for David a faithful house so long as David himself lives a faithful life.

That the faithfulness is dependent upon David's faithful living is manifest in 2 Sam 11–18. Immediately after David's sin with Bathsheba and Uriah in 2 Sam 11–12, the narrative begins to present his house as unfaithful before the Lord by focusing on Amnon and Absalom's conduct (chs. 13–18). Prior to this, the narrative had nothing negative to say about David's house, but once David ceased to live faithfully, so too did his house. As David spiritually falters, so his house spiritually falters. How then will David's house ever be faithful?

The answer to this question is found in 2 Sam 7:11b–17. David will receive a faithful house (v. 16), but this will occur only after God has raised up David's seed (vv. 11b–15). As we saw, as soon as David ceased living faithfully, the text began to depict his direct descendants negatively. Since verse 16 says that David will have a faithful house, the implication is that David's house will again be faithful because it will once again have a faithful ruler reigning over it. In the words of Abigail, the Lord will make for David a faithful house because its ruler will be "fighting the battles of the LORD, and evil shall not be found in [him]" so long as he lives.

When this promised royal seed has lived a faithful life, this seed's house will be faithful. In this way David will have a faithful house because the house of the seed of David is also David's house.[37] The Lord will make for David a faithful house by raising up David's offspring. For these reasons, it is best to not understand David as the faithful priest.

36. Bergen, 1, 2 Samuel, 250. Likewise, Alter states concerning the verb "found" (מצא) in 1 Sam 25:28: "Abigail exploits the temporal ambiguity of the Hebrew imperfective verb to make a statement that is both descriptive of the way David has conducted himself and predictive of the way he will, or should, conduct himself" (Alter, The David Story, 157).

37. The following chapter will buttress the assertion that David's royal seed will live a faithful life and thereby bring about a faithful house by arguing in detail that David's promised seed in 2 Sam 7:11b–17 is the faithful priest from 1 Sam 2:35.

Identifying Zadok, Samuel, a priestly line, or David as the faithful priest does not fit the biblical material. Though one is tempted to say with Fokkelman that the text "leaves us utterly in the dark as to the identity of the priest,"[38] in the following chapter we will provide positive arguments suggesting that the faithful priest of 1 Sam 2:35 is the Messiah, the son of David.

Returning now to our larger point, this means that David's sin with Bathsheba in 2 Sam 11 has the function of showing that David is not the faithful Messiah. The reason the text immediately dispels the notion that David might be the Messiah is because the reader ought to have considered if David was the Messiah when he defeated Hanun, a serpentine individual.[39]

The David and Bathsheba story not only demonstrates that David is not the Messiah, but it also shows that he is not the seed of the woman who will defeat the serpent. As seen already within the David and Bathsheba narrative, Samuel presents David's sin with Bathsheba in the likeness of the first woman's sin in the garden. There is strong irony that while the text presents David as the seed of the woman defeating Hanun, the serpent's seed, along with his allies (10:1—11:1 + 12:26–31), David sins in the likeness of the woman who joined the serpent's insurrection (11:2—12:25).

Like the first woman before him, David needs a seed to defeat the serpent. Also, just like that first transgression caused sin to spread throughout all peoples—as seen by Cain killing his brother Abel—so too David's transgression caused sin to spread through his royal house—as seen by Absalom murdering his brother Amnon. Thus, David's entire house is failing to do justice and righteousness. They are all in need of the woman's seed to defeat the serpent. In sum, because David defeated the serpent in 2 Sam 10, the narrative proceeds to reference other elements from Genesis's early chapters in order to show that David is not the seed of the woman. Rather he needs the woman's seed to conquer the serpent on his behalf as the first man and woman did.

5.2. THE SIGNIFICANCE OF THE NAHASH, GOLIATH, ABSALOM, AND AMASA STORIES

We have seen that the author of Samuel connected David's decline after conquering Hanun to the book's messianism. If the various serpentine passages function together as part of a unified literary motif, one would expect

38. Fokkelman, *Vow and Desire*, 149.

39. In chapters 6–7 of this book, we will present evidence that seeks to demonstrate that Samuel presents the seed of David, the Messiah, to be the seed of the woman from Gen 3:15.

the other serpent stories within Samuel to likewise contribute to the book's messianism. In this section we will see how the Nahash, Goliath, Absalom, and Amasa stories each contribute toward Samuel's messianic message.

5.2.1. The Messianic Significance of the Nahash Story

In chapter four we demonstrated the compositional unity between Judges and Samuel. We also noted that 1 Sam 11 inverses the imagery from Judg 19–21. These two elements converged to cast Saul in a messianic light as he defeated Nahash. This messianic light causes the reader to wonder if Saul is the Messiah as Hannah and the man of God respectively prophesied about in 1 Sam 2:10 and 35.

Intriguingly, the narrative portrays Saul far more negatively after he defeats Nahash. Lee W. Humphrey's notes this and writes, "Saul appears first as a man apparently set apart by his god for greatness, one for whom a special fate has been fixed, and for whom events seem to work to bring out and utilize his best qualities (11:1–11). But then events turn, and he is set on a course of destruction."[40] Though one could point out narrative clues preceding chapter 11 that highlight Saul's deficient character,[41] Humphrey is right to assert that the narrative begins to present Saul markedly worse after he defeats Nahash.[42]

Thus, a pattern emerges. Just like the narrative presented David negatively after he defeated Hanun the serpent, so too the narrative presents Saul negatively after he defeats Nahash the serpent. Sternberg—though noticing different similarities between David and Saul's falls—concurs. He writes that David's decline is "reminiscent of Saul's decline."[43] The narrative provides both David and Saul's falls immediately after they defeat someone associated with the serpent in order to show that neither of them are the anticipated Messiah from 1 Sam 2:10 and 35. Furthermore, when one

---

40. Humphreys, "The Rise and Fall of King Saul: A Study of an Ancient Narrative Stratum in 1 Samuel," 79.

41. Scholars note that the narrative never presents Saul completely positively. See Long, *The Reign and Rejection of King Saul*, 239; Hamilton, *God's Glory in Salvation through Judgment*, 164. One significant clue that Saul is not godly is that the narrative calls Saul "tall" (גבה) in 9:2 and 10:23. See Polzin, *Samuel and the Deuteronomist*, 34.

42. Sam Dragga argues that the Samuel narrative routinely presents Saul as less godly than the judges before him. All of the examples he cites occur after 1 Sam 11 (see Dragga, "In the Shadow of the Judges: The Failure of Saul," 39–46). David Jobling notes that in 1 Sam 14, the narrative presents Saul as foolish (see Jobling, "Saul's Fall and Jonathan's Rise," 367–76, esp. 368).

43. Sternberg, *The Poetics of Biblical Narrative*, 356.

notices how David's fall mirrors Saul's fall, one can deduce that Saul is not the promised seed of the woman just as David was not the promised seed of the woman.

5.2.2. The Messianic Significance of the Goliath Story

To see how David's victory over Goliath contributes to Samuel's messianism, we must first note the similarities between Saul's battle against Nahash and David's battle against Goliath. To begin, both Nahash and Goliath are Saul and David's first respective battles in Samuel. Both Saul and David enter into battle right after Samuel anointed them (10:1; 16:13). After Samuel anoints them, the Spirit of the Lord comes down on both of them (11:6; 16:13). Thus, both are victorious on account of the Spirit's aid. In the MT, both narratives connect Saul and David to animals immediately before their battles. Saul "was coming from the field behind the oxen," when men told him about Nahash (11:5), and the narrative states that before David entered into battle, he was going "back and forth from Saul to feed his father's sheep" (17:15).[44] Both Saul and David have to fight because the enemy is attempting to make Israel "serve" (עבד) their nation as a vassal (11:1; 17:9). In both cases, Nahash and Goliath intend to make Israel a "reproach" (חרף/חרפה; 11:2; 17:10, 25–26, 36, 45).[45]

These parallels suggest that one should read Saul's battle with Nahash and David's battle with Goliath together. This further suggests that the messianic import of Saul's victory over Nahash will be present in David's victory over Goliath. Despite the parallels, there is one connection that contrasts rather than compares. After Saul defeated Nahash, the narrative presented him negatively. In contrast, after David defeated Goliath, the narrative presents him remarkably positively.

That is not to say that before David's victory over Goliath, the narrative presented David poorly. The narrative just did not present him in such a perfect fashion. David was merely a short/young (קטן) and handsome shepherd boy who could play the harp well (16:11–18).[46] After defeating Goliath, the nation knows that David has slain his ten thousands (18:7). He is Saul's

44. The OG is missing this material because it lacks 1 Sam 17:15.

45. The OG does not contain 1 Sam 17:25–26. Still, McCarter notes a connection between the reproach Nahash and Goliath attempt to bring on Israel (McCarter, *I Samuel*, 203).

46. Since Samuel consistently connects being "tall" (גבה) with pride, David being "young/short" (קטן) is a subtle clue that he is humble. Garsiel contrasts David's small stature with Saul's height (see Garsiel, *The First Book of Samuel*, 115–16).

rival to the throne, and he is more righteous than Saul (24:17). Abigail says that David fights the Lord's battles and that "evil shall not be found in [him] so long as [he] lives" (25:28). She then immediately connects this persuasion to David's victory over Goliath when she says that the Lord "will sling out as from the hollow of a sling" David's enemies (v. 29).[47] In fact, we have already noted that 1 Kgs 15:5 says that David always did what was right in the Lord's eyes except for his dealings with Uriah. First Kings apparently understands Samuel to present David as unblemished prior to 2 Sam 11. After David defeats Goliath, he is no mere boy. He is the heir apparent to the throne who can do no wrong until the narrative demonstrates that he is not the seed of the woman in 2 Sam 11–20.

Thus, in all three of these serpent battles, the narrative begins to present the character markedly different immediately after the battle. Unlike when Saul beat Nahash and unlike when David defeated Hanun, the narrative presents David in an increasingly positive light after he defeats Goliath. Why this stark difference?

Since Samuel presents Saul and David's falls in order to communicate that they are not the seed of the woman or the Messiah, it is reasonable to infer that Samuel presents David's rise and moral purity after defeating Goliath in order to cast him as the Messiah and the seed of the woman.[48] Within the literary flow, when David conquered Goliath the serpent, the reader should wonder if David is the serpent-slayer from Gen 3:15, who is the Messiah within Samuel's narrative. Instead of falling like Saul did, David's rise further suggests that he is the Messiah. The narrative uses David's victory over Goliath to present David as though he were the Messiah.

This means that within Samuel, there is a literary strategy that explains David's positive portrayal (David might be the Messiah) and his negative portrayal (David is not the Messiah). Scholars have noticed how the narrative presents David both positively and negatively. Still, many of them often fail to provide a literary explanation for why one would arrange pre-existing documents or write a new document in order to present David both negatively and positively.[49]

47. Bergen, *1, 2 Samuel*, 250.

48. The reason the narrative demonstrates that David is not the seed of the woman in 2 Sam 11–20 is because it assumes that when David slays the serpent, the reader will have warrant to identify him with the seed from Gen 3:15. This suggests that the narrative intends to cast David as the woman's seed when he defeats Goliath the serpent.

49. Brueggemann notes how in David's rise (1 Sam 16:1—2 Sam 5:5), the narrative first presents David positively, and then in the so-called "succession narrative" (2 Sam 9—1 Kgs 2) the narrative presents him negatively (Brueggemann, *David's Truth*, 19–65). According to Brueggemann, the reason for these two different portrayals is not to be found within the book of Samuel as we are attempting to do. Rather, it is because

Gillian Keys and Carlson are exceptions to this. Keys argues that 2 Sam 10–20 presents David negatively to provide a theological biography showing the "inevitable consequences of transgression."[50] This is true, but it begs the question of why the narrative feels the need to inform the reader that inevitable consequences accompany transgression. For what literary reason does the narrative communicate that transgressions lead to ruin?

Carlson has argued that David is a man "under blessing" in 2 Sam 2–5, and that he is a man "under curse" in 2 Sam 13–24. The "blessing" and the "curse" refer back to Deuteronomy's covenantal language regarding obedience and disobedience.[51] Carlson himself notes that David's sin with Bathsheba in chapters 10–12 "inaugurates a pattern of cause and effect which is thoroughly Deuteronomic in character."[52]

We are arguing that the reason the narrative presents David both positively and negatively has everything to do with the book's messianism. Immediately after David defeats his first serpent, the narrative takes the opportunity to show the reader what the Messiah is like (i.e., faithful).[53] After this, David defeats his second serpent, and the narrative reveals to the reader that David is not the Messiah.[54]

---

in the Succession Narrative "we have a different storyteller" (Brueggeman, *David's Truth*, 43).

50. Keys, *The Wages of Sin*, 180.

51. Carlson, "David, the Chosen King," 25.

52. Carlson, "David, the Chosen King," 25.

53. Brettler convincingly argues that 1 Sam 14:52–2 Sam 8:18 is pro-David and that 2 Sam 9–20 presents David negatively, but for what literary purpose (see Brettler, *The Creation of History in Ancient Israel*, 97–110)? If one accepts Brettler's divisions, then additional reasons emerge for believing that 1 Sam 14:52–2 Sam 8:18 functions to present David in a messianic light. We have already seen that Samuel's Messiah is a priest-king. In 1 Sam 14:52–2 Sam 8:18, David is both a king and a priest. The text presents him as a priest when he eats the holy bread (1 Sam 21:1–6), offers sacrifices as a priest (2 Sam 6:12–15), and has his sons serving as a priest beneath him (8:18). Interestingly, in 2 Sam 9–20 the text does not present David as a priest, and it does not present his sons as priests either. This is the case because in 1 Sam 14:52–2 Sam 8:18 the narrative intends to present David as the messianic priest-king while in 2 Sam 9–20 the narrative intends to demonstrate that David is not the longed-for Messiah.

54. DeRouchie has also argued that the Samuel narrative presents David's sin in order to demonstrate the need for a greater David, though he does not connect his observation to Samuel's serpent motif (see DeRouchie, "The Heart of YHWH and His Chosen One in 1 Samuel 13," 487). In addition, noticing that a single literary technique explains the narrative's positive and negative portrayal of David decreases the likelihood that different authors created the "History of David's Rise" (1 Sam 16:14–2 Sam 5:10) and the "Succession Narrative" (2 Sam 9–20 + 1 Kgs 1–2) as Brueggemann—who is following Leonhard Rost—argues (Brueggemann, *David's Truth*, 43; Rost, *Succession to the Throne of David*). Since a drastic change in a prominent character's portrayal

5.2.3. The Messianic Significance of the Absalom and Amasa Stories

The final serpent stories to consider are Joab slaying Absalom and Amasa. The purpose of these accounts is to further demonstrate that David is not the Messiah. The narrative does this by presenting Joab as a foil to David. In order to begin to see how Joab foils David, first notice how in 2 Sam 19:13b (ET v. 14b) David sends Zadok and Abiathar to tell Amasa that he is the "commander of [David's] army (צבא) from now on in the place of Joab (תחת יואב)." By saying this, David echoes 2 Sam 17:25a. That text states that Absalom "set Amasa over the army instead of Joab (תחת יואב על-הצבא)." Fokkelman explains the significance of this shared language: "By appointing Amasa 'in the place of Joab' . . . David comes into alignment with the Absalom of 17:25a."[55] The narrative does not present David well in this instance.

To make matters worse, Joab—and not David—slew both Amasa the serpent (20:10) and Absalom the serpent (18:14). In both of these instances, Joab did not have David's permission. When David tells Joab, Abishai, and Ittai to spare Absalom, David is seeking to prevent a serpent from undergoing judgment (18:5).[56] Also, when David appoints Amasa as his general, he is following Absalom's steps and positioning a serpent over his army. Instead of slaying two serpents (Goliath and Hanun), David now seeks to protect and promote two serpents (Absalom and Amasa). When Joab kills these two serpents, he is doing what David previously did in the narrative (i.e., kill two serpents).[57] David has fallen far indeed. No longer can Abigail say that David is "fighting the Lord's battles." The narrative uses Joab as a foil to show that David is not the ultimate serpent-slayer.[58]

---

immediately follows three different serpent stories it is reasonable to think that a single consciousness shaped these different narratives.

55. Fokkelman, *King David*, 293.

56. Though one might be tempted to think that the narrative casts David as a serpent because he fathered Absalom like Nahash fathered Hanun, one must remember that genealogy alone does not make one a serpent (cf. 2 Sam 17:27–29). Also, though David appears similar to Absalom when he appoints Amasa as his general, the narrative never explicitly attaches serpentine language or imagery to David.

57. One should not think that the narrative casts Joab as the Messiah simply because he defeats the serpent. Since Joab is not a king, he cannot be the messianic (1 Sam 2:10) serpent-slayer (Gen 3:15; cf. 49:8–12).

58. Eschelbach has argued that Joab foils David, though he does not link this to Samuel's serpent motif. See Eschelbach, *Has Joab Foiled David?*. Filip Čapek Prague agrees in large part with Eschelbach's findings. See Prague, "David's Ambiguous Testament in 1 Kings 2:1–12 and the Role of Joab in the Succession Narrative," 4–26.

5.3. A SUMMARY OF SAMUEL'S SERPENT MOTIF

Saul first slays a serpent in 1 Sam 11. He momentarily appears to be the Messiah who will invert the problems Israel faced in Judg 19–21 because they lacked the messianic king. After his victory over Nahash, the narrative consistently presents him as failing to lead Israel well in order to demonstrate that Saul is not the Messiah. In this way, the reader is forced to hope for another who will defeat the serpent and then not proceed to act so foolishly. A ray of hope comes when God promises to replace Saul with his neighbor who is "better than him" (1 Sam 15:28). In this way, Saul is a foil for David.[59]

After David defeats Goliath, the reader's hopes are high. Perhaps he is the Messiah. He has beaten a serpent. He then becomes Israel's king—which makes him look like the Messiah (1 Sam 2:10). Instead of living foolishly like Saul, David acts like a priest (2 Sam 6:13–14), and he continues to live blamelessly (1 Sam 24:17; 25:28b)—which the Messiah must do (2:35). In this unit,[60] the narrative presents David as the Messiah.

David then defeats Hanun, the seed of Nahash, who is a serpent. The reader thinks that David is surely the serpent-slaying seed of the woman at this point. He has defeated two serpents. Yet, just as the narrative presented Saul markedly more negatively after he conquered Nahash, so too it presents David negatively after he defeats Hanun, Nahash's son. As Sternberg writes about David, "The onetime darling of fortune, with an unbroken record of

59. Scholars widely agree that Saul is a foil for David. See Hamilton, *God's Glory in Salvation through Judgment*, 164.

60. There is no scholarly consensus regarding Samuel's structure. The present author finds Brettler's structural divisions the most convincing. Brettler understands 1 Sam 7—14:51 to be the Saul narratives. First Samuel 14:52—2 Sam 8:18 are the positive David narratives. Second Samuel 9–20 are the negative David narratives. A summary statement (1 Sam 14:47–51; 2 Sam 8:15–18; 20:23–26) concludes each of these various sections (Brettler, *The Creation of History in Ancient Israel*, 97–110). By adopting Brettler's divisions, we understand the "positive David" narratives to present David positively because these narratives are specifically presenting David messianically. The "negative David" narratives present David negatively because they are showing the reader that David is not the Messiah. Brettler's structure compliments this book's findings. If Brettler's divisions are correct, then the first battle in the Saul, positive David, and negative David sections are all serpent battles. Unlike Brettler, many scholars start a new unit at 1 Sam 16 (see Dorsey, *The Literary Structure of the Old Testament*, 129; McCarter, *I Samuel*, 57; Keil and Delitzsch, *Biblical Commentary on the Books of Samuel*, v–viii; Smith, *A Critical and Exegetical Commentary on the Books of Samuel*, ix; Brueggemann, *First and Second Samuel*, vii–ix; Klein, *1 Samuel*, vii–viii; Gehrke, *1–2 Samuel*, 23–25; McKane, *I & II Samuel*, 5–12; Tsumura, *The First Book of Samuel*, viii).

success as both private and public figure, now suffers one catastrophe after another, in all spheres of life and with no end in sight."[61]

The narrative presents David's fall as a repeat of the first woman's sin. Accordingly, David is not the ultimate seed of the woman who fulfills Gen 3:15. Rather, in 2 Sam 11–14 the narrative presents him to be more like Eve than her seed. Just as sin entered the world through the first man and woman and spread to others, so too do the effects of David's sin infiltrate his house. After David sinned like Eve, his son, Absalom, murdered Amnon like Cain murdered Abel. Both David and his house need the true serpent-slaying seed of the woman.

Noticing the order of David's serpent victories is vital. The narrative first presents David as though he were the seed of the woman, and only then does it present David as though he needs the seed of the woman. Thus, the narrative ends saying that David is not the ultimate seed of the woman who will defeat the serpent and evil. This encourages the reader to identify the woman's seed with someone besides David.

Joab then proceeds to slay two serpents (Absalom and Amasa). In so doing, the narrative presents Joab as a foil to further demonstrate that David is not the one for whom the reader should hope. Rather than slaying two serpents—like when David slew Goliath and Hanun—now David seeks to protect Absalom, and he promotes Amasa over his army. Instead of David purging the kingdom of serpents, Joab has to do David's job much like David did Saul's job when David defeated Goliath.[62] At this point in the narrative, Joab appears more like the seed of the woman than David does.

Though Saul, David, and Joab all slay the serpent, none of them fulfills the serpent-slaying promise from Gen 3:15 nor do they fulfill the two messianic promises from 1 Sam 2:10 and 35. The reader is forced to look beyond Saul, David, and Joab. Who then will defeat the serpent? The narrative provides the reader a clue to answer this question when it casts David as Eve. Genesis promised that Eve's seed would defeat the serpent. Does Samuel present evidence that David's seed will defeat the serpent? The next chapter will answer that question in the affirmative.[63] In this way, as Saul was a foil for David, so too David is a foil for his seed, the Messiah who fulfills Gen 3:15.

61. Sternberg, *The Poetics of Biblical Narrative*, 357.

62. For a detailed explanation of how David was doing Saul's job for Saul when he conquered Goliath see Kuruvilla, "David V. Goliath (1 Samuel 17)," 495–97.

63. Dempster agrees that the Samuel narrative presents David's shortcomings so that the reader concludes that "the hope for the future lies in a *descendant* of David." See Dempster, *Dominion and Dynasty*, 147, (emphasis his).

6

THE SEED OF DAVID AS THE SEED OF THE WOMAN

This book's thesis argues that the Samuel narrative contains a serpent motif and that this motif's significance within Samuel is to present the seed of David as the promised seed of the woman from Gen 3:15 who will defeat the serpent and reign as king in the new creation. We demonstrated the first half of this thesis by showing in chapters 3–4 that Samuel does employ a serpent motif. We have also partially demonstrated the second half of this thesis in chapter 5 by noting that Samuel employs this serpent motif in order to demonstrate that neither Saul nor David are the longed-for seed of the woman who will defeat the serpent.

This chapter and the following chapter intend to finish the second half of this thesis by demonstrating that Samuel presents David's seed to be the woman's seed who will defeat the serpent and reign as king in the new creation. In order to prove this, in this chapter we will seek to accomplish four goals and then summarize our findings. First, we will argue that Samuel does not understand Solomon to be the promised messianic seed of 2 Sam 7:11b–17. Second, we will see that the faithful priest from 1 Sam 2:35 is the promised messianic seed of 2 Sam 7:11b–17. Third, we will bolster this interpretation by considering Zechariah and Hebrews's priest-king theology. Fourth, having established that the messianic priest-king is the promised seed of David from 2 Sam 7:11b–17, we will argue that this Messiah is the seed of the woman from Gen 3:15. In this chapter's conclusion, we will summarize our findings.

6.1. SOLOMON AS DAVID'S SEED
IN 2 SAMUEL 7:11B–17?

In this portion of the chapter, we will argue that Samuel does not under-stand Solomon to be the seed of David in 2 Sam 7:11b–17.[1] In order to do this, we will first argue that 2 Sam 7:11b–17 expects David's seed to be a single offspring. Then we will argue that though Solomon claims to be Da-vid's seed in 1 Kings and 2 Chronicles, the authors of these two books do not fully agree with Solomon's assessment. We will finish this section by noting that within Samuel there is little to no reason to conclude that Solomon is the seed the Lord promised David.

6.1.1. The Singular Seed of 2 Samuel 7:11b–17

After David desired to build a house (בית; i.e., temple) for the Lord (7:1–4), God gave two messages to Nathan. After the Lord made it clear that he did not want David to build him a house (vv. 5–7), the Lord told David what he had done and would do for David (vv. 8–16). With a play on words, the Lord tells David that he will build a house (בית; i.e., dynasty) for David, rather than David building a house (בית; i.e., temple) for the Lord (v. 11b). Then, in verses 12–16 God explains to David how he will accomplish building this house for David. In order to build David's house, God will raise up a "seed" (זרע) when David dies (v. 12). It is of paramount importance to identify who this seed is.

In verses 12–15 of the MT, the text routinely modifies this "seed" with third masculine singular (3ms) modifiers. God will establish "his kingdom" (ממלכתו; v. 12). "He" (הוא) will build a house for the Lord, and the Lord will establish the throne of "his kingdom" (ממלכתו) forever (v. 13). The Lord will be a father to "him" (לו), and "he" (הוא) will be a son to the Lord (v. 14). Also, the Lord's steadfast love will never depart from "him" (ממנו; v. 15).[2] The text consistently refers to the "seed" with 3ms modifiers.

This observation is important because Collins has demonstrated that "when *zera'* denotes a specific descendant, it appears with singular verb inflections, adjectives, and pronouns."[3] Collins explicitly mentions that the

---

1. Scholars frequently divide the Samuel text to make 2 Sam 7:11b–17 a section. See Bergen, *1, 2 Samuel*, 339; Firth, *1 & 2 Samuel*, 385.

2. As we discuss below, the OG continues to refer to this seed with 3ms modifiers in verse 16: "And I will make his house endure/faithful and his kingdom will be forever before me, and his throne will be made upright forever" (AT).

3. Collins, "A Syntactical Note (Genesis 3:15): Is the Woman's Seed Singular or Plural?," 144.

grammar of 2 Sam 7:12–15 indicates that the seed is singular.[4] Following Collins's insights, 2 Sam 7:11b–17 anticipates a single, male descendant from David. Even though the Samuel narrative mentions that David had multiple descendants (5:14–16), 2 Sam 7:11b–17 only anticipates a single descendant.

Who then is this singular seed? The majority of scholars understand Solomon to be this promised seed of David. Regarding verses 12–15, Bruce Waltke writes, "The first set of future promises pertain to Solomon."[5] Robert P. Gordon writes, "The reference is to Solomon" or an equivalent phrase more than once.[6] Morrison writes in a matter of fact manner that 1 Kings reveals the identity of the seed who will build a temple in 2 Sam 7:13.[7] By this, he clearly means that Solomon fulfills verse 13.

6.1.2. Does 1 Kings Present Solomon as the Seed of 2 Samuel 7:11b–17?

Understanding Solomon to be the promised seed in 2 Sam 7:11b–17 initially makes sense because Solomon understood himself to be the seed of the Davidic covenant. In 1 Kgs 5:4–5 Solomon says that the Lord gave him rest on every side and that he has no enemies (cf. 2 Sam 7:10–11). Thus, he intends to build a house for the name of the Lord in accordance with the Lord's promise to David: "[Your seed] shall build a house for my name" (2 Sam 7:13). Though Solomon understands himself to fulfill the Davidic covenant, this does not require that the narrator agrees.

There are reasons to believe that the author of 1 Kings does not believe Solomon to be the promised seed of the Davidic covenant. The first reason is structural, and the second is lexical. Concerning the structural reason, Jerome T. Walsh has argued that 1 Kgs 1–11 is a chiastic structure with its focal point being Solomon building the temple.[8] If correct, this struc-

---

4. Collins, "A Syntactical Note (Genesis 3:15): Is the Woman's Seed Singular or Plural?," 144.

5. Waltke and Yu, *An Old Testament Theology*, 661.

6. Gordon, *I & II Samuel*, 238–39.

7. Morrison, *2 Samuel*, 100–01.

8. Walsh, *1 Kings*, 151. Walsh's chiasm without its sub-points is as follows:
A. A prophet intervenes in the royal succession: 1:1—2:12a
 B. Solomon eliminates threats to his security: 2:12b–46
  C. The early promise of Solomon's reign: 3:1–15
   D. Solomon uses his gifts for the people: 3:16—4:34
    E. Preparations for building the temple: 5:1–18
     F. Solomon builds the temple: 6:1—7:51

ture would certainly suggest that the author of 1 Kings believed Solomon
to fulfill 2 Sam 7:13. However, Waltke has revised Walsh's structure noting
that the center of the chiasm is actually Solomon building his own build-
ings.[9] Between Solomon beginning to build the temple (1 Kgs 6:1–38) and
finishing the temple (7:13–51), the text mentions that Solomon built his
own house (7:1), the house of the forest of Lebanon (v. 2), the hall of pil-
lars (v. 6), the hall of the throne (v. 7), and a house for Pharaoh's daughter
(v. 8). It is hard to miss the narrator's pessimistic stance toward Solomon
building these houses. After mentioning that Solomon spent seven years
building the Lord's house (6:38), in the next verse the narrator informs the
reader that Solomon spent thirteen years on his own house (7:1). By placing
Solomon's personal building projects in the center of this chiastic structure,
Solomon's efforts building the Lord's house revolve around his own personal
projects. If Waltke's chiastic structure is correct, then building the Lord's
house comes across as a side project for Solomon. The author of Kings does
not ultimately identify Solomon as the one who builds the Lord's house.
Rather, Kings primarily presents Solomon as the man who builds his own
house. This suggests that the reader should look for another one to build a
different temple for the Lord.

First Kings also provides a key lexical link to Samuel that suggests
the author of 1 Kings does not think that Solomon is the seed of the Davidic covenant. Once the author of 1 Kings makes Solomon's sins apparent (11:1–13), he writes in verse 11 that the Lord said to Solomon that

---

F′. Solomon dedicates the temple: 8:1—9:10
E′. After building the temple: 9:11–25
D′. Solomon uses his gifts for himself: 9:26—10:29
C′. Tragic failure of Solomon's reign: 11:1–13
B′. Lord raises up threats to Solomon's security: 11:14–25
A′. A prophet determines the royal succession: 11:26–43.

9. Waltke and Yu, *An Old Testament Theology*, 693. Waltke's chiasm without its sub-
points is as follows:

A. A prophet intervenes in the royal succession: 1:1—2:12
  B. Solomon eliminates threats to his security: 2:13–46
    C. The early promise of Solomon's reign: 3:1–15
      D. Solomon uses wisdom for the people: 3:16—4:34
        E. Preparations for building the temple: 5:1–18
          F. Solomon begins building the temple: 6:1–38
            X. Solomon builds "rival" buildings: 7:1–12
          F′. Solomon completes building the temple: 7:13–51
        E′. Solomon dedicates the temple and is warned by God: 8:1—9:9
      D′. Solomon uses wisdom for himself: 9:10—10:29
    C′. Tragic failure of Solomon's reign: 11:2–13
  B′. Lord raises up threats to Solomon's security: 11:14–25
A′. A prophet determines the royal succession: 11:26–43.

he would "tear the kingdom from [him] and will give it to [his] servant
(אקרע את־הממלכה מעליך ונתיה לעבדך)."[10] The servant to whom the Lord
gives the kingdom is Jeroboam (vv. 11, 26). The Lord illustrates that he is
tearing the kingdom from Solomon and giving it to Jeroboam by having
Ahijah the prophet tear a garment into twelve pieces. Jeroboam then took
ten pieces because the Lord had torn the "kingdom from the hand of Solomon and [given him] ten tribes" (vv. 30–31).

First Samuel 15 serves as the background for this entire scene in
1 Kgs 11. After Saul sinned yet again (1 Sam 15:9), and Samuel declared
God's rejection of Saul as king (vv. 10–26), Saul seized Samuel's robe as
Samuel turned to leave, and he tore it (קרע; v. 27). Samuel then responded,
"The LORD has torn the kingdom of Israel from you this day, and has given
it to a neighbor of yours (קרע יהוה את־ממלכות ישראל מעליך היום ונתנה לרעך),
who is better than you" (v. 28). In both instances the Lord uses a prophet
with a torn garment to declare to a king that the Lord has torn the kingdom
from him immediately after mentioning that king's sin.[11] That 1 Sam 15
serves as 1 Kgs 11's background is made more certain because the Lord only
"tears" (קרע) a "kingdom" (ממלכה) from a king within the OT in these two
instances. First Kings patterns Solomon's fall after Saul's.

This point is crucial because in the MT the Lord explicitly promised
David that he would never remove his "steadfast love" (חסד) from David's
seed as he removed it from Saul (2 Sam 7:15). Though there are variants in
this verse that do not mention Saul, the MT seems to only make explicit
what the other variants imply.[12] In the context of 2 Sam 7:14–16, the Lord's

10. We can know that the author thought it important that the Lord tore the kingdom from Solomon because the text mentions this "tearing" four times in this chapter
(11:11, 12, 13, 31).

11. Martin J. Mulder notes that "tearing the kingdom" connects Solomon's fall to
Saul's: "Aside from in our chapter the act of 'tearing up' is reported both with reference
to a king's realm and to the symbolic act of tearing one's clothes also in 1 Sam. 15:27f.;
28:17. In 1 Sam. the reference is to the rejection of Saul as Israel's king." Despite this
connection, he does not consider how Saul and Solomon's rejections relate. See Mulder,
1 Kings, 1:561.

12. McCarter identifies three slightly different readings of 2 Sam 7:15. The MT
reads, "But my steadfast love will not depart from him, as I took it from Saul, whom I
put away from before you." First Chronicles 17:13 represents a second reading. It says,
"But my steadfast love will not depart from him, as I took it from him who was before
you." The OG represents the third reading. It reads, "But my steadfast love will not
depart from him whom I removed from before me." In this case, the MT is probably not
original. Someone has probably historicized the text in order to make clear the identity
of the one the Lord removed from being king before David. Still, the MT's interpretation is true. The Lord will not remove the kingdom from the seed as he removed it from
"him who was before" David or the Lord (i.e., Saul). For this discussion see McCarter,
II Samuel, 194–95.

"steadfast love" is equivalent to allowing David's seed to be king over his own kingdom.[13] The Lord promised that he would never remove the kingdom from David's seed as he removed it from Saul. So, when 1 Kings shows that the Lord removed the kingdom from Solomon remarkably similar to how he removed the kingdom from Saul, this strongly suggests that the author of 1 Kings does not think Solomon is the seed of David whom the Lord promised in the Davidic covenant. Within 1 Kings, the author disagrees with Solomon's assessment. The author does not think that Solomon is the seed the Lord promised David.[14]

6.1.3. Does 2 Chronicles Present Solomon as the Seed of 2 Samuel 7:11b–17?

Unlike 1–2 Kings, 1–2 Chronicles contains its own adapted form of the Davidic covenant (1 Chr 17:11–14).[15] This means that 1–2 Chronicles may use the Davidic covenant and/or Solomon differently than Samuel or 1–2 Kings did. As was the case in 1 Kings, in 2 Chronicles Solomon understands himself to be the promised seed of David. In 2 Chr 6:10 Solomon says, "Now the LORD has caused his word—which he spoke—to stand, and I have risen in the place of David my father, and I sit on the throne of Israel just as the LORD spoke, and I have built the house for the name of the LORD, the God of Israel" (AT). Once again, we must ask if the narrator agrees with Solomon.

Admittedly, the Chronicler does not seek to dissuade the reader from understanding Solomon to be David's promised seed as clearly as 1 Kings did. This is mainly because 2 Chronicles does not include Solomon's fall as 1 Kgs 11 did. Nevertheless, the Chronicler provides evidence that he does not believe Solomon to completely fulfill the Davidic covenant.

To begin, some have argued that the very reason the Chronicler does not mention David or Solomon's fall narratives is because he is presenting

13. McCarter understands the "steadfast love" also to be ruling over the Lord's people. While explaining what it means for the Lord to remove steadfast love in this context, he references 1 Sam 13:7b–15a and 15:22–28. In both of these texts the Lord is removing the kingdom from Saul to one degree or another. See McCarter, *II Samuel*, 208.

14. That 1–2 Kings's author does not understand Solomon to be a fulfillment of 2 Sam 7:11b–17 does not preclude the idea that 1–2 Kings presents Solomon as a type of the true seed of the Davidic covenant. In fact, the author uses Solomon's failures in order to show the reader the need for a better Davidic descendant.

15. The differences between 2 Sam 7:11b–17 and 1 Chr 17:11–14 are striking. Most notably, the Chronicler does not include material comparable to 2 Sam 7:14b: "When he commits iniquity, I will discipline him with the rod of men, with the stripes of the sons of men."

Judah's kings in the best light possible in order to foreshadow the messianic king to come. Shepherd notes that the Chronicler is not trying to write a "revisionist history." This is because the Chronicler cites his sources and all history comes from one perspective or another.[16] Rather, much like a modern-day highlight reel would only show Michael Jordan's best moments to demonstrate his greatness, so too the Chronicler emphasizes the highlights of the various kings in order to help the reader understand the coming Messiah's greatness.[17] Even David and Solomon's positive portrayal anticipates a greater David and Solomon to come. This suggests that the Chronicler views Solomon as a partial fulfillment of his own version (1 Chr 17:11–14) of the Davidic covenant.

The Chronicler presents Solomon in such a way that the reader should anticipate the Messiah to be a greater Solomon. This resonates nicely with 1–2 Chronicle's "new Solomon" motif. Multiple scholars have noted that Chronicles presents Hezekiah as a new Solomon.[18] H. G. M. Williamson argues this most persuasively noting multiple similarities between Hezekiah and Solomon.[19] Williamson summarizes the Chronicler's purpose in treating Hezekiah as a new Solomon when he writes, "Thus in Hezekiah's recapitulation of Solomon's achievements it is as though the Chronicler is taking us back prior to the point of division where the one Israel is united around a single temple under the authority of the Davidic king."[20]

Noting that a "new Solomon" is one who unites "Israel around a single temple under the authority of the Davidic king" suggests that Cyrus's decree in 2 Chr 36:23 anticipates a final "new Solomon." This is because 2 Chr 36 ends by citing Cyrus's decree in an abbreviated form. Ezra 1:2–4 provides a longer form of Cyrus's decree. The result of 2 Chronicles providing a shorter decree than Ezra is that the decree of Cyrus in 2 Chronicles anticipates that an individual male from among exiled Israel will build the temple in

---

16. Shepherd, *Daniel in the Context of the Hebrew Bible*, 112–13.

17. Shepherd, *Daniel in the Context of the Hebrew Bible*, 113.

18. See Dillard, *2 Chronicles*, 228–29; Klein, *2 Chronicles*, 412; Williamson, *1 and 2 Chronicles*, 351.

19. Some of the many reason Williamson argues that Hezekiah is a new Solomon is because the material the Chronicler adds to Hezekiah that is absent in 2 Kings frequently likens Hezekiah to Solomon. Also, 2 Chronicles heavily associates both monarchs with the temple and the Passover. Both Hezekiah and Solomon appoint priests, and the text emphasizes the wealth of both. In addition, the text links Hezekiah and Solomon through their Gentile dealings. Also, Hezekiah restores the land to the same geographical size over which Solomon reigned. For additional similarities see Williamson, *Israel in the Books of Chronicles*, 119–25.

20. Williamson, *1 and 2 Chronicles*, 351.

Jerusalem, rather than the corporate rebuilding we see in Ezra. This focus on a single male temple builder fosters a messianic reading.

Postell further supports this messianic interpretation. Cyrus's decree ends saying, "May the LORD his God be with him, and let him go up!" Postell mentions that the phrase "may the LORD his God be with him" (יהוה אלהיו עמו) is "only used two other times in Chronicles, both of which refer to a Davidic king (2 Chr 1:1; 15:9)."[21] He then notes that the only other time this phrase occurs in the OT is in Num 23:21, which is "in the context of Balaam's eschatological oracles (Num 24:14)."[22] Postell's observations further encourages the reader to understand the single male temple builder at the conclusion of 2 Chronicles to be a royal figure.

Thus, 2 Chronicles ends anticipating a royal son of David to come and fulfill the Davidic covenant by building a temple for the Lord.[23] This single male who will rebuild the temple would rebuild Solomon's destroyed temple. As Hezekiah was an initial "new Solomon," this new temple builder is the book's final, climactic "new Solomon." Within 1–2 Chronicles, Solomon, a son of David who built a temple, anticipates the Messiah, the son of David who will build the temple. This suggests that once again Israel will be reunited in Jerusalem around the temple under the authority of the Davidic king. Chronicles does not regard Solomon as the complete fulfillment of the Davidic covenant.

We have seen that both 1–2 Kings and 1–2 Chronicles use Solomon to heighten messianic expectations, but each does it in a different way.[24] The narrator of 1 Kings consciously demonstrates that Solomon does not fulfill 2 Sam 7:11b–17, and thus the reader should anticipate one besides Solomon who will fulfill the covenant. We will see below that the text of Samuel does not present Solomon as one who fulfills the Davidic covenant in any way.

21. Postell, *Adam as Israel*, 165.

22. Postell, *Adam as Israel*, 165.

23. Sailhamer also recognizes the probable messianism of the conclusion of 2 Chronicles. See Sailhamer, "Biblical Theology and the Composition of the Hebrew Bible," 35.

24. We are arguing that the Chronicler relates Solomon to the Davidic covenant differently than the author of 1–2 Kings did. It is not unusual for the Chronicler to use material differently than the author of 1–2 Kings. For example, in 1 Kgs 10:26–29 the author recounts Solomon's chariots, horseman, silver, and dealings with Egypt in order to show that he violates Deut 17:16–17. These violations show Solomon's disregard for the law and lead naturally into Solomon's fall (1 Kgs 11). The author of 1 Kings uses 1 Kgs 10:26–29 to show that Solomon's fall did not come out of the blue. Conversely, the Chronicler uses the same exact material in 1 Kgs 10:26–29 in 2 Chr 1:14–17. Surprisingly, the Chronicler uses this parallel text to prove that the Lord had blessed Solomon financially because Solomon asked for wisdom instead of riches (1:8–13). The biblical authors at times use similar texts in different ways. Likewise, the biblical authors can use the same character in different ways depending on their literary purposes.

Based on this interpretation, the Messiah fulfills 2 Sam 7:11b–17 by way of direct prophetic fulfillment.

The author 2 Chronicles presents Solomon as a partial fulfillment of the Davidic covenant as recorded in 1 Chr 17:11–14. Thus, the reader should long for the Messiah to come and completely fulfill the Davidic covenant. We must be careful to note that this does not necessarily mean that 2 Chronicles believes Solomon to be a partial fulfillment of the text of 2 Sam 7:11b–17. When 2 Chronicles presents Solomon as a partial fulfillment of the Davidic covenant, the Chronicler most directly understands Solomon to be a partial fulfillment of 1 Chr 17:11–14. Both 1 Kings and 1–2 Chronicles use Solomon to heighten messianic anticipation, but each book (Samuel, 1–2 Kings, and 1–2 Chronicles) must be allowed to have its own, complementary voice.

6.1.4. Does Samuel Present Solomon as the Seed of 2 Samuel 7:11b–17?

Neither 1 Kings nor 2 Chronicles seem to understand Solomon to be the ultimate seed whom the Lord promised to David in 2 Sam 7:11b–17. Most intriguingly, there appears to be no evidence within Samuel that would cause one to conclude that Solomon is the promised seed of 2 Sam 7. The Samuel narrative mentions Solomon only two times. In 2 Sam 5:14 he is merely the fourth son of David in a list of David's sons. In 12:24 Bathsheba gives birth to him, and the text mentions that the Lord loves him. The narrative presents him positively, but there are no apparent textual links between Solomon and the Davidic covenant promises of chapter 7. In fact, the Samuel narrative stops in chapter 24 immediately before one would expect to see Solomon assume the throne and begin building the temple. One could understand the Samuel narrative to stop short of Solomon's reign and temple building in order to dissuade the reader from thinking Solomon is the seed the Lord promised to raise up after David. Even if Samuel originally stretched through 1 Kgs 2 or if Samuel and 1–2 Kings were originally one book, we have already shown 1 Kings's author ascribes language to Solomon to demonstrate that he does not fulfill 2 Sam 7:11b–17.[25]

25. Samuel's final form suggests that it is a completed book in its own right. It is unlikely that Samuel–Kings was originally a single work for at least five reasons. First, we will note in the following chapter that scholars understand 2 Sam 21–24 to conclude the book with a theological appendix. These final chapters (2 Sam 21–24) form a clear chiastic structure (see chapter 7 below). This means that Samuel's final story concludes a section. Structurally speaking, Samuel's conclusion does not end awaiting completion. Second, Samuel also displays signs that the author finished the book's narrative (2

6.2. THE FAITHFUL PRIEST AS THE SEED
OF DAVID IN 2 SAMUEL 7:11B–17

Samuel does not connect Solomon to the Davidic covenant in any notice-
able way. This being the case, one should wonder if the Samuel narrative
provides textual links between the promised seed of the Davidic covenant
and someone else. This section argues that the Samuel narrative presents
the messianic faithful priest in 1 Sam 2:35 as the promised seed of David
in 2 Sam 7:11b–17. We will attempt to identify the faithful priest as the
Davidic seed by first noting shared language and concepts between 1 Sam
2:35 and 2 Sam 7:11b–17. We will then defend this reading by practicing
textual criticism on verse 14 and consulting how Ps 89 reads 2 Sam 7. At
the end of this chapter and in the following chapter we will argue that the
Samuel narrative presents this promised seed of David as the fulfillment of
Samuel's serpent-slayer motif.

Sam 20)—and not just the book's theological conclusion (chs 21–24). Multiple scholars
understand 2 Sam 20:23–26 to parallel 8:15–18 because the two passages share so much
language (see Brettler, *The Creation of History in Ancient Israel*, 97–110; Smith, *The
Fate of Justice and Righteousness during David's Reign*, 102). Both passages conclude
large portions of narrative, as well. Childs writes that 2 Sam 8:15–18 is one of the few
"obvious summaries of literary sections" (Childs, *Introduction to the Old Testament as
Scripture*, 267). His comments apply equally to 20:23–26, which concludes the book's
narrative flow. Samuel's narrative does not end awaiting completion either. Third, because of significant lexical overlap scholars agree that Hannah's prayer in 1 Sam 2:1–10
and David's psalm in 2 Sam 22 frame 1–2 Samuel (see Fokkelman, *Throne and City*,
354; Polzin, *Samuel and the Deuteronomist*, 33). This framing strongly suggests that we
should read 1–2 Samuel as a single, completed work. Fourth, if 1 Kings is the same literary work as Samuel, then why is there such a large temporal gap between the different
books? Samuel's narrative ends with David returning to Jerusalem and beginning his
reign anew. Kings begins with David practically on his death bed. The narrative apparently skips many years between 2 Sam 20 and 1 Kgs 1. Fifth, in our biblical theology of
the serpent in chapter 2, we followed Scheumann's reading of 1–2 Kings. Scheumann
persuasively argued that 1–2 Kings mentions the mothers of the kings of Judah to show
that the seed of the woman from Gen 3:15 is in their line. He also argued that for
this reason 1 Kings emphasizes that Bathsheba is Solomon's mother (see Scheumann,
"Mothers of Offspring in 1–2 Kings," 48). If one person originally authored Samuel
and 1–2 Kings as one document, it is exceedingly odd that the Samuel narrative says
nothing about David's mother. Moreover, even if Samuel and 1–2 Kings were originally
one book, we have argued that the author of 1 Kings intentionally associates language
with Solomon to lead the interpreter to not identify him as the promised seed in 2 Sam
7:11b–17. We conclude that Samuel's author provides little to no reason within Samuel
to associate Solomon as the promised seed of the Davidic covenant.

6.2.1. Faithful Priest Language in 2 Samuel 7:11b–17

If one had to identify the seed of the Davidic covenant with someone from within Samuel, the best option is the faithful priest of 1 Sam 2:35. First Samuel 2:35 and 2 Sam 7:11b–17 share much language in common. Just as God said he would "raise up" (והקימתי) the faithful priest (1 Sam 2:35), so too God will "raise up" (והקימתי) David's seed (2 Sam 7:12). Within the MT of Samuel, the Lord does not raise up (קום in the *hiphil*) any single person except for this faithful priest and David's seed.[26] That the Lord only raises up the faithful priest and David's seed should at least cause one to wonder if the priest might be David's seed.

Another link connecting the faithful priest of 1 Sam 2:35 and the royal seed of David is the presence of a faithful house. The Lord promised the faithful priest that he would "build him a sure house" (ובניתי לו בית נאמן 1 Sam 2:35). This language is remarkably similar to 2 Sam 7:16. In this verse God tells David, "And your house (בית ונאמן) and your kingdom shall be made sure forever before me." In the previous chapter we argued that David's house and kingdom will only become sure/faithful (v. 16) after his seed comes in verses 11b–15.[27] We can now strengthen this argument. David's house will be faithful because his coming royal seed is the faithful priest who will have a faithful house. David's house will be faithful in and through his faithful offspring's house.[28]

The OG makes the link between the faithful priest's house and the seed's house more apparent. While the MT explicitly states that the house, kingdom, and throne in verse 16 belong to David, the OG translates 2 Sam 7:16 to read, "And [the seed's] house and his kingdom will be made faithful forever before me, and his throne will be caused to stand aright forever" (AT). Thus, the OG explicitly mentions that David's seed will have a "faithful house."[29] This creates

26. A possible exception to this is the textual variant in 2 Sam 23:1. We will consider this issue below.

27. For this argument refer to section 5.1.2.

28. There is evidence within 2 Sam 7 itself that suggests that David's house and his seed's house are coextensive. In verse 16 David's throne will endure forever (עד־עולם). Yet, in verse 13 the Lord said that he would establish the throne of the seed's kingdom forever (עד־עולם). David's throne and his seed's throne both last forever because they are the same throne (cf. Luke 1:32–33). Just as David's throne will endure forever because his seed's throne will endure forever, so too David's house will be faithful because his royal seed is the faithful priest who will have a faithful house.

29. Determining whether the OG or the MT is original is a difficult decision. First Chronicles 17:14a does not agree with either the OG or MT of 2 Sam 7:16a. First Chronicles 17:14b does agree with the OG of 2 Sam 7:16b, though. Psalm 89:5 (v. 4 ET) and verse 15 (v. 14 ET) seems to agree with the MT's version of 2 Sam 7:16b when it says "your throne" to David, as opposed to "his [the seed's] throne." Still, Ps 89:37 (v. 36

an even tighter lexical link with 1 Sam 2:35 than we saw in the MT.[30] Both the OG and the MT indicate that God builds a faithful house for David's royal seed from 2 Sam 7:11b–17, but the OG makes this more explicit.

A final link between the faithful priest and the seed of David is that both are said to serve as a priest or a king for an extended period of time. The messianic priest will serve before the Lord "all the days" (כל־הימים). Though the expression "all the days" need not mean "forever," in this context understanding it to mean "forever" makes the most sense.[31] This priest will serve as a priest forever. This implies that he will be eternal (cf. Ps 110:4). Likewise, the Lord will establish the seed's throne "forever" (עד־עולם; 2 Sam 7:13). Furthermore, God will never remove his "steadfast love" (i.e., the kingship) from this seed. This further suggests that unlike Saul, he will remain king forever.

The Lord will raise up the faithful priest and the seed of David. The Lord will also give the seed of David and the faithful priest a faithful house. Moreover, both the faithful priest and the seed of David will serve as a priest and a king forever. Noting this shared language Fokkelman writes, "The similarities are striking."[32]

ET) agrees with the OG's version of 2 Sam 7:16b because it refers to the Davidic throne as belonging to the seed. Thus, like 2 Sam 7, Ps 89 understands the house/kingdom and throne of David to also be the seed's house, kingdom, and throne. The kingdom belongs to both of them.

30. Mary Rose D'Angelo also notes how the OG of 2 Sam 7:16 provides a tighter lexical link to 1 Sam 2:35. See D'Angelo, *Moses in the Letter to the Hebrews*, 79–80.

31. The phrase "all the days" (כל־הימים) occurs ten times within Samuel (1 Sam 1:28; 2:32, 35; 18:29; 20:31; 23:14; 27:11; 28:2; 2 Sam 13:37; 19:14). In three of these ten times (1 Sam 1:28; 18:29; 28:2), the phrase seems to basically mean "until one's death" or "for one's whole life." Three times (1 Sam 23:14; 2 Sam 13:37; 19:14 [ET v. 13]) the phrase basically means "continually." Two times (1 Sam 20:31; 27:11) the author qualifies the phrase in such a way so that the reader knows that the author is not using the phrase to say "forever." This suggests that the phrase can mean forever. One time (1 Sam 2:32) the phrase seems to clearly mean "forever." It is this last usage that is most important for interpreting 1 Sam 2:35. There is indeed a day coming when Eli's priesthood will forever be without an old man (v. 32), but there is a day coming when the priest will serve "forever" because he is replacing Eli and his father's priestly line. Contextually, the phrase "all the days" (כל־הימים) probably means "forever" in 1 Sam 2:35. Thus, 1 Sam 2:35 anticipates an eternal high priest who is not from the line of Aaron.

32. Fokkelman, *Throne and City*, 233–34. Firth also notes these lexical links though he does not connect the faithful priest to the Davidic seed: "Here we return to direct address to David, with specific focus on the establishment of a sure dynasty and kingdom for him, though describing this as confirmed (*ne'man*) evokes the promise of the faithful priest of 1 Sam. 2:35" (*1 & 2 Samuel*, 386). Likewise, Tsumura—though noting that Samuel ascribes Davidic language to the faithful priest—fails to identify the faithful priest as David's seed (see Tsumura, *The First Book of Samuel*, 17).

Besides these lexical links, there are conceptual links. We argued that the faithful priest in 1 Sam 2:35 would be a high priest with priestly offspring replacing the Aaronic line.[33] This means that the faithful priest cannot be of Aaronic descent. This fits nicely with the seed of David because he does not descend from Aaron. In addition, we argued that the faithful priest is the Messiah because no one else fulfills the prophecy of 1 Sam

33. Jeremiah 33:14–26 seems to challenge our interpretation of 1 Sam 2:35 that the Messiah's priesthood would coincide with the end of the Aaronic priesthood. This is the case because Jer 33:15 connects the coming "Branch" (i.e., the Messiah; see Dearman, *Jeremiah, Lamentations*, 304), with the ongoing Levitical priesthood in verses 17–18. Dearman even suggests that the Levitical priests of Jer 33:15 fulfill the prophecy of 1 Sam 2:35 (Dearman, *Jeremiah, Lamentations*, 304, n. 31). Despite Dearman's suggestion, we have already seen that this is an unlikely interpretation of 1 Sam 2:35.

Still, what then is one to make of Jer 33:14–26's plain statement that the Levitical priests will serve alongside the Messiah? There are two basic approaches. The first is to understand that "the Levitical priesthood was taken up and fulfilled by Jesus Christ" (Wright, *The Message of Jeremiah*, 353; see also Huey, *Jeremiah, Lamentations*, 302). In this reading, Jeremiah's prophecy is not to be read literally, but interpreted to mean that the Levitical priests will serve forever, so to speak, through the Messiah's ministry.

The second option, and more likely in the present author's opinion, is to regard Jer 33:14–26 as secondary and unoriginal material on textual, theological, and structural grounds. Regarding the textual grounds, Ronald E. Clements points out "this whole section [i.e., Jer 33:14–26] is missing in the Greek (Septuagint) translation of the Hebrew Bible and this should certainly be taken as an indication that the unit is a late addition to the book" (Clements, *Jeremiah*, 199). Also, verse 18 "is the only reference in the book where the revival of the priesthood is mentioned" (Thompson, *The Book of Jeremiah*, 602). Lastly, Jer 33:18 is the only place within Jeremiah that the term "Levite" occurs (see Hill, "The Book of Jeremiah [MT] and Its Early Second Temple Background," 161).

Concerning theological grounds, there is evidence within Jeremiah that suggests the book does not envision a future Levitical priesthood. In Jer 3:16–17 the prophet anticipates the day when God's people will forget about the ark of the covenant, which held the Ten Commandments and represented God's presence, and yet God's presence will be in all of Jerusalem. Apparently, the ark will be obsolete because the commandments it held will be written on his people's hearts and God's people will be forgiven forever, which implies his continuing presence with them (Jer 31:33–34). Why then would the Levitical priests need to offer sacrifices (Jer 33:18; cf. Heb 10:17–18)?

Lastly, Jer 33:14–26 appears to be a later addition on structural grounds. It breaks the symmetry between the two connected oracles of 32:1–44 and 33:1–13. Without Jer 33:14–26, both of these oracles would begin and end similarly. That one is supposed to read 32:1–44 and 33:1–13 in conjunction is seen in how Jer 33:1 presents 33:1–13 as the "second time" the word of the Lord came to Jeremiah. This implies that Jer 32:1 is the first oracle and that one should read these two oracles together. (For a similar reading see Allen, *Jeremiah: A Commentary*, 374). Both oracles begin by mentioning that the word of the Lord came to Jeremiah (32:1; 33:1). Without 33:14–26, both oracles would end similarly, as well. Both Jer 32:42–43 and 33:12–13 end their respective oracle, and these verses contain much identical language. Jeremiah 32:1–43 and 33:1–13 are constructed so as to have similar introductions and conclusions. That 33:14–26 prevents these two parallel oracles from having similar conclusions suggests that it is not original.

2:35. We also mentioned that there is reason to believe the faithful priest is the Messiah because the text seems to call him the "anointed one" (משיח), and because the previous time the term "anointed one" (משיח) occurred in Samuel (2:10), the Messiah was in view. Seeing the faithful priest as the Messiah mentioned in 1 Sam 2:10 would mean that the priest is actually a priest-king because the Messiah in 1 Sam 2:10 is a king. This also fits nicely with seeing the faithful priest as the promised Davidic offspring because 2 Sam 7:11b–17 promises that David's seed would be a king.

In sum, the Samuel narrative provides multiple lexical links ("raised up," "faithful house," "all the days"/"forever") that suggest the faithful priest is the Davidic seed. Furthermore, we have already come to expect that this faithful priest would not descend from Aaron and that he would be the messianic king. This also corresponds nicely with the Davidic seed. He descends from Judah, and he is a king. Within Samuel, there is ample reason to interpret the faithful priest as the seed of David. Conversely there is little to no reason within Samuel to believe that Solomon is the promised seed of 2 Sam 7:11b–17. After addressing a text critical issue in 7:14, we will buttress this interpretation by arguing that other texts understand the Davidic seed to be a priest who will build a temple.

6.2.2. Textual Variant of 2 Samuel 7:14

Besides Solomon's declarations that he is the promised seed of David who builds a temple for God, perhaps the main reason scholars understand the seed of 2 Sam 7:11b–17 to be Solomon is because of verse 14. In the ESV the text reads, "I will be to him a father, and he shall be to me a son. When he commits iniquity (אשר בהעותו), I will discipline him with the rod of men, with the stripes of the sons of men." How can the faithful priest of 1 Sam 2:35 be the messianic seed of David when 1 Sam 2:35 presented the faithful priest as one who will glorify God and live faithfully?

The present author resolves this difficulty by arguing that the OG contains the superior reading in this instance. The OG reads, "I myself will be to him a father, and he himself will be to me a son, and if his unrighteousness comes (ἐὰν ἔλθη ἡ ἀδικία αὐτοῦ), then I will reprove him with the rod of men and with the attacks of the sons of men" (AT). The OG primarily differs from the MT in that it suggests that the seed of David might not sin. "If his unrighteousness comes" (i.e., if he sins), then the Lord will punish him, but the OG does not suggest that the seed of David will necessarily sin. McCarter prefers the OG in this case.[34] Also parallel passages of 2 Sam 7:11b–17

34. McCarter, *II Samuel*, 194.

read "if" and not "when" in both the MT and the OG (Ps 89:29–31 [ET vv. 30–32]; 132:12). It seems that McCarter's conclusion is well founded.[35]

Preferring the OG leaves open the possibility that this seed of David will not sin. As the previous chapter argued, within Samuel it is unlikely that this messianic priest who is the seed of David will commit iniquity. The text calls him a "faithful" priest. He seems to act in accord with what is in the Lord's heart and soul without exception (1 Sam 2:35). He is the one whom the Lord will glorify because he glorifies the Lord (v. 30). In the previous chapter we also argued based on Abigail's statement to David in 25:28 that the Messiah will fight the Lord's battles and evil will never be found in him. Surely David will have sons who fail to keep the Lord's covenant stipulations, but 2 Sam 7:11b–17 coupled with 1 Sam 2:35 suggest that the seed is not one of those sinful sons.

Psalm 89 seems to agree that the promised seed of David will not sin. Before we consider that seed in Ps 89, we must understand the overall message of the psalm. Gerald Henry Wilson summarizes his interpretation of Ps 89 saying, "At the conclusion of the third book . . . the impression left is one of a covenant remembered, but a covenant *failed*. The Davidic covenant introduced in Ps 2 has come to nothing and the combination of the three books concludes with the anguished cry of the Davidic descendants."[36] Goldingay agrees with Wilson's pessimistic reading of Ps 89: "It is astonishing that Book III of the Psalter comes to an end with two psalms that terminate with Yhwh's having abandoned Israel. They recall the books of Kings or the books of Chronicles without their hopeful last paragraphs."[37] Wilson and Goldingay agree that David's sons have broken the Davidic covenant. It is a failed covenant.

Pohl challenges this reading. Pohl—like others—notes that verses 31–33 (ET vv. 30–32) heavily allude to 2 Sam 7:14.[38] Pohl then notices another allusion that Wilson failed to observe. Not only does Ps 89:31–33 (ET vv. 30–32) allude to 2 Sam 7:14, but Ps 89:34 (ET v. 33) alludes to 2 Sam 7:15.[39] Pohl observes that in verse 34 (ET v. 33) the Lord promises to not break off his steadfast love from the singular seed of the Davidic covenant. Though

35. See "Excursus: Textual Criticism of 2 Sam 7:14" at this chapter's conclusion.

36. Wilson, *The Editing of the Hebrew Psalter*, 213, (emphasis his).

37. Goldingay, *Psalms: Psalms 42–89*, 691.

38. Pohl IV, "A Messianic Reading of Psalm 89," 513.

39. Pohl IV, "A Messianic Reading of Psalm 89," 513. The parallel between these two texts is suggestive. Second Samuel 7:15a reads as follows: וחסדי לא־יסור ממנו (but my steadfast love will not turn aside from him) [AT]. Psalms 89:34a (ET v. 33a) reads as follows: וחסדי לא־אפיר מעמו (but my steadfast love I will not break off from him) [AT].

David's sons have sinned,[40] the Lord says, "But my steadfast love I will not remove from him" (AT). Notice the switch from David's plural "sons" (בֶּן; vv. 31–33 [ET vv. 30–32]), to David's singular "seed" (זֶרַע; vv. 30, 33–37 [ET vv. 29, 32–36]). Despite the sin of David's sons—which has temporarily stalled the Davidic covenant—the Lord has promised that a single seed will come from David.[41] The hope of the Davidic covenant rests on this seed. All of this suggests that Ps 89 understands that the promised seed of David had not yet come at the time of its writing. Psalm 89 also contrasts David's singular seed with David's plural sons who violate 2 Sam 7:14. This suggests that David's seed will not violate the Lord's covenant stipulations and that the Lord will not discipline him. Rather than sinning and the Lord punishing this seed (i.e., removing his kingship), this seed will "endure forever" (cf. 2 Sam 7:13, 16; לְעוֹלָם יִהְיֶה), and his throne will last as long as the sun appears before God (Ps 89:37 [ET v. 36]).[42]

40. Psalm 89 applies language from 2 Sam 7:14 to David's descendants. This need not mean that 2 Sam 7:14 refers to a collective "offspring." Collins's syntactical note has demonstrated that 2 Sam 7:11b–17 anticipates a single offspring. We will shortly see that Psalm 89 does understand that 2 Sam 7 has promised a particular messianic seed to come from David. Why then does Ps 89 apply language about this coming seed to David's descendants? Apparently, Ps 89 understood that 2 Sam 7 anticipated a single Messiah (v. 34 [ET v. 33]), and yet thought that the ethical components of the Davidic covenant also applied to David's sons who reigned before the Messiah appeared. This logic seems natural. God promised that he would punish the promised messianic seed if he sinned. Surely then God would also punish David's other kingly descendants when they sin.

41. Psalm 132 shares the same basic view of the Davidic covenant that Ps 89 did. Though David has had many sons who must heed 2 Sam 7:14 (cf. Ps 132:11–12), there is one son on whom Israel's salvation rests (vv. 17–18). Though verse 12—which alludes to 2 Sam 7:12 and/or 1 Chr 17:11—seems to understand the "fruit of [David's] loins" (מִפְּרִי בִטְנְךָ) in a collective sense, this is unlikely. We have already seen that 2 Sam 7:11b–17 anticipates an individual seed. First Chronicles 17:11 promises that David's seed will come from his sons (זַרְעֲךָ אַחֲרֶיךָ אֲשֶׁר יִהְיֶה מִבָּנֶיךָ). Thus, the seed of 1 Chr 17:11 is an individual from among David's multiple descendants. Also, Peter quotes Ps 132:10 in Acts 2:30. Peter understands the "fruit of [David's] loins" (καρποῦ τῆς ὀσφύος αὐτοῦ) in Ps 132:10 to be the single messianic son of David from Ps 16:10. Thus, the present author understands Ps 132 to teach that God promised David he would have a descendant come from him (v. 11). Other sons descended from David (v. 12), but these are not the sons whom the Lord promised. This promised son is the Messiah, who is the horn God will make sprout for David, and he is the anointed one (v. 17; cf. 1 Sam 2:10). The Lord will put to shame the enemies of this anointed one, and the anointed one's crown will shine/flourish like a plant (וְעָלָיו יָצִיץ נִזְרוֹ; vv. 17–18; cf. 2 Sam 23:5). For some who interpret verses 17–18 messianically see Kruse, "Psalm 132 and the Royal Zion Festival," 289–90; Sailhamer, NIV Compact Bible Commentary, 345. Others note messianic imagery and language, yet still manage to conclude verses 17–18 do not anticipate the Messiah (see Hossfeld and Zenger, Psalms 3: 459; Goldingay, Psalms: Psalms 90–150, 558).

42. In the next chapter we will note the importance of comparing the seed's reign to the sun (cf. 2 Sam 23:4; Ps 72:16–17).

6.3. THE MESSIANIC PRIEST-KING OF ZECHARIAH AND HEBREWS

In this section, we will seek to buttress the previous exegesis by arguing that both Zechariah and Hebrews understand that a priest-king is the promised seed of David. Demonstrating this increases the likelihood that the author of Samuel intended his readers to understand the faithful priest of 1 Sam 2:35 to be the royal seed of David.

6.3.1. The Messianic Priest-King of Zechariah

Zechariah 6:9–15 concludes the second major portion of the book, and contains an oracle from the Lord.[43] In the oracle, the Lord tells Zechariah to take gold and silver from Heldai, Tobijah, and Jedaiah and to make crowns (עֲטָרוֹת; vv. 10–11).[44] According to Carol L. Meyers and Eric M. Meyers, the root word used for "crowns" (עֲטָרה) "is frequently used as a term for royal power."[45] The Lord instructed Zechariah to put the crown(s)[46] on the head of Joshua the high priest (v. 11b).[47] This effectively makes the high priest appear kingly. The text presents him as though he were a priest and a king.[48]

43. Meyers and Meyers, *Haggai, Zechariah 1–8*, xi.

44. For a discussion on the plural "crowns" see Sweeney, *The Twelve Prophets*, 2:630–31; Meyers and Meyers, *Haggai, Zechariah 1–8*, 350–53.

45. Meyers and Meyers, *Haggai, Zechariah 1–8*, 351.

46. The Hebrew of Zech 6:11 literally reads, "And take silver and gold and make crowns and set on head of Joshua (וְשַׂמְתָּ בְרֹאשׁ יְהוֹשֻׁעַ), the son of Jehozadak, the high priest." Since the text does not provide an explicit direct object for the verb "set" (וְשַׂמְתָּ), one cannot be certain if Zechariah placed one crown or more than one crown on Joshua the high priest's head, though it is hard to imagine how one man could wear two or more crowns simultaneously.

47. Sweeney disagrees with this reading. He understands "Joshua" to be the object of "set." He translates the text to say, "You shall place Joshua ben Jehozadak at (the) head." To place Joshua at the head means to make Joshua the authority figure over Heldai, Tobijah, Jedaiah, and Josiah (see Sweeney, *The Twelve Prophets*, 2:631). This reading is unlikely because the passage nowhere else stresses Joshua's authority over these individuals. Sweeney even notes that the weighty and authoritative words in verses 12–13 apply "to someone other than Joshua" (Sweeney, *The Twelve Prophets*, 2:631). Moreover, Meyers and Meyers demonstrate that Sweeney has misread the Hebrew and that the text "is quite explicit in stating that the 'crown' was placed on Joshua's head" (see Meyers and Meyers, *Haggai, Zechariah 1–8*, 354).

48. Meyers and Meyers disagree with this reading. They understand that while it is true that the crown on Joshua's head "signifies the increased judicial powers of the high priest," one is mistaken to think that this text presents him as a though he were a king. This is so even though the crown on Joshua's head communicates "strong . . . royal associations." Meyers and Meyers argue that Joshua is presented as having only

Thus a priest-king of sorts immediately precedes and thereby introduces the proclamation given in verses 12–13. The text presents Joshua as though he were a priest-king in order to help the interpreter understand that the oracle in verses 12–13 anticipate the messianic priest-king.

After presenting Joshua the high priest as though he were a priest-king, the ESV says that Zechariah said to him, "Thus says the LORD of hosts, 'Behold, the man whose name is the Branch: for he shall branch out from his place, and he shall build the temple of the LORD. It is he who shall build the temple of the LORD and shall bear royal honor, and shall sit and rule on his throne. And there shall be a priest on his throne (והיה כהן על־כסאו), and the counsel of peace shall be between them both" (vv. 12–13). Though most scholars understand this "Branch" to be Zerubbabel,[49] this is unlikely. In a book that has already mentioned Zerubbabel's name four times (4:6, 7, 9, 10), why does the text not say his name in this passage if it is prophesying about him? Meyers and Meyers note this problem, and they point out that scholars frequently emend the text so that it is actually Zerubbabel who wears the crown in 6:11. They suggest that scholars have no basis for these emendations and they emend the text to fit their assumed interpretation.[50]

Scholars agree that this "Branch" (צמח) is a royal figure because of the normal usage of that title.[51] The text seems to present him as the fulfillment of the Davidic covenant because he will "build the temple of the LORD." This is an allusion to 2 Sam 7:13—which said that the seed of David will

"semiautonomy but no monarchy." This is so because Zechariah placed only one crown on Joshua's head while it is the other crown "which is intended to accommodate traditional attachments to the monarchic model of governance" (see Meyers and Meyers, *Haggai, Zechariah 1–8*, 370). They reason thusly because they understand that Joshua wore the silver crown instead of the gold crown. Wearing the silver crown demonstrates royal power but not to the same degree that wearing the gold crown would symbolize. Thus, they conclude that the golden crown is "reserved for the true Davidic monarch" (Meyers and Meyers, *Haggai, Zechariah 1–8*, 354). Much can be said about their view. To begin, the text does present Joshua as a royal priest to at least some degree. How could it not when he is wearing a kingly crown? Second, the text does not explicitly state that there are two crowns. The text does not also explicitly state that one crown was silver and the other was gold, though this seems like a reasonable assumption. Furthermore, the text does not say which crown Joshua wore. Meyers and Meyers conjecture about much to arrive at their conclusion. Lastly, even if Joshua merely wore the silver crown in order to show that the gold crown is for the true Davidide, the text could still present Joshua as a priest-king in order to anticipate the true priest-king who fulfills the Davidic covenant.

49. See Petersen, *Haggai and Zechariah 1–8*, 276–77.

50. Meyers and Meyers, *Haggai, Zechariah 1–8*, 350.

51. Sweeney, *The Twelve Prophets*, 2:641; Petersen, *Haggai and Zechariah 1–8*, 276.

build a house (i.e., temple) for the LORD.[52] We know that the one building the temple is a king—like the seed of David—because he will sit on his throne (Zech 6:13; cf. 2 Sam 7:13).[53]

The text then says that this king "will be a priest on his throne" (והיה כהן על־כסאו). Admittedly, most translations understand the subject of the verb "will be" (והיה) to be the "priest" (כהן), instead of the king from the previous clause. Understanding the priest to be the subject of the verb "will be" (והיה) is certainly grammatically possible, but there are contextual factors that make this unlikely. Remember, one presented as a priest-king served as the illustration and introduction to this oracle. Thus, one should not be surprised to see in this oracle a priest-king. Also, though some desire to render the words "על־כסאו" to mean "beside his throne,"[54] Sweeney is right to say that the preposition "more commonly means 'upon.'"[55] Not only does על normally mean "upon" but the prepositional phrase "על־כסאו" seems to mean "on his throne" without exception.[56] The best explanation for why the priest sits on the king's throne is because the priest is the king.[57]

Most take the following phrase—"and the counsel of peace shall be between them both"—to mean that the respective priest and the respective

52. Shepherd, *Daniel in the Context of the Hebrew Bible*, 48. In the following chapters we will see that additional language from this oracle derives from 2 Samuel.

53. Through personal correspondence DeRouchie informed the present author that "his throne" in Zech 6:13 could be the "LORD's throne." If the "LORD" is the antecedent to "his," then this would suggest that the messianic priest-king (see below) would reign on the LORD's throne. This could suggest that the priest-king may be divine (cf. Isa 9:5–6 [ET vv. 6–7]).

54. Petersen, *Haggai and Zechariah 1–8*, 277.

55. Sweeney, *The Twelve Prophets*, 2:632.

56. The prepositional phrase "על־כסאו" occurs 16 times in the MT and without exception means "on his throne" rather than "beside his throne." For these references see Exod 11:5; 12:29; 1 Kgs 2:19; 3:6; 16:11; 22:10, 19; 2 Kgs 13:13; 2 Chr 9:8; 18:9, 18; Jer 13:13; 22:4; 33:21; Zech 6:13.

57. Though Meyers and Meyers think that the priest will sit "upon" a throne/chair, they do not understand this priest to be royal because in Hebrew the word "throne" (כסא) "is the basic word for 'chair' and takes on the meaning of throne only in royal contexts. It can just as easily be understood to designate the seat of any high official" (Meyers and Meyers, *Haggai, Zechariah 1–8*, 361). Thus, Meyers and Meyers understand the "throne/chair" that the priest sits on to be a different "throne" than the one mentioned in the immediately preceding clause. This understanding fails to convince because Zech 6:12–13 is a royal context. Scholars agree that the title "Branch" is a term for a royal king. This royal context decreases the likelihood that the reader should understand the second "throne/chair" in v. 13 to be merely a "chair" and not a throne. The most natural reading seems to be to understand the second כסא and the first כסא to be one and the same. The Bible infrequently if ever uses כסא to mean "throne" and "chair" in the same sentence without making this difference in meaning clear.

king will be at peace with each other.[58] If the king is the priest, what could this phrase possibly mean? There are two options. The first is that there is peace between both the priestly and the kingly offices because they are united in one priest-king. The second option is that there will finally be peace between the Lord and his king because this king is the righteous seed of David.[59] This reading is certainly possible because if the king is the priest, then verses 12–13 only mention two parties (i.e., the LORD and the priest-king). This reading also gains plausibility when one considers how most of Israel and Judah's kings' ways were antithetical to their God's ways. In sum, the Branch is a priest-king. Zechariah 6:12–13 anticipates a priest-king to fulfill the Davidic covenant by building a temple for the Lord.

6.3.2. The Messianic Priest-King of Hebrews

Hebrews 3:1–6 also understands the faithful priest of 1 Sam 2:35 to be the seed of David in 2 Samuel 7:11b–17. Understanding 1 Sam 2:35 to be a prophecy about a messianic priest who is David's royal seed explains seven different elements in this text.[60]

First, both Samuel and Hebrews present God's anointed one to be a faithful priest. The author of Hebrews calls Jesus a "faithful" (πιστὸν; v. 2) "high priest" (ἀρχιερέα; v. 1). We have already seen that the Lord promised to raise up a faithful priest (ἱερέα πιστόν) in 1 Sam 2:35. It is not concerning that Hebrews calls Jesus a "high priest" while 1 Sam 2:35 merely calls him a "priest" because in the context of 1 Sam 2:27–36 this faithful priest will be a high priest with a priesthood functioning under his authority.

Following D'Angelo,[61] William L. Lane agrees that "the form of the allusion in v 2a reflects a modification of the Nathan oracle under the influence of the oracle to Eli in 1 Sam 2:35. . . . As modified, the Nathan oracle became a testimony for a royal messianic figure, providing a parallel to the oracle to Eli and its testimony to a faithful priest."[62] We agree with Lane, though we wonder why Lane does not explain which elements the author of Hebrews modified from 1 Sam 2:35.[63]

58. Meyers and Meyers, *Haggai, Zechariah 1–8*, 362.

59. Baron, *Commentary on Zechariah*, 201–02.

60. The present author has come to these conclusion independently, though Mary Rose D'Angelo has argued similarly in *Moses in the Letter to the Hebrews*, 65–94.

61. D'Angelo, *Moses in the Letter to the Hebrews*, 78–89.

62. Lane, *Hebrews 1–8*, 76.

63. We can interpret the OG of 1 Sam 2:35 messianically if we simply take the "faithful house" (οἶκον πιστόν) to be the subject of the verb "it will go" (διελεύσεται). The

Noticing how infrequently the biblical material calls priests and high priests "faithful" strengthens Lane and D'Angelo's proposal that Heb 3:1–2 alludes to 1 Sam 2:35. In the Greek NT and in the OG, Heb 2:17 is the only verse that explicitly calls a high priest "faithful"—though one can deduce this same truth from Heb 3:1–2. Also, only 1 Sam 2:35 and Neh 13:13 call a priest(s) "faithful." It is unlikely that Hebrews is alluding to Neh 13:13 because it is not a prophetic text. Following D'Angelo and Lane, the author of Hebrews understands Jesus to be the faithful priest from 1 Sam 2:35.

Second, in both Samuel and Hebrews the faithful priest builds God's house. In 1 Sam 2:35 God builds a faithful house, but in 2 Sam 7:13 the Davidic seed who is the faithful priest builds God's house. This corresponds nicely with Heb 3:3: "For Jesus has been counted worthy of more glory than Moses—as much more glory as the builder of a house has more honor than the house itself."[64] The idea within Hebrews is that Jesus has built the house of God—the temple of people in which God dwells by his Spirit (cf. v. 6). Moses on the other hand, did not create the people of God. Rather, he was a member of the house of God (i.e., Israel), and he served in that house as a servant (cf. Num 12:7).

Third, the authors of both Samuel and Hebrews claim that not only does the faithful priest build the temple, but they also claim that God builds the temple. In Heb 3:1–6 Jesus builds God's house, and yet the author still says that God has built all things—which includes the house (v. 4). This is a jarring statement because the reader is left wondering if Jesus (v. 3) or God (v. 4) built the house. The author of Hebrews seems to say that the answer is that both built God's house. This reading accords with interpreting the faithful priest to be the seed of David within Samuel. This is the case because though the royal, faithful priest would build God's faithful house (2 Sam 7:13, 16), God also promised that he would build a faithful house (1 Sam 2:35).

---

sense of this translation would be that the faithful house will go before the Lord's Christ all the days. Kaiser has proposed reading the Hebrew in this same way. Translated in this way—which is apparently how the author of Hebrews read the Greek—the faithful priest is most naturally the anointed one (χριστοῦ). We can assume that the author of Hebrews was reading the OG because the OT citations within Hebrews "are taken from the LXX. The author never employs the MT" (see Allen, *Lukan Authorship of Hebrews*, 135). This reading of the Greek is likely because of the parallel in 1 Sam 2:30. In that verse the Lord promised that the house of Eli and Eli's father "would go before me [the Lord] forever" (ὁ οἶκός σου καὶ ὁ οἶκος τοῦ παρτός σου διελεύσεται ἐνώπιόν μου ἕως αἰῶνος). One does not need to modify the original sense of the Greek or Hebrew of 1 Sam 2:35 to arrive at a messianic reading—though the present author has followed Deenick in slightly emending the vowel pointings in the MT.

64. See Lane, *Hebrews 1–8*, 77; O'Brien, *The Letter to the Hebrews*, 132–33.

Fourth, Samuel and Hebrews understand the house that the faithful priest will build to be a non-physical temple consisting of people among whom God will dwell. That the house that Jesus builds in Heb 3:1–6 is a non-physical temple consisting of people is quite clear. Hebrews 3:6 reads, "But Christ is faithful over God's house as a son. And we are his house, if indeed we hold fast our confidence and our boasting in our hope." In Hebrews, God's house is a non-physical temple, but can the same be said of the house of God that the faithful priest will build in Samuel?

To understand that David's royal seed will build a non-physical temple consisting of people for the Lord to dwell within one must first notice three important terms in 2 Sam 7:12–13. These terms are "house" (οἶκον), "kingdom" (βασιλείαν), and "throne" (θρόνον). The royal seed of David, who is the faithful priest, will build a "house" for God and will possess his own "kingdom" and "throne." What is essential to notice is that these same three terms appear again in verse 16. In this verse the Lord will make the seed of David's "house" (οἶκος) faithful, and the seed will possess his own "kingdom" (βασιλεία) and "throne" (θρόνος). Since the "kingdom" and "throne" in verse 16 are the same "kingdom" and "throne" in verses 12–13, the "house" in verse 16 is most likely the same "house" in verse 13.

By linking the house of verse 13 with the house of verse 16, Samuel's author presents intentional ambiguity concerning the meaning of the word "house" within 2 Sam 7. David wanted to build a "house" (i.e., temple build-ing) in which the Lord would dwell, and so it is right to interpret the "house" that David's messianic seed will build to be a dwelling place for God. Yet, we have seen above that the "house" that David's messianic, priestly seed will build in verse 13 is the same "house" that appears in verse 16. This "house" in verse 16 refers to a group of people, the descendants of David's messianic son.[65] This is similar to how the house that God will build in 1 Sam 2:35 for the faithful messianic priest also referred to a group of people. Taking all the evidence together, Samuel anticipates that David's son, the messianic priest-king, and God will build a dwelling place for God consisting of those people who belong to the house of David's messianic, priest-king son.

Fifth, in both Samuel and Heb 3:1–6 the faithful high priest is the "Christ." Hebrews 3:6 refers to the faithful high priest as "Christ." This cor-responds to our exegesis of 1 Sam 2:35 that understood the faithful priest

---

65. As mentioned before, the OG identifies the faithful house in 2 Sam 7:16 to be the house of David's royal seed. Though the MT says that the faithful house in 2 Sam 7:16 is David's house, we argued in section 5.1.2. that Samuel's larger context indicates that David's faithful house in 2 Sam 7:16 is only faithful on account of his messianic seed's faithful house. Previously in this chapter we also noted evidence from within 2 Sam 7 that suggested that David and his seed's house are coextensive.

to be the anointed one (i.e., Christ/Messiah) mentioned previously in that same verse. Interestingly, O'Brien notes that "the title *Christ* is used here for the first time in Hebrews."[66] Though one cannot be certain, it is possible that the author of Hebrews waits to use the word "Christ" until this point in his letter so that he can imitate 1 Sam 2:10 and verse 35. These are the first places that Scripture calls the royal eschatological deliverer the Christ/Messiah. As the OT used the title "Christ" to refer to the royal eschatological deliverer for the first time when speaking of the messianic, faithful priest in Samuel, so too the author of Hebrews ascribes the title "Christ" to Jesus for the first time when identifying him as the messianic, faithful priest.

Sixth, both Samuel and Hebrews identify the faithful, messianic priest to be the Son of God. In Hebrews 3:6 the author of Hebrews says, "But Christ is faithful over God's house as a son."[67] Within Hebrews, the faithful high priest who builds the house for God, Jesus, is the Son of God. Once again, this accords nicely with how we previously identified the faithful priest from 1 Sam 2:35 with David's royal seed in 2 Sam 7:11b–17. God says concerning this faithful priest from 1 Sam 2:35, "I will be to him a father and he will be to me a son" (2 Sam 7:14a).[68]

Seventh, in both Samuel and Hebrews the house that the messianic faithful priest builds is a faithful house. Hebrews 3:6 says, "And we are [Jesus's] house if indeed we hold fast our confidence and our boasting in our hope." Hebrews's point is that only those who persevere in their faith in the Christ are part of the faithful priest's house. In other words, Jesus's house consists exclusively of those who faithfully maintain their belief in him. Lane agrees with this: "According to 1 Sam 2:35 God promised not only that he would raise up a faithful priest but that he would build a faithful house. This latter promise is taken up in v. 6b."[69] We have already argued that the faithful priest from Samuel will replace the Aaronic priesthood with his descendants, his house. This would mean that those who "hold fast" their confidence and their "boasting" until the end are priests. It is no surprise then that Hebrews twice refers to Christians as priests offering sacrifices to the Lord (see 12:28; 13:15).

66. O'Brien, *The Letter to the Hebrews*, 134.

67. Though "faithful" is not in the Greek text in verse 6, it is assumed because of the comparison with Moses from the previous verse.

68. One may object to this by saying that it is too subtle to think the author of Hebrews alluded to 2 Sam 7:14 when he calls the Christ a "son over God's house." In response, Hebrews's author need not make his allusion explicit because he has already alluded to this text in Heb 1:5. Regarding the quotation of 2 Sam 7:14 in Heb 1:5 see O'Brien, *The Letter to the Hebrews*, 66.

69. Lane, *Hebrews 1–8*, 79, (emphasis his).

In sum, the author of Hebrews understands the Son of God from 2 Sam 7:14 to be the faithful priest from 1 Sam 2:35. Hebrews identifies this faithful high priest as Jesus. He is the Messiah, and he has built a house for God consisting of his faithful offspring.[70] Samuel, Zechariah, and Hebrews all understand the faithful priest of 1 Sam 2:35 to be David's seed. This confirms that David's seed in 2 Sam 7:11b–17 is the Messiah. Having finally identified the seed of David, we are now in a position to begin to argue that this seed will defeat the serpent.

6.4. SAMUEL'S MESSIAH AND GENESIS'S SEED

As mentioned, for this study to successfully argue that Samuel understands the Messiah to reign as king over the defeated serpent, it must demonstrate that Samuel understands its Messiah to be the seed of the woman from Genesis. Such an understanding is present in 2 Sam 7.[71]

The covenant the Lord made with David in 2 Sam 7 contains allusions to the Abrahamic covenant. The two most obvious allusions are in verses 9 and 12. In verse 9, the Lord tells David, "I have been with you wherever you went and have cut off all your enemies from before you. And I will make for you a great name (ועשׂתי לך שׁם גדול), like the name of the great ones of the earth."[72] When the Lord promises to make for David a "great name," the text alludes to Gen 12:2. There God promises Abram, "I will make of you a great nation, and I will bless you and make your name great (ואגדלה שׁמך), and

---

70. We can strengthen Lane's point that Heb 3:6b alludes to the faithful priest's faithful house by noting that the Christ's house must "hold fast" (κατάσχωμεν) to their hope. The author of Hebrews uses the verb "hold fast" three times in his letter (3:6, 14; 10:23). Of these three times, he uses it two times in close proximity with the word "faithful" (πιστός; 3:5–6; 10:23). This suggests that the author of Hebrews closely connects "holding fast" with the idea of "faithful." This increases the likelihood that the author of Hebrews wrote 3:6b with the reference to the faithful priest and his faithful house.

71. Our previous chapter provided us with evidence that David's seed is the expected seed from Gen 3:15, as well. There we noted that the text presented David as though he were the first woman when he saw that Bathsheba was good and took her. Like the first woman, David sinned, and like the first woman whom God promised a seed, God also promised David a royal seed. Since David's royal seed and the first woman's promised seed are in parallel relationship with each other, this suggests that these two seeds are actually one in the same. The following chapter will likewise marshal evidence that Samuel presents David's seed to be the royal eschatological deliverer promised in Gen 3:15.

72. In 2 Sam 7:9, there is some debate about whether one should translate certain verbs as referring to the future or past. For a discussion see Fokkelman, *Throne and City*, 223–26. Fokkelman concludes that 2 Sam 7:9c–16 refers to the future.

you are to be a blessing" (AT). As the Lord promised to make a great name for Abram, so too the Lord promised to make David a great name. Morrison agrees that Samuel alludes to Genesis. He writes, "God will make David's name great (2 Sam 7:9b), echoing language of the covenantal promise to Abraham in Genesis 12:2."[73]

Second Samuel 7:12 also alludes to the Genesis narrative. God promised that when David dies, he will raise up David's seed. This seed "will go out from [David's] inward parts" (אשר יצא ממעיך) [AT]. This awkward sounding phrase alludes to a promise God made with Abraham. On this allusion Fokkelman writes, "The combination of 'your seed after you' itself takes us back to the Torah and God's promises to the patriarchs, and the idiom denoting 'the offspring of your body' becomes even more specific. It stems from Gen. 15, its sole occurrence except for here and [2 Sam] 16:11!"[74]

The specific verse that Fokkelman says Samuel quotes is Gen 15:4. In Gen 15:3 Abram tells the Lord that he has not given him a "seed" (זרע) and that Eliezer, his servant, will gain his inheritance. God then replies, "This man [Eliezer] will not be your heir, but the one whom will go out from your inward parts (אשר יצא ממעיך)—that one will inherit you" (v. 4; AT).

On account of these connections, both Dempster and Fokkelman understand the Davidic covenant to further develop the covenant that God made with Abram.[75] What God promised to do through Abram, he is now promising to continue to bring about through David and his seed.

Since the Lord's covenant with David develops the covenant he made with Abram, one should ask what did the Lord promised to do through Abram. Though one could write at length about that question, we will try to simply and briefly argue that God made promises to Abram to restore God's blessing to the world. Since the first man and woman lost this blessing because of their sin with the serpent, God made promises to Abram to restore the blessing to the world, and this would seem to necessarily involve overcoming the serpent.

James Mckeown provides support for thinking that the promises made in the Abrahamic covenant necessitate the serpent's defeat. He has noted that the Lord spoke his promises to Abram in Gen 12:1–3 in such a way to

---

73. Morrison, 2 Samuel, 100. Bergen likewise concurs: "And the Lord was not finished adorning his earthly dwelling place; he would make David's 'name great, like the names of the greatest men of the earth'—a covenant promise not made by the Lord to an individual since the days of Abraham (cf. Gen 12:2)." See Bergen, 1, 2 Samuel, 339.

74. Fokkelman, Throne and City, 230. Firth agrees with Fokkelman's assessment. He writes, "The promise [to David] is rich in Abrahamic allusions, especially in language concerning the 'seed' to come from David's own body" (see Firth, 1 & 2 Samuel, 385).

75. See Dempster, Dominion and Dynasty, 143; Fokkelman, Throne and City, 230.

show that Abram will restore the blessing that was lost in Gen 3. McKeown writes,

> This promised blessing in 12:1–3 is clearly intended as a contrast to the cursing that is mentioned in the primeval history (3:14, 17; 4:11; 5:29; 9:25). It is probably not coincidental that cursing occurs five times in chs. 1–11 and the Hebrew root conveying the idea of blessing appears five times in the 'call of Abram' (12:1–3). . . . The underlying message in this passage is that God now counters the power of cursing with blessing.[76]

Schreiner further elaborates on how the Lord plans to restore the blessing on humanity. He writes, "The blessing was universal so that it encompassed all the peoples of the world (12:3). The serpent, then, would be defeated by the children of Abraham, and so it is now clear in the story that the children of the woman (Gen 3:15) would come from the family of Abraham. . . . Blessing for the world would come from a royal figure."[77]

This royal figure is the seed of the woman. By defeating the serpent, the seed of the woman would bring about the fulfillment of the Abrahamic covenant. Hamilton concurs: "When the Lord promises to bless Abraham, and when he declares that all the families of the earth will be blessed in Abraham (Gen. 12:3), he is promising victory to the seed of the woman over the seed of the serpent."[78] Hamilton shows his agreement with our argument that the seed of David will defeat the serpent when he writes, "The seed of David is seed of Judah, seed of Abraham, and the genealogies in Genesis 5 and 11 show us that he is also seed of the woman."[79]

Through the allusions in 2 Sam 7 with the Abrahamic covenant, one can infer that the Davidic covenant develops the Abrahamic covenant. This means that the Lord's promises to David about his seed imply the destruction of the serpent. We will see this implication made explicit when we consider 2 Sam 23:1–7 in the following chapter. Within Samuel, the seed of David is the promised Messiah, and he is also the seed of the woman.

6.5. SUMMARY

This chapter sought to demonstrate that Samuel presents the seed of David in 2 Sam 7:11b–17 to be the woman's seed from Gen 3:15. In order to

---

76. McKeown, *Genesis*, 74.

77. Schreiner, *The King in His Beauty*, 17.

78. Hamilton, *God's Glory in Salvation through Judgment*, 81–82.

79. Hamilton, "The Seed of the Woman and the Blessing of Abraham," 268.

accomplish this goal, we argued that neither Samuel, 2 Kings, nor 2 Chronicles understood Solomon to be the ultimate fulfillment of the seed that the Lord promised he would raise up when David dies. Instead of Solomon, we proposed that Samuel presents the faithful priest in 1 Sam 2:35 as the seed of the Davidic covenant on account of multiple lexical and conceptual links. Though we have argued that Samuel presents the faithful priest as one who will be righteous and always glorify the Lord, this priest can still fulfill the Davidic covenant because 2 Sam 7:14 did not originally say "when [the seed] sins" but "if [the seed] sins." We then noted that Ps 89 also seems to understand the seed of David as one who will obey the Lord's commands and avoid the punishment of 2 Sam 7:14.

In order to substantiate our interpretation that Samuel understands a priest to be David's royal son, we argued that both Zech 6:9–13 and Heb 3:1–6 present a similar understanding. Both of these texts say that the priest-king builds the house for the Lord and thereby fulfills the Davidic covenant. Finally, we concluded that David's seed in 2 Sam 7:11b–17 fulfills the Abrahamic covenant. The Lord gave the Abrahamic covenant to restore the blessing that humanity lost on account humanity's sin with the serpent. This means that for the blessings of the Abrahamic covenant to come about, the serpent must be defeated. Since David's seed fulfills the Abrahamic covenant, we concluded that this necessarily implies that he will defeat the serpent. In the following chapter, we will further demonstrate that Samuel presents David's messianic seed as the one who will defeat the serpent.

Excursus: Textual Criticism of 2 Samuel 7:14

An analysis of ἐάν within Samuel confirms McCarter's conclusion that the OG contains the original reading for 2 Sam 7:14. Ἐάν occurs sixty-seven times within Samuel. Ἐάν translates אשר seventeen times (1 Sam 2:14; 9:6; 10:7; 14:7; 16:3; 19:3; 22:23; 23:13; 25:8; 28:8; 2 Sam 7:14; 15:4, 21, 35, 36, 17:12; 18:4), while it translates אם thirty-eight times (1 Sam 1:11; 2:16, 25a, 25b; 3:9, 17; 6:9; 11:3; 12:14, 15, 25; 14:9, 10, 39; 17:9a, 9b, 9d; 19:11; 20:6, 7a, 7b; 9a, 21, 22; 2 Sam 3:35; 10:11a, 11b; 11:20; 15:8, 21b, 21c, 25, 26, 33, 34; 17:13; 18:3a, 3b). Three times ἐάν translates כי (1 Sam 23:3; 27:1; 2 Sam 7:12). There are five times that ἐάν does not translate any particular word within the Hebrew text. In these instances, ἐάν tends to translate implied potentiality within the Hebrew text (1 Sam 1:22; 19:3b; 20:9b, 14; 2 Sam 18:23). Ἐάν translates מה once (1 Sam 20:10), and one time there is material missing in the MT so one cannot know for certain which word ἐάν would have translated (1 Sam 12:41). Lastly, there are two times when ἐὰν μὴ translates כי אם (1 Sam 26:10; 2 Sam 3:13).

What is most relevant for our purposes is that every time ἐὰν translates אשר in Samuel, the pattern is relative pronoun (or relative adjective) + ἐὰν. The relative adjective + ἐὰν pattern only occurs once (1 Sam 10:7). There are fifteen instances of the relative pronoun + ἐὰν pattern. The only exception for this relative pronoun/adjective + ἐὰν pattern is in 2 Sam 7:14. Thus, either 2 Sam 7:14 is simply an exception to this pattern, or a relative pronoun/adjective has dropped out of the OG, or the OG was not translating a Hebrew text that looks like the MT as we now have it. Inserting a relative pronoun or relative adjective into the Greek does not make sense. Thus, it is unlikely that the relative pronoun or relative adjective has dropped out. Also, if the MT is original, there seems to be no reason why the Hebrew of 2 Sam 7:14 is that different from the other constructions so as to cause the established pattern to differ. There seems to be no reason for 2 Sam 7:14 to be an exception, though that does not mean that it cannot be one. With that said, a pattern that holds sixteen out of seventeen times is significant. Thus, it is unlikely that the OG was translating a Hebrew text that resembles the MT as we now have it. It seems most likely that someone has changed the original Hebrew by inserting אשר into 2 Sam 7:14.

Since a scribe(s) has probably altered the MT text by inserting אשר, then other alterations are possible. It seems probable that someone has changed the MT by adding in the ב + infinitive construct "when he commits iniquity" (בהעותו). This is a reasonable assertion for a few reasons. First, the parallel text in Ps 89:31–33 (ET v. 30–32) is significant here. That text clearly parallels 2 Sam 7:14 and uses אם. It does not contain any temporal clause or infinitive construct. It simply says, "If (אם/ἐὰν) they forsake my law and do not walk in my judgments; if (אם/ἐὰν) they violate my statutes and do not keep my commandments, then I will punish their transgression with the rod and their iniquity with stripes." These verses support the "if" reading, and they help cast doubt on the "when" reading.

Psalm 132 corroborates this, but not as strongly as Ps 89:31–33 (ET vv. 30–32) did. Psalm 132:11 seems to allude to 2 Sam 7:12, which mentions that David's seed "will go out from your inner parts." Psalm 132:11 reads, "The LORD has sworn truth to David. He will not turn back from it: 'I will set from the fruit of your womb/body on your throne for you'" (AT). Verse 12 then alludes to 2 Sam 7:14. Instead of saying, "When the seed sins, I will punish him," Ps 132:12 reads, "If (ἐὰν/אם) your sons keep my covenant and my testimony which I will teach them, then your sons will sit upon your throne forever." Once again, that portion of Scripture which corresponds to 2 Sam 7:14 does not mention "when" or an infinitive construct at all. Both the MT and the OG of Ps 89 and 132 contain readings similar to the OG of 2 Sam 7:14. This suggests that the MT of 2 Sam 7:14 is a corrupted text.

Also, the syntactical pattern we see in the OG of 2 Sam 7:14 is ἐὰν + verb + article + noun. This pattern occurs eight times in Samuel (1 Sam 10:7; 12:14; 20:10; 25:8; 2 Sam 7:12, 14; 11:20; 15:21). Twice when this pattern occurs (1 Sam 12:14; 2 Sam 11:20), ἐὰν translates אם. Thus, there are two instances where the syntactical pattern displayed in the OG matches a clause beginning with אם. This shows that the OG as it presently stands could have been translating an אם clause and need not have been translating a clause with a temporal infinitive construct.

Also, one must ask which contains the harder reading. The greater temptation would be for a scribe to change a text agreeing with the message of the OG to the message of the MT rather than the other way. This is true for two reasons. First, it is a bit jarring to read "if" he sins. That seems to suggest that a son of David could actually not sin even though texts like 1 Kgs 8:46 say that everyone sins. Secondly, since scribes tend to historicize texts, a scribe could have been tempted to change the text to align more closely to what he knew about Solomon. For the scribe it was not a matter of "if" Solomon would sin. The scribe would know that Solomon sinned egregiously at his life's end (1 Kgs 11). Furthermore, we have already seen the MT historicize the OG in 2 Sam 7:15. There the MT provided the historical referent to David's unstated royal predecessor (i.e., Saul). It seems that someone has once again altered the MT by historicizing the text.

In sum, we have noted that someone has likely altered the MT. When the OG translates אשר in Samuel, it always follows a relative pronoun/adjective + ἐὰν pattern. The only exception to this pattern is in 2 Sam 7:14. This suggests that either the OG has lost a relative pronoun/adjective or that the OG was not translating a Hebrew document that looks like 2 Sam 7:14 as the MT now presents it. Since inserting a relative pronoun/adjective into the OG makes little sense, it is more likely that the OG was not translating a Hebrew clause that contained אשר. Since this suggests that someone has altered 2 Sam 7:14 in the MT, other alterations become more probable. We concluded that the original text also did not have the MT's "when he commits iniquity" (בהעותו) but that it originally had the OG's "if" (ἐὰν/ אם). We came to this conclusion because the MT and OG in both of 2 Sam 7:14's closest parallel texts (Ps 89:29–31 [ET v. 30–32]; 132:12) agree with the OG's translation of 2 Sam 7:14.

7

THE MESSIANIC HOPE OF THE NEW CREATION IN 2 SAMUEL 23:1–7

THIS BOOK HAS A two-fold purpose: (1) demonstrate that Samuel contains a serpent motif and (2) demonstrate that this motif's significance within Samuel is to present the seed of David as the promised seed of the woman from Gen 3:15 who will defeat the serpent and reign as king in the new creation. We demonstrated the first purpose of this book in chapters 3–4 by showing that Samuel does employ a serpent motif. In order to demonstrate the second purpose of the book, we argued in chapter 5 that the serpent motif reveals that neither Saul nor David are the complete fulfillment of the promised seed of the woman who will one day defeat the serpent from Gen 3:15. We then argued in chapter 6 that Samuel identifies the seed of David as the Messiah and as the fulfillment of the promised seed of the woman from Gen 3:15.

In this chapter we will seek to complete the second purpose of this book by showing that Samuel presents David's messianic seed as the one who will reign as king in a new creation and defeat all opposition including the serpent. We will try to accomplish this goal in four steps by (1) locating 2 Sam 23:1–7 within its larger context and explaining its structure, (2) briefly exegeting 2 Sam 23:1–7, (3) considering how other Scriptures read 2 Sam 23:1–7, and (4) noting how this passage reveals that the Messiah will reign in the new creation and defeat all of his enemies.

7.1. THE CONTEXT AND STRUCTURE
OF 2 SAMUEL 23:1–7

Scholars agree that 2 Sam 23:1–7 forms half of the center of a chiasm that stretches from 2 Sam 21 to chapter 24. Morrison confidently states, "Scholars have long been in agreement that these episodes, despite their apparent disaggregation, are carefully crafted into a concentric, three-tiered structure."[1] Morrison is representative of scholarship when he presents the following structure:

A. National crisis (21:1–14)

    B. Lists of David's warriors and accounts of heroic deeds (21:15–22)

        C. Poem (22:1–51)

        C'. Poem (23:1–7)

    B'. Lists of David's warriors and accounts of heroic deeds (23:8–39)

A'. National crisis (24:1–25).[2]

One can see that 2 Sam 23:1–7 is at the center of Samuel's chiastic conclusion.

Furthermore, it is important to see that 2 Sam 22:1–51—the poem immediately preceding 2 Sam 23:1–7—concludes by referring to the Lord's "steadfast love to his anointed, to David and his seed forever" (v. 51) [AT]. Concerning this verse Fokkelman notes, "The words 'his king' and 'his anointed' carry us back to the song of Hannah once again: Her final cola

---

1. Morrison, *2 Samuel*, 276.

2. Morrison, *2 Samuel*, 276. For a similar chiastic understanding see van Wijk-Bos, *Reading Samuel*, 236. Though Morrison and van Wijk-Bos have correctly divided their chiastic structures, perhaps one can provide more precise titles for each section by emphasizing what David does or says. For example, the text presents David as a priest in both (A) 21:1–14 and (A') 24:1–25. In 21:1–14, David asks the Gibeonites how he can "make atonement" and appease God's anger (v. 3). Chapter 24:1–25 concludes with David stopping another national crisis through offerings. The final verse of 2 Samuel reads, "And David built there an altar to the LORD and offered burnt offerings and peace offerings. So, the LORD responded to the plea for the land, and the plague was averted from Israel." Once again, David saves Israel through priestly activity. The text then highlights David's military successes in 21:15–22 (B) and 23:8–29 (B'). These military victories are fitting for a king. Thus, it seems that David as priest (21:1–14 and 24:1–25) and David as military conqueror (i.e., king; 21:15–22 and 23:8–39) frame the two central poems (22:1–51 and 23:1–7). We have seen thus far that Samuel contains a prominent priest-king motif. It seems that the text presents David as a priest-king to frame the messianic poems in the chiasm's center. If this understanding is correct, then the structure would encourage the reader to understand David's messianic seed in the two central poems to also be a priest-king.

ended on the same rhyming pair!"[3] For Fokkelman, "the large number of words [Hannah and David's poems] have in common require our making an explicit connection between the poetic opening and the poetic close of the books of Samuel."[4] Noticing these same similarities, Polzin writes that "the Song of Hannah [is] a proleptic summary of David's final hymn."[5]

Polzin and Fokkelman's observations about Hannah's song and David's poem are important because we have already seen that Hannah's song ends by expecting the coming messianic king (1 Sam 2:10). This king is the faithful priest in 1 Sam 2:35, and he is also the seed of David in 2 Sam 7:11b–17. Thus, one can conclude that—like Hannah's song—David's poem in 2 Sam 22:1–51 ends anticipating the messianic seed of David. Because 2 Sam 23:1–7 is structurally parallel to 2 Sam 22:1–51, one can reasonably infer that the king of 2 Sam 23:1–7 is the messianic seed of David. In addition, 2 Sam 23:1 begins with a *waw*, and this suggests that 2 Sam 23:1–7 continues to discuss the messianism at the conclusion of 2 Sam 22:1–51.[6] The structural location of 2 Sam 23:1–7 encourages a messianic reading.

Scholars understand the structure of 2 Sam 23:1–7 in two different ways. The disagreement revolves around if verses 6–7 are part of David's prophecy or if they are David's comments about his prophecy. Most scholars seem to prefer the former option,[7] but others do prefer the latter.[8] The present author finds the former option most persuasive. For this reason, we will approach 2 Sam 23:1–7 as an introduction (vv. 1–3a) and an oracle (vv. 3b–4, 6–7) with an interjection (v. 5).

7.2. EXEGESIS OF 2 SAMUEL 23:1–7

In this section, we briefly exegete 2 Sam 23:1–7 by considering the text's introduction (vv. 1–3a), oracle (vv. 3b–4, 6–7), and interjection (v. 5). We will note select textual variants along the way, but will mainly explain the MT. As Auld states, "The LT [Lucianic text] largely makes good sense; but that need not imply that the underlying Hebrew is always superior to the MT's."[9]

3. Fokkelman, *Throne and City*, 354.

4. Fokkelman, *Throne and City*, 354.

5. Polzin, *Samuel and the Deuteronomist*, 33.

6. Likewise, the OG begins with καὶ. It is worth noting that the apostle Paul also apparently understood 2 Sam 22's conclusion messianically (cf. Rom 15:9; 2 Sam 22:50).

7. Morrison, *2 Samuel*, 297; Olmo Lete, "David's Farewell Oracle (2 Samuel 23:1–7)," 424.

8. Anderson, *2 Samuel*, 267.

9. Auld, *I & II Samuel*, 593. Another reason for choosing to prioritize the MT over

7.2.1. The Introduction of 2 Samuel 23:1–7: Verses 1–3a

The introduction to 2 Sam 23:1–7 reads,

> And these are the last words of David: The oracle of David, the
> son of Jesse, the oracle of the man who was raised on high,[10] the
> anointed of the God of Jacob, the delightful one of the songs[11]

---

the OG is because—as we will see below—when the rest of Scripture alludes to 2 Sam
23:1–7, it interprets it in such a way that accords with the MT and not with the OG.

10. The textual critical difficulties regarding 2 Sam 23:1–7 are immense. H. Neil
Richardson goes so far as to say that "although the text presents a number of difficulties it cannot be said that the ancient versions provide much help in solving them.
As the reader no doubt is well aware, the textual situation especially in regard to the
books of Samuel is highly complex" (Richardson, "Last Words of David," 258). Each of
the three major text traditions (Dead Sea Scrolls, MT, and OG) differ in verse 1. The
Dead Sea Scrolls differ from the MT by understanding the word "on high" (עָל) to have
been "God" (אֵל). 4QSam[a] also has "raised" as a *hiphil* instead of as a *hophal* like the
MT. Thus, 4QSam[a] reads, "And these are the last words of David: The oracle of David,
the son of Jesse, the oracle of the man whom God raised (הקים אל), the anointed of
the God of Jacob, the delightful one of the songs of Israel." The LXX[B] slightly differs
from both: "And these are the last words of David: The faithful David, the son of Jesse
and the faithful man whom the Lord raised—concerning/over the anointed one (ἐπὶ
χριστὸν) of the God of Jacob and the fair songs of Israel." Apparently, the translator of
LXX[B] read עַל as "concerning" (עַל) as opposed to the MT, which read עַל as "high" (עָל).
According to Julius A. Bewer (see Bewer, "Notes on 1 Sam 13:21; 2 Sam 23:1; Psalm
48:8," 47–48) the LXX[L] revised this text by omitting the "concerning/over" (ἐπί) from
the LXX[B]. Thus, the LXX[L] differs by saying, "The man whom God raised, the Christ,
the God of Jacob." Of particular interest is the reading found in LXX[B]. That text suggests that in 2 Sam 23:1–7 David prophesies specifically about the Christ. Following
Sailhamer (see Sailhamer, *Introduction to Old Testament Theology*, 221), Rydelnik has
argued for such a position (see Rydelnik, *The Messianic Hope*, 39–41). This reading
faces a significant challenge because it says that David was prophesying concerning
the "Christ of God and the fair songs of Israel." It is difficult to see within 2 Sam 23:1–7
where David prophesied about Israel's "fair songs." Also, the LXX[B] renders "utterance"
(נאם) as "faithful" (πιστὸς/נאמן). Though confusing "faithful" (נאמן) and "utterance"
(נאם) may have been an accident, it could be a sign that those translating the LXX[B] were
reading 2 Sam 23:1–7 with 1 Sam 2:35 because in that text the Lord "raises up" (*hiphil*
of קוּם) a faithful (נאמן) priest. Similarly, in the LXX[B] of 2 Sam 23:1 the Lord "raises up"
the faithful David.

11. Many scholars no longer understand זמיר to mean "song." These scholars (see
Cross, *Canaanite Myth and Hebrew Epic*, 234; Richardson, "Last Words of David,"
261; Olmo Lete, "David's Farewell Oracle [2 Samuel 23:1–7], 416) translate the word
as "protection" based on a possible parallel with the "Arabic *dhamara* 'protect'" (see
Gaster, "Notes on 'the Song of the Sea,'" 45). Fokkelman maintains that translating the
word as "song" still makes sense (Fokkelman, *Throne and City*, 357–58). The word occurs in Exod 15:2, Isa 12:2, Ps 118:14 (OG 117:14), and 2 Sam 23:1. In Exodus, Moses
immediately proceeds to sing a song after using the word in question. Likewise, in Isa
12:2, Isaiah breaks out in song in 12:5 praising the Lord. Since the word tends to occur
in contexts containing songs, the traditional translation makes good sense.

of Israel.[12] The Spirit of the Lord spoke by me and his word was
on my tongue. The God of Israel has spoken; the Rock of Israel
has said to me (AT).

These are David's last words. Since he speaks later in Samuel (2 Sam 24:2),
it is best to understand these "last words" not as his final words in the book,
but as the words that David spoke shortly before he died. After the narrator
informs the reader that these are David's "death bed" words, David himself
introduces the poem.

David begins by saying that his poem is in fact an "oracle" (נאם). He is
prophesying by the Spirit of the Lord (23:2–3).[13] When David states, "The
oracle of David, the son of Jesse, the oracle of the man who was raised on
high," scholars agree that David is modeling this prophetic introduction after Balaam's remarkably similar introductions in Num 24:3 and 15. Agur in
Prov 30:1 also introduces an oracle in the same way that David does here.[14]
The similarities between these prophecies are that Balaam, David, and Agur
each speak the "oracle" (נאם) of Balaam/David/Agur who is the son of Beor/
Jesse/Jakeh. They then parallel this initial line by saying that they are giving
the "oracle" (נאם) of the "strong man" (הגבר).

Significantly, though Balaam gives seven distinct prophecies,[15] he only
introduces his two messianic prophecies with the introduction that David
copies.[16] Also, an increasing number of scholars are beginning to argue that
Agur prophesied about the Messiah with this same prophetic introduction.[17] Since the three other prophecies that use David's particular introduction prophesy about the Messiah, it is likely that David intended to prophesy
about the coming Messiah, his seed (2 Sam 22:51).

Perhaps it is for the reasons above that two ancient translations rendered David's prophecy as a messianic oracle. The *Targum Jonathan* reads,

12. One can understand the phrase "the delightful one of the songs of Israel" (ונעים
זמרות ישראל) in two ways. It is either a genitive of reference or production. In the MT,
David is either saying that he produces Israel's songs or that the songs are about him.
The former option seems more likely than the latter.

13. van Wijk-Bos, *Reading Samuel*, 244.

14. A few scholars noting the similarities between David, Balaam, and Agur's prophetic introductions are Morrison (see *2 Samuel*, 298), Auld (see *I & II Samuel*, 594),
and Richardson (see "Last Words of David," 260).

15. Balaam's seven different prophecies occur in Num 23:7–10, 18–24; 24:3–9;
15–19, 20, 21–22, 23–24.

16. For a defense of Num 24:3–9 and 15–19 as messianic prophecies see Sailhamer,
The Meaning of the Pentateuch, 476–80; Hamilton, "The Seed of the Woman and the
Blessing of Abraham," 262–68.

17. See Sailhamer, *NIV Compact Bible Commentary*, 354; Shepherd, *Daniel in the
Context of the Hebrew Bible*, 59.

"David said, 'The God of Israel spoke unto me; the powerful one of Israel who has dominion among the sons of man, judging the truth, said to appoint for me the king, that is the Messiah to come who will arise and rule by fear of the Lord.'"[18] Likewise, the LXX[B] says that David prophesied "concerning the Christ of God and the fair songs of Israel" (AT). Both of these translations clearly understood David's oracle to be messianic. It is to this oracle that we now turn.

7.2.2. The Oracle of 2 Samuel 23:1–7: Verses 3b–4 and 6–7

Scholars translate David's oracle in 2 Sam 23:3b–4 in various ways, though most agree on the basic meaning of the verses. The present author woodenly translates these verses from the MT as follows: "The one who rules[19] over humanity is righteous, who rules with respect to the fear of God—even like the light of the morning the sun will rise, a morning without clouds: from brightness: from rain [the] grass from the land."[20]

Though the translation is cumbersome, the sense is basically clear.[21] David is prophesying that a king will reign righteously and in the fear of God. This king will not be wicked, and he will be like a morning sun ending the darkness of night. He will shine brightly on the grass, his people. He shines so brightly that he is like a day without clouds. The king is probably also not just the sunlight but also the rain upon the grass (cf. Ps 72:5–6).[22] This king is the light and rain that causes his people to flourish as they benefit from his righteous rule.

After David's interrupts his own prophecy (v. 5), he resumes the prophecy in verses 6–7. These verses read, "But worthlessness is/are[23] all

18. Harrington and Saldarini, *Targum Jonathan of the Former Prophets*, 203.

19. The LXX[B] misunderstood משל to mean "parable" or "wise saying" instead of "to rule." Perhaps the LXX[B] thought that David was continuing to copy Balaam's oracle (cf. Num 24:3, 15).

20. The New English Translation of the Septuagint (NETS) translates 2 Sam 23:3–4 like this: "The God of Israel speaks; Israel's keeper spoke to me: Speak a parable. How might you strengthen fear of God by a human? And by God may the sun rise at the light of dawn; the morning did not pass from splendor, and it was as if from rain for tender grass from the earth." See McLean, "The Kaige Text of Reigns," 295.

21. Cross states that perhaps some of the material in verse 4 is hopelessly corrupt (Cross, *Canaanite Myth and Hebrew Epic*, 235). We maintain that though there are challenges, one can discern the general idea of the passage.

22. van Wijk-Bos, *Reading Samuel*, 244. In contrast, McCarter does not understand the ideal king to be the rain. He only understands the ideal king to be the sun that shines upon grass that just happens to have rain upon it (see *II Samuel*, 481).

23. We will explain the subject-verb agreement below.

like thorns being chased away for they cannot be taken in hand. But the man who strikes against them will be filled with reference to iron and the shaft of a spear and they will be completely burned where they lie" (AT).[24]

Though this king causes his own subjects to grow through his light and rain, he destroys others. Reading verses 6–7 together, it is best to understand the "man" (אִישׁ) in verse 7 to be the one who disposes of the thorns in verse 6. These thorns are a manifestation of the "worthlessness" (בְלִיַּעַל) mentioned in verse 6. Using botanical imagery, "worthlessness" and its accompanying "thorns" are antithetical to the "sun" causing the "grass" to grow. Since the grass stands in contrast to the thorns, and since the grass represents the king's subjects, this suggests that the "thorns" are the wicked subjects of a wicked king. This wicked king then would be personified "worthlessness" (בְלִיַּעַל). It is best to interpret "worthlessness" as the identity of a rival king opposing the "sun" who shines down righteousness for his subjects' good. This reading is in keeping with commentators who understand "worthlessness" to be a king opposing the righteous "sun."[25]

By personifying this rival king as "worthlessness" the narrative presents him in a profoundly negative light. Firth explains, "The personification is evident from the fact that in the noun's nine previous occurrences it always described someone as a son (1 Sam 2:12; 10:27; 25:17), daughter (1 Sam 1:16) or man (1 Sam 25:25; 30:22; 2 Sam 16:7; 20:1; 22:5) of Belial."[26] Samuel routinely calls people sons, daughters, and men of worthlessness. This rival king is "worthlessness" personified. It is as if he is the father of worthlessness. Those who practice worthlessness are his seed. In Firth's words, this king who is worthlessness is "embodied wickedness."[27]

As mentioned, this king and those aligning with him are "thorn-like."[28] The text notes that fire will burn them in their "sitting" (בְּשָׁבֶת; v. 7).[29] Within the context, this fire is probably a poetic allusion to the heat from the sun mentioned in verse 4. McCarter agrees saying, "[The fire] is the blaze of the

24. NETS translates these verses to say, "They are all like a thorny plant, thrust out, for not by hand shall they be taken, and a man shall not grow weary among them—and full of iron also is a shaft of a spear—and with fire, with burning, they shall be burned by their shame." See McLean, "The Kaige Text of Reigns," 295.

25. See Morrison, *2 Samuel*, 300; Fokkelman, *Throne and City*, 360; Firth, *1 & 2 Samuel*, 528.

26. Firth, *1 & 2 Samuel*, 528.

27. Firth, *1 & 2 Samuel*, 528.

28. Below we will further investigate the relationship between the king of worthlessness and those aligned with him, the thorns.

29. Firth understands the "sitting" of the thorns to refer to their royal status. As kings sit on thrones, so too "worthlessness" and the thorns sit on thrones (see Firth, *1 & 2 Samuel*, 524).

sun. The rule of a lawful king is like the life-giving warmth of the sun for crops (= the king's loyal subjects), but it is like the death-dealing heat of the sun for thorny weeds (= the disloyal)."[30] If this reading is correct, then the man who burns the thorns in verse 7 is the king shining down righteousness and the fear of God on his subjects in verse 4. This king's righteousness brings life to some and destroys others.

7.2.3. David's Interjections: Verse 5

David interrupts his own oracle in verse 5 by making three different causal statements that all begin with כִּי. These three statements are all parallel to one another, and they all provide an explanation for why God spoke the message in verses 3b–4 to David.[31] We will consider each of these three כִּי clauses in turn.

7.2.3.1. David's First Interjection: Verse 5a

The first reason that God told David that a righteous and God-fearing king blesses his people (vv. 3b–4) is because David's house has failed to meet this standard (v. 5a). We translate David's first כִּי clause to read, "For my house is not thus with God" (כִּי־לֹא־כֵן בֵּיתִי עִם־אֵל).[32] Translated in this way, one of the reasons that the Lord told David that a king should reign in righteousness

---

30. McCarter, *II Samuel*, 483.

31. For some examples of asyndetic parallel causal (כִּי) clauses see 2 Sam 22:22–23; Ps 22:12 (ET v. 11); 49:17 (ET v. 16); 71:24; 92:10 (ET v. 9); 96:13; 102:14 (ET v. 13); 147:1; Isa 6:5; 15:1; 59:11–12; 60:1–2; Jer 6:4; 9:19. Two of these references are especially noteworthy. Isaiah 6:5 reads, "And I said: Woe is me! For (כִּי) I am lost; for (כִּי) I am a man of unclean lips, and I dwell in the midst of a people of unclean lips; for (כִּי) my eyes have seen the King, the LORD of hosts.'" Here Isaiah provides three asyndetic parallel כִּי clauses. Each provides a different reason for why Isaiah said, "Woe is me." Likewise, in 2 Sam 23:5 David provides three asyndetic parallel כִּי clauses that provide three different reasons for David's prophetic statement in verses 3b–4. The other noteworthy example is 2 Sam 22:22–23. There David says, "For (כִּי) I have kept the ways of the LORD and have not wickedly departed from my God. For (כִּי) all his rules were before me, and from his statutes I did not turn aside." Both of these כִּי clauses provide the reason for why in verse 21 David says, "The LORD dealt with me according to my righteousness; according to the cleanness of my hands he rewarded me." This example is noteworthy because it is apparently an example of asyndetic parallel כִּי clauses within Samuel's poetry. We are suggesting that 23:5 is another example.

32. For those with a similar translation see Rydelnik, *The Messianic Hope*, 40–41; Sailhamer, *NIV Compact Bible Commentary*, 248. The NETS translates verse 5a as follows: "For is my house not so with Someone Strong?" (McLean, "The Kaige Text of Reigns," 295).

and the fear of God is because David's house has not been meeting this standard. One could state it the other way. It is because David's house has failed to practice righteousness and fear God (v. 5a) that the Lord told David that the ideal king should live righteously for the good of his people (vv. 3b–4). Read in this way, in David's first כִּי clause he understands God's statement about the righteous and God-fearing king to be a rebuke against the conduct of his house. He has not lived up to God's ideal kingly standard.

In contrast to this understanding, most scholars translate David to be saying in this first כִּי clause that his house is in keeping with the kingly ideal that God expressed in verses 3b–4.[33] The primary problem with this understanding is that these scholars fail to take into account the Samuel narrative's previous negative portrayal of David.[34] For example, though the

33. Our translation of the clause above, "For my house is not thus with God," does not reflect the majority of scholarship. Many understand the phrase to be a rhetorical question with an implied interrogative particle expecting a positive answer: "For is my house not so with El?" (Auld, *I & II Samuel*, 585; see also Gordon, *I & II Samuel*, 311). Others suggest that לֹא should be repointed to the asseverative particle לְא. (For possible evidence for the asseverative particle לְא see Lewis, "An Asseverative לֹא in Psalm 100 ?," 216; Richardson, "A Critical Note on Amos 7₃,₁₄," 89). This repointing would mean that David's house is in keeping with the ideals of verses 3b–4. This amounts to the following translation: "Truly, my house is established by God" (see Richardson "Last Words of David," 259, 263; see also McCarter, *II Samuel*, 483; Anderson, *2 Samuel*, 267). Those who translate the disputed phrase as a rhetorical question or an assertion interpret David to be saying that his house is in keeping with God's pronouncement in verses 3b–4. For the problems with these approaches see below.

34. Besides neglecting the Samuel narrative's previous negative portrayal of David's house, there are additional problems with interpreting David's first interjection as affirming that David's house lives righteously. Concerning the asseverative interpretation, one should notice that 2 Sam 23:6 shares the same construction (כִּי־לֹא) that scholars dispute the meaning of in verse 5a and 5c. In verse 6, it is clear that the כִּי grounds a previous clause while לֹא negates a finite verb. We understand the two כִּי־לֹא constructions in verse 5a, c to have the same function. Given the proximity of these three identical constructions in verse 5a, c, it is preferable to render them all in the same way if possible. In addition, within the MT the asseverative particle of לֹא is infrequent at best. Within Samuel the כִּי־לֹא construction occurs 36 times in 34 verses (1 Sam 2:9; 4:7; 6:9; 8:7; 9:13; 12:5, 22; 13:14; 15:29; 16:7, 11; 17:39, 47; 20:26; 21:7 [ET v. 6]; 22:15; 23:17; 26:21; 28:20; 29:6, 8; 30:12; 2 Sam 1:10; 3:37; 7:6; 12:12, 13; 15:14; 17:17, 23; 19:7 [ET v. 6], 29 [ET v. 28]; 23:5, 6). In this construction, לֹא consistently functions as a negation. Besides the two disputed כִּי־לֹא constructions in 2 Sam 23:5, the only other possible exception is 2 Sam 19:7 (ET v. 6), which is a *kethib* (לֹא) and *qere* (לֹ) issue. In this case, the OG (εἰ) agrees with the *qere*. In this text it is more likely that the *qere* is correct than it is that the לֹא is an asseverative particle. Given the consistency of the כִּי־לֹא function within Samuel, one should seek to keep its regular meaning if at all possible. Concerning seeing an implied interrogative particle in verses 5a, c, this approach also fails to understand the כִּי־לֹא phrases in verses 5a, c, and 6 in the same way, which is preferable if possible. Also, the author could have prefixed the interrogative particle to the כִּי if he desired to mark a question as he did in 2 Sam 9:1 and 23:19, though admittedly such

narrative says that David did at one time reign in righteousness (2 Sam 8:15), the parallel text drops this phrase (20:23) because David fails to reign righteously in 2 Sam 11–20.[35] In fact, Smith devotes an entire book arguing that the narrator presents David as not practicing justice and righteousness in 2 Sam 11–20.[36] While discussing 2 Sam 23:5a, Sailhamer writes, "We have seen that the narratives that follow God's promise to the house of David in ch. 7 have focused on the failure of David and his house."[37]

In addition, we have pointed out that like Eli and Samuel before him, David also has two wicked sons. One of these sons was a rapist and the other was a treasonous murderer in the likeness of Cain. We argued above that the motif of two wicked sons functions within Samuel to designate a family as failing to live according to the ideal of messianic faithfulness as prophesied about in 1 Sam 2:35. We previously concluded that though David's house is unfaithful, one day he will have a faithful house that meets the Lord's messianic standard of conduct when the faithful messianic priest, David's son, lives a faithful life and has a faithful house.[38]

Given the above, it is difficult to know in what meaningful way David could say that his house is living righteously and fearing God.[39] Feeling the tension between David's prior failings and interpreting verse 5 to say that David and his house had upheld God's standards in verses 3b–4 causes Morrison to write, "Perhaps David can be accused of being a revisionist as he writes his final testament, which forgets some of his crimes and missteps."[40]

---

particles are implied more frequently in poetry than in narrative. With that said, if it is possible, it is preferable to interpret each of the כִּי־לֹא phrases as signaling a negation and not having an implied interrogative particle. This is the case since כִּי־לֹא more regularly signals a negation rather than a rhetorical question even in poetic texts. For example, within Psalms, the construction occurs 19 times (5:5 [ET v. 4]; 9:11, 19 [ET vv. 10, 18]; 16:10; 22:25 [ET v. 24]; 28:25; 35:20; 41:12 [ET v. 11]; 44:4, 7 [ET vv. 3, 6]; 49:18 [ET v. 17]; 51:18 [ET v. 16]; 55:13 [ET v. 12]; 71:15; 75:7 [ET v. 6]; 78:22; 94:14; 125:3; 143:2), and not once does it pose a question.

35. Firth makes this same point from 2 Sam 20:23 about David failing to reign righteously in *1 & 2 Samuel*, 98–99.

36. Smith, *The Fate of Justice and Righteousness During David's Reign*.

37. Sailhamer, *NIV Compact Bible Commentary*, 248.

38. For a defense of the claims made in this paragraph see sections 5.1.2. and 6.2.1. above.

39. If the translation of 2 Sam 23:5a that we have argued for above is not correct, then this does not necessarily derail the larger argument we are making. Our larger argument in this chapter is that the Messiah will defeat evil and reign as king in the new creation forever. If David is claiming in 2 Sam 23:5a that his house is in keeping with the prophecy in verses 3b–4, then we would understand the text to mean that David's house would eventually produce the ideal king of verses 3b–4, the Messiah.

40. Morrison, *2 Samuel*, 300.

We conclude that David is not guilty of revisionist history nor is he claiming that his house will not one day produce the promised king he is prophesying about. Rather, he transparently admits his present failings to live up to the same standard that the future king he is prophesying about will one day meet. The first reason David interrupts his prophecy is to inform the reader that his house is not presently living in accord with the righteousness that this future promised king will exhibit.

7.2.3.2. David's Second Interjection: Verse 5b

David again interrupts his prophesy about the future righteous king who will bless the Lord's people. This time he interrupts the prophecy because God "set to [David] an eternal covenant, secured in all things and kept" (v. 5b).[41] Based on this statement, it is evident that David understands God's promises to him in 2 Sam 7 as a covenant.[42] This covenant is also unconditional since it is "secured in all things and kept."[43] In addition, this covenant is "eternal" (עולם). The reason this covenant is "eternal" is because in 7:13, 16 the Lord promised to raise up for David his messianic son who will "forever" (עולם) reign.[44]

Having understood the meaning of David's interjection, we can now state the logic of this second כי clause. God revealed to David that the ideal king will reign in righteousness and the fear of God to bless his people (vv. 3b–4) because he made an irrevocable covenant with David to raise up his seed to eternally reign on David's throne (v. 5b). If one understands the ideal king who reigns righteously and in the fear of God to be David's promised messianic son, then the logic fits nicely. We have already seen that evidence

41. The NETS translates verse 5b as follows: "For he made with me an everlasting covenant, ready in every season, kept safe" (McLean, "The Kaige Text of Reigns," 295).

42. Though the narrator did not use the word "covenant" in 2 Sam 7, we have already seen that Ps 89 identifies God's promises to David in 2 Sam 7 as a covenant. Scholars commonly recognize the covenant in 2 Sam 23:5b to be a reference to the promises of 2 Sam 7. See Bergen, *1, 2 Samuel*, 466; Baldwin, *1 and 2 Samuel*, 227; Morrison, *2 Samuel*, 300.

43. For the Davidic covenant being unconditional see Anderson, *2 Samuel*, 269; Chisholm, *1 & 2 Samuel*, 303. That David understands God's covenantal promises in 2 Sam 7 to be unconditional agrees with our reading of Ps 89 above. There we argued that though David's sons disobey, God will not renege on his promise to bring about the seed of David who will reign forever.

44. As mentioned, the "eternal" (עולם) covenant of 2 Sam 23:5b is an allusion to the son of David who would reign "forever" (עולם) from 7:13, 16. On account of this, it is better to not translate "eternal" as a reference to God (i.e., the Eternal One) as Gordon does (see *I & II Samuel*, 311).

from David's introduction and the larger context encourages the reader to understand David's prophecy to be about the Messiah. That this second כי clause refers back to God's covenant with David in 7:11b–17 further increases the messianism of this passage since we have seen above that David's promised seed is the messianic faithful priest from 1 Sam 2:35. Thus, David interrupts his prophecy about a future ideal ruler for a second time to inform the reader that this ruler will come about to fulfill the covenant promises that God made to him.

7.2.3.3. David's Third Interjection: Verse 5c

Lastly, David provides a third כי clause explaining why God told him that the ideal king reigns in righteousness and the fear of God for the good of his people. David stated, "For all my salvation and all desire,[45] he will not make it grow" (AT).[46] In context it is best to understand the words "my salvation" to be an objective genitival relationship signifying the salvation that God enabled David to accomplish on Israel's behalf by defeating foreign nations.[47] Using a botanical metaphor, David presents his salvation and desire as a

45. The present author has not translated this כי because he understands it to be resumptive (see Driver, *Notes on the Hebrew Text of the Books of Samuel*, 360). A few manuscripts have בי instead of כי. This is less likely than the MT's rendering for two reasons. First, it is more likely that someone would change the כי to בי than the other way around. This is the case because changing the כי to בי would produce tighter parallelism within the line. Second, it is possible that the reason the Syriac is lacking the second כי in this verse is because it understood the כי to be resumptive and for this reason omitted it.

46. As was the case when considering 2 Sam 23:5c, our translation of the clause above does not reflect the majority of scholarship. For why it is best to not translate 23:5c as a rhetorical question or a positive assertion about David, see our comments on verse 23:5a above. If our approach is wrong and either of these alternate translations is correct, then this does not nullify this chapter's larger argument that David prophesies that the Messiah will defeat the serpent and reign in the new creation forever. This is the case because one can still interpret the passage messianically even if one understands 23:5a, c to be positive statements about David and his house. Alter, who translates these two clauses as rhetorical questions with implied positive replies, writes, "Because of the everlasting covenant with David, God will make his house blossom" (Alter, *The David Story*, 347). Read in this way, we understand this future blossoming to refer to the Lord raising up the Messiah from David's house. This same messianic interpretation is possible if 23:5a, c are positive assertions about David and his house rather than rhetorical questions. Concerning the Old Greek, the NETS translates verse 5c as follows: "For my whole salvation and total will is that the lawless shall not sprout" (McLean, "The Kaige Text of Reigns," 295).

47. For others who understand the words "my salvation" in 2 Sam 23:5c to be an objective genitival relationship see Olmo Lete, "David's Farewell Oracle [2 Samuel 23:1–7]," 422; Bergen, *1, 2 Samuel*, 466.

plant that the Lord will not cause to "grow" (צמח). The salvation David has wrought for his people is like a seedling or young plant. David's salvation was only a beginning, and God's people are still in need of a greater salvation to grow. God will not cause the plant of David's salvation to grow. In context, this means that David will soon perish since these are his last words (v. 1). God will not prolong David's days, and when David perishes, he will no longer bring about salvation for the Lord's people. Read in this way, David is again interrupting his prophecy to admit his failings and insufficiencies as he did in his first interjection. Since David is dying, who then will cause Israel's salvation and desire to grow into a mature plant?

The immediate and wider context provide us with the answer to this important question. In the immediate context, the one who will bring about growth is the ideal king that David has just finished initially prophesying about. The Lord will use this king's righteous and God-fearing reign to be like sunlight and rain upon the Lord's people causing them to grow up from the land like grass (vv. 3b–4). The wider context has informed us that the Lord will raise up the promised messianic king after David dies (7:12). When David dies, he will no longer be able to cause Israel's salvation to grow, but the ideal king, his messianic son, will.

Interestingly, this reading understands the coming of David's seed to bring about the growth of Israel's salvation. Below we will tease out the significance of this point, but for now we simply note that Dempster astutely observes that "David thus looks to the future assured of hope, having seen the initial growth of God's salvation. The word 'sprouted up' (*yaṣmîaḥ*) is a theologically charged word whose cognate noun ('growth') is employed by later writers to describe a Messiah to come (Jer. 23:5; Zech. 3:8; cf. Isa 4:2)."[48] We will consider some of these passages and others below. For now, we note that David interrupted his prophecy about a future ideal ruler for a third time to let the reader know that he is not Israel's promised savior. God's people must look elsewhere. They must look David's messianic son.

7.2.4. Synthesizing the Findings

Within 2 Sam 23:1–7, David's introductory words, which are verses 1–3a, suggest that his prophecy will concern the Messiah. In verse 1 David introduced his prophecy similarly to how Balaam introduced his two messianic prophecies. This suggests to the reader that as Balaam predicted the coming royal eschatological deliverer, so too David predicted the Messiah's coming. The introduction also connected to the larger context in such a way so as

48. Dempster, *Dominion and Dynasty*, 145.

to encourage one to interpret David's last words messianically. David's song in chapter 22 came immediately before 23:1–7. This psalm and David's last words in 23:1–7 constituted the two halves of a chiasm. David's psalm in chapter 22 ended by anticipating the Messiah—whom the text identifies as David's seed (22:51). The juxtaposition between these two poems, the initial *waw* in 23:1 linking these two passages, and the fact that 23:1–7 corresponds to chapter 22 within the larger chiasm all encourage the reader to interpret 2 Sam 23:1–7 as a prophecy of David about his messianic seed.

The prophecy itself (vv. 3b–4, 6–7) speaks of a coming king with messianic language and imagery.[49] This king shines righteousness and the fear of God down on his subjects causing them to flourish as the morning sun and rain cause the grass to grow. Being like a morning sun, this king will also bring about the end of darkness and night. This king will also destroy wickedness (i.e., thorns) and the personification of evil itself. Given the nature of this prophecy, it was not surprising to see that *Targum Jonathan* and the LXX[B] both understood David's prophecy to be about Israel's Messiah.

David's interjection (v. 5) also contributes to this passage's messianism. David provided three reasons why God revealed to him that one day an ideal king would bless the Lord's people through righteous and God-fearing ways. The first reason David interrupted his prophecy was to instruct the reader that his house was not living in accord with the righteousness that this future promised king would exhibit. In order to prevent one from thinking that David was saying that his house would not eventually produce the Messiah, he clarified with a second interjection. In this second interruption he informed the reader that the prophesied righteous ruler would fulfill God's covenant promises to David. His third interjection was similar to his first one. He interjected so the interpreter would know that David is not Israel's promised savior and that one should look to David's messianic son to bring about a fully blossomed salvation.

7.3. SCRIPTURE'S USE OF 2 SAMUEL 23:1–7

In this section we will consider how five different books (Psalms, Isaiah, Jeremiah, Zechariah, and Malachi) apply the language and imagery from 2 Sam 23:1–7 to the Messiah. In so doing, these texts further demonstrate that 2 Sam 23:1–7 anticipates the coming Messiah.

---

49. The following section will demonstrate that the OT applies the language and imagery in 2 Sam 23:1–7 to the Messiah.

THE MESSIANIC HOPE OF THE NEW CREATION 157

7.3.1. Psalm 72 and 2 Samuel 23:1–7

Scholars regularly recognize Ps 72 to be a messianic psalm.[50] It is no accident then that this psalm contains several allusions to 2 Sam 23:1–7.[51] Van Wijk-Bos notices that in Ps 72:1–4 "the picture of the ideal king who partakes of God's 'justice' and 'righteousness'" is comparable to the ideal king who rules in righteousness from 2 Sam 23:3.[52] She also notes that the righteousness of the ideal king in Ps 72 consists of giving "deliverance (ישׁע) to the needy" (v. 4).[53] Likewise, the ideal king from Samuel will cause "salvation" (ישׁע) to grow as a healthy plant (2 Sam 23:5).

Van Wijk-Bos then proceeds to notice that after Ps 72 and 2 Sam 23 describe the ideal king's righteousness, both texts use an analogy to compare the ideal king's righteousness to light and rain that help the grass grow from the earth (2 Sam 23:4; Ps 72:5–6).[54] For this reason, it follows that Ps 72 presents the subjects of this ideal king as vegetation growing healthily under his reign as does 2 Sam 23:4. Concerning this plant metaphor in Ps

50. David C. Mitchell mentions Jewish and Christian interpreters who have interpreted Ps 72 messianically (see Mitchell, *The Message of the Psalter*, 251–52). Others interpreting Psalm 72 messianically are Robertson, *The Flow of the* Psalms, 118–19; Cole, *The Shape and Message of Book III*, 138–39; and Sailhamer, *NIV Compact Bible Commentary*, 330–31.

51. The presents author understands Solomon to have written Ps 72. If this is the case, a straightforward reading would make the composition of Ps 72 subsequent to the composition of 2 Sam 23:1–7 since these are David's last words. This would mean that Ps 72 borrowed from David's last words. Psalm 72 begins by saying, "Of Solomon" (לשׁלמה). This most likely indicates that Solomon is the author. (For some who understand the superscription to signal Solomon's authorship see Sailhamer, *NIV Compact Bible Commentary*, 331; VanGemeren, *Psalms*, 64; Robertson, *The Flow of the Psalms*, 118, n. 25). The primary reason some understand the superscription to mean "for Solomon" instead of "by Solomon" is because verse 20 supposedly says that David wrote the psalm. Verse 20 reads, "The prayers of David, the son of Jesse, are ended." Against this interpretation Cole effectively argues that verse 20 is mistranslated, and it should read, "The prayers of David, the son of Jesse, are perfected (כלו)." Rather than asserting David's authorship of Ps 72, verse 20 is an editorial comment concluding book II of Psalms, and it suggests that the ideal kingship that Ps 72 depicts is the fulfillment (i.e., perfection) of David's prayers, which are his psalms (see Cole, *The Shape and Message of Book III*, 138–39). That verse 20 functions as the conclusion of book II of Psalms and not Ps 72 is likely since verse 19 is also an editorial comment concluding book II (cf. 41:14 [ET v. 13]; 89:53 [ET v. 52]; 106:48). For another scholar who translates Ps 72:20 similarly to Cole see Mitchell, *The Message of the Psalter*, 66–69.

52. van Wijk-Bos, *Reading Samuel*, 244.

53. van Wijk-Bos, *Reading Samuel*, 244.

54. van Wijk-Bos, *Reading Samuel*, 244. See also deClaissé-Walford, *The Book of Psalms*, 578.

72:16, Marvin E. Tate writes, "It is because the king is truly God's agent, giving hope and fullness to their lives, that the people flourish."[55]

Besides these messianic links between Ps 72 and 2 Sam 23:1–7, there are two additional links that emerge when one views 2 Sam 23:1–7 within its wider context of Samuel as a whole. First, the enemies of the ideal king of Ps 72 will "lick the dust" (v. 9). Hamilton notes, "The licking of the dust calls to mind the fact that the serpent was told that he would eat dust (Gen 3:14)."[56] In a psalm that is littered with allusions to 2 Sam 23:1–7, it is significant to our purposes that Ps 72 presents the messianic ruler of 2 Sam 23:1–7 as one who reigns over the defeated nations as the seed of the woman will reign over the serpent. This observation supports our contention below that the Messiah of 2 Sam 23:1–7 is the seed of the woman who will bring Samuel's serpent-slaying motif to its consummation by defeating the serpent and its hosts.

Second, the ideal king of Ps 72 will also fulfill the Abrahamic covenant. Psalm 72:17 reads, "May his name endure forever, his fame continue as long as the sun! May people be blessed in him, all nations call him blessed."[57] These blessings on Ps 72's ideal king "will be the visible sign [of] the promise God has given to the patriarchs,"[58] and they are "in accordance with the promise of the Abrahamic covenant."[59] We noted in the previous chapter that David's messianic son in 2 Sam 7:11b–17 would fulfill the Abrahamic covenant.[60] Since the ideal ruler of whom David prophesies about in 2 Sam 23:1–7 is this same messianic son, it is reasonable that Ps 72 presents the promised ideal king from David's last words as the fulfillment of the Abrahamic covenant. The ideal ruler of 2 Sam 23:1–7 and Ps 72 will fulfill the Abrahamic covenant because these texts speak of the same ruler.

55. Tate, *Psalms 51–100*, 225.

56. Hamilton, "The Skull Crushing Seed of the Woman," 39.

57. Whether one understands ויתברכו as a reflexive (may people bless themselves) or passive (may people be blessed) in Ps 72:17 has little bearing on the present discussion. Either way, the language of Ps 72:17 is an allusion to Gen 22:18, which is part of God's covenantal promises to Abraham. We briefly argued above that Gen 22:18 is about God's singular eschatological deliverer, and one should understand this verse to be connected to the Abrahamic covenant because of its likeness to Gen 12:3. Genesis 22:18 reads, "And in your offspring shall all the nations (כל גויי) of the earth be blessed (והתברכו), because you have obeyed my voice." Notice how similar this is to Ps 72:17: "May his name endure forever, his fame continue as long as the sun! May people be blessed (ויתברכו) in him, all nations (כל־גוים) call him blessed."

58. Weiser, *The Psalms*, 504.

59. VanGemeren, *Psalms*, 555. See also Hamilton, "The Seed of the Woman and the Blessing of Abraham," 270.

60. See section 6.4.

7.3.2. Isaiah and 2 Samuel 23:1–7

Isaiah presents the Messiah similarly to what we have seen in Samuel. In 4:2, Isaiah refers to the Messiah as the Branch (צמח).[61] By mentioning a "shoot" from the "stump" of Jesse, Isaiah communicates that this Branch will descend from Jesse and David (11:1) and he will be a king (vv. 3–4). By using botanical language again, Isaiah asserts that this kingly Branch is the suffering servant who "grew up . . . like a young plant, and like a root out of dry ground" (53:2).

In addition, to using botanical language to describe the Messiah, Isaiah also compares the Messiah to a dawning sun that ends darkness. Though the people have no dawn and are in the dark (8:20–22), they will see a great light (9:1; ET v. 2). This great light is the morning sun. Isaiah 9:6 (ET v. 7) then clarifies that this morning sun is the Messiah who fulfills the Davidic covenant by alluding to 2 Sam 7:13 and 16.[62] For Isaiah, the messianic son of David is like the morning sun ending the darkness of night.

Isaiah's Messiah is also a priest like Samuel's Messiah is. The messianic Branch is the same individual who "sprinkles (יזה) many nations" as priests would sprinkle the tabernacle (Lev 4:6, 17; 5:9).[63] This messianic Branch also "intercedes" (פגע) for sinners like priests do (Isa 53:12). The result of the Messiah's ministry is that all Israel will become priests of the LORD (61:6).[64] Within Isaiah, there is a new priest with a new priesthood.

The last verse to consider is Isa 55:3. That verse reads, "Incline you ear, and come to me. Hear, and your soul will live, and I will cut for you an eternal covenant (ברית עולם), the faithful covenant loyalties of David (חסדי דוד הנאמנים)" (AT). Recently Peter J. Gentry has argued that the "faithful covenant loyalties of David" should be understood as a subjective genitival relationship. These "faithful covenant loyalties" are actually "the kindnesses performed by David—a rubric for the future king in this text."[65] Gentry un-

---

61. See Childs, *Isaiah*, 35–36.

62. For the link between the light of Isa 9:1 and the Messiah see Motyer, *The Prophecy of Isaiah*, 100; Shepherd, *Daniel in the Context of the Hebrew Bible*, 36. For a messianic interpretation of Isa 9:5–6 (ET vv. 6–7) see Motyer, *The Prophecy of Isaiah*, 103; Oswalt, *The Book of Isaiah*, 248. For Isa 9:6 (ET v. 7) being an allusion to 2 Sam 7:13 and 16 notice that these are the only verses that contain the words "throne" (כסא), "kingdom" (ממלכה), and "establish" (כון).

63. For a defense of reading "sprinkle" instead of "startle" see Motyer, *The Prophecy of Isaiah*, 425–26. This reading may imply that because of the servant's sacrifice, the nations become the temple of the Lord, which would be sprinkled by priests (cf. Lev: 4:17; 8:11).

64. See Shepherd, *The Text in the Middle*, 75; Motyer, *The Prophecy of Isaiah*, 502.

65. Gentry and Wellum, *Kingdom through Covenant*, 421.

derstands Isa 55:3 to be saying that the Lord's eternal covenant (ברית עולם) with David is that the new David, the Messiah, will act faithfully. Though Gentry does not connect Isa 55:3 to 2 Sam 23:1–7, the verse may allude to that passage. Besides Isa 55:3, only 2 Sam 23:5 explicitly links the words "eternal covenant" (ברית עולם) with the Davidic covenant. In addition, we have already argued that in 2 Sam 23:1–7 David prophesies that his seed, who is the faithful (נאמן) priest, will come and fulfill the Davidic covenant. Thus, when Isaiah anticipates that the new David will come and act faithfully to bring about the Davidic covenant, he could be alluding to both 1 Sam 2:35 and 2 Sam 23:1–7 in a messianic fashion since within Samuel these verses expect the Messiah to act faithfully and fulfill the Davidic covenant.[66]

Regardless of whether Gentry's proposal about Isa 55:3 is correct, both Isaiah and Samuel present the Messiah as the growing Branch, who is the son of David. This son of David ends the night by being like a morning sun, and he is also a priest-king. Lastly, those who benefit from his ministry will serve as priests of the Lord.

7.3.3. Jeremiah 23:5–6 and 2 Samuel 23:1–7

In Jer 23:5–6, the prophet combines multiple elements from Samuel and applies them to the Messiah.[67] Jeremiah begins this oracle in verse 5 with the oft stated, "Behold the days are coming (הנה ימים באים)." Though Jeremiah may be using this is as a stock expression to refer to the future, he may also be alluding to 1 Sam 2:31, which is where the phrase first occurs. Strikingly, immediately after Jeremiah says "behold, the days are coming," he says, "the [Lord] will raise up (והקמתי) for David a righteous Branch" (v. 5). Besides a defectively written *hireq yod*, the word "raise up" is identical to the word "raise up" (והקימתי) in 1 Sam 2:35 and 2 Sam 7:12. Jeremiah tells the reader

---

66. Further support for our claim that 1 Sam 2:35 and 2 Sam 23:5 may be the intended background for Isa 55:3 is that verses 4–5 allude to 2 Sam 22:44–45. By alluding to these messianic texts within Samuel, Isaiah effectively recalls the messianic texts that bracket the book of Samuel. Strengthening this claim is the observation that other texts have done the same thing. We have already noted that Hab 3:18–19 alluded to 1 Sam 2:1 and 2 Sam 22:34. Also, Ps 132:17 combines the "horn" 1 Sam 2:10 with the "growth/ sprout" of 2 Sam 23:5 to describe the Messiah. This tendency to combine the messianic passages that bracket the book of Samuel supports the recent scholarship that sees these bracketing passages as interconnected and intentional to the shape of Samuel (see Fokkelman, *Throne and City*, 354; Polzin, *Samuel and the Deuteronomist*, 33; Cole, *The Shape and Message of Book III*, 42, n. 9).

67. For an understanding of Jer 23:5–6 as a messianic passage see Calvin, *Jeremiah*, 138–46. Kruse also understands this passage to be messianic (see Kruse, "Psalm 132 and the Royal Zion Festival," 288–89).

to "behold the days are coming" when the LORD will "raise up" the Messiah, and 1 Sam 2:31–35 said, "behold the days are coming" when the Lord will "raise up" the faithful, messianic priest.

Like Isaiah did, Jeremiah calls the Messiah the "Branch" (צמח). Because of the other potential allusions to Samuel, one may understand this to be a reference to the Messiah who in 2 Sam 23:4–5 will cause salvation and desire to "grow" (צמח). This Branch in Jeremiah will do justice and righteousness. This is in keeping with our findings in 2 Sam 23:1–7 because we saw that David's seed who will cause David's salvation and desire to branch out is like a sun shining down righteousness on his people. Lastly, the Branch in Jeremiah will bring about "salvation" (תושע) for God's people. This may also be an allusion to 2 Sam 23:5 because we understood that passage to say that when the seed of David comes, this seed will cause salvation (ישע) to grow and branch out. Samuel and Jer 23:5–6 both compare the Messiah to a growing plant that the Lord will raise up from David's line who will do righteousness and bring about salvation in the days to come.

7.3.4. Zechariah 6:9–15 and 2 Samuel 23:1–7

We have already seen in the previous chapter that Zechariah understands the one who will build the temple in fulfillment of the Davidic covenant to be the promised priest-king from 1 Sam 2:35 and 2 Sam 7:11b–17. We are now capable of seeing that Zechariah also describes the Messiah with language found in 2 Sam 23:1–7. Zechariah 6:12b–13a reads, "Behold, the man (איש) whose name is Branch (צמח), for he shall branch out from his place, and he shall build the temple of the LORD. It is he who shall build the temple of the LORD and shall bear royal honor, and shall sit and rule (משל) on his throne" (Zech 6:12b–13a). For Zechariah the messianic priest-king from Samuel is a "man" (איש) called "Branch" (צמח) who will "reign" (משל). Likewise, the messianic priest-king from David's last words will be a "man" (איש; 2 Sam 23:7) who "reigns" (משל; 23:3) and causes salvation for the Lord's people to "grow" (צמח; v. 5).[68]

68. Although it is common for scholars to suggest that Zechariah depends on Jeremiah for his "Branch" theology, Jeremiah does not seem to say that the Branch will be a priest like Zechariah claims. It is more likely that Zechariah is dependent upon Samuel. See Petersen, *Haggai and Zechariah 1–8*, 276; Meyers and Meyers, *Haggai, Zechariah 1–8*, 355.

7.3.5. Malachi 3:20 (ET 4:2) and 2 Samuel 23:1–7

Malachi also appropriates language and imagery in 2 Sam 23:1–7 and applies it messianically. Malachi 3:20a (ET 4:2a) says, "But for you who fear my name, the sun of righteousness shall rise with healing in its wings." While commenting on 2 Sam 23:4 and noting links with Mal 3:20a (ET 4:2a), McCarter writes, "'Sun' may also mean 'king' in Mal 3:20 [4:2], which prophesies the coming of a 'rightful Sun' . . . a legitimate king (!). Indeed, Mal 3:19–20a [4:1–2a], though a post-exilic passage looking forward to the coming of a future king, displays many parallels to our passage."[69] The most obvious link between the two passages is the "sun of righteousness." In 2 Sam 23:3b–4, the text compared the messianic king to a sun who shines righteousness down on his subjects. This same sunshine burns away his enemies with fire. Likewise, this king in Mal 3:20 (ET 4:2), is a "sun of righteousness." This king also shines down on his subjects and they benefit (3:20) [ET 4:2], but a fire burns up the wicked (3:19 [ET 4:1]; cf. 2 Sam 23:6–7).

Within the context, it is best to understand this "sun" as the Messiah because Malachi has already linked the coming of the Messiah to the day of the Lord—a day characterized by burning (cf. 3:1–2). Since Elijah the prophet comes before the day to prepare the Messiah's coming (3:23; ET 4:5), and since the king who is the sun of righteousness is not Elijah (3:20; ET 4:2), this suggests that the sun is the Messiah.[70] Zechariah, John the Baptist's father, seems to agree. Though scholars are not unanimous, many understand Zechariah to apply language from Mal 3:20 (ET 4:2) in Luke 1:78 to Jesus when he says that the "sunrise that shall visit us from on high."[71]

Malachi appropriates language and imagery in 2 Sam 23:1–7 and applies it to the coming Messiah. For both Malachi and 2 Sam 23:1–7, the Messiah is the sun of righteousness who is bringing salvation to his subjects but burning destruction to his enemies.

Psalms, Isaiah, Jeremiah, Zechariah, and Malachi all borrow language within 2 Sam 23:1–7 and apply the language messianically. Some of these even combine elements from 1 Sam 2:35 and 2 Sam 7:11b–17 with 2 Sam 23:1–7. They read all three of these texts together and messianically.

---

69. McCarter, *II Samuel*, 484, (punctuation his).

70. Kaiser, *Malachi*, 105.

71. See Wolf, *Haggai & Malachi*, 120; Kaiser, *Malachi*, 105; Carroll, *Luke*, 61; Fitzmyer, *The Gospel According to Luke I–IX*, 387.

7.4. THE MESSIAH AND THE NEW CREATION IN 2 SAMUEL 23:1–7

Thus far in the chapter we have seen that 2 Sam 23:1–7's context, content, and intertextual links demonstrate that David prophesied about his messianic seed's reign. In this final section, we will seek to demonstrate that Samuel understands that the Messiah will reign in the new creation over a defeated serpent by considering the significance of the passage's creation language and the identity of the one who personifies evil in verses 6–7.

7.4.1. The Creation Language in 2 Samuel 23:1–7

David's messianic prophecy in 2 Sam 23:1–7 contains imagery pertaining to plants. The Lord will one day cause salvation to "grow" or "sprout" (צמח) through David's messianic son. This Messiah will also shine down righteousness and the fear of God on his royal subjects causing them to grow like "grass from the land" (v. 4; דשא מארץ). Though the subjects grow in his light, he will completely burn every "thorn" (vv. 6–7).

What is most essential to see about this plant language is that it derives from the first three chapters of Genesis. When Samuel says that the Messiah will shine down on his subjects so that they grow like "grass from the land," this alludes to Gen 1:11–12a. Those verses read, "And God said, 'Let the earth sprout vegetation (תדשא הארץ דשא), plants yielding seed, and fruit trees bearing fruit in which is their seed, each according to its own kind, on the earth.' And it was so. The earth brought forth vegetation (הארץ דשא)." Second Samuel 23:4 and Gen 1:11–12 are the only verses that bring together "grass" (דשא) and "earth" (ארץ) this closely. As grass came forth from the earth within God's original creation, so too God's salvation will "grow" or "sprout" (צמח) through the Messiah causing his subjects, the grass, to flourish.[72] By employing language that harkens back to the original creation, David's last words present the Messiah's subjects as being part of a new creation just as the grass from the earth in Gen 1:11–12 was part of God's original creation.

As is the case in 2 Sam 23:6, thorns are also present in Gen 1–3. Within Genesis, thorns came about because of the first man and woman's rebellion

---

72. "To grow" (צמח) is a description of what the Messiah will do in 2 Sam 23:5, and also a key word within the creation narrative occurring in Gen 2:5, 9; 3:18. The messianic ruler of 2 Sam 23:1–7 will also rule over "men" (אדם). Given the other allusions to Gen 1–3 in this passage, it is likely that the mention of "men" (אדם) also alludes to Genesis's mention of "humanity" (אדם; Gen 1:26–27; 2:5, 7–8, 15–16, 18–23, 25; 3:8–9, 12, 17, 20, 22, 24) and "Adam" (אדם; 2:20; 3:17, 21).

against God under the serpent's influence. The Lord told Adam that because of his sin, the ground will produce "thorns (קוֹץ) and thistles" (3:18). Within Gen 1–3, thorns are the result of rebellion against the Lord. We have already seen that 2 Sam 23:6–7 poetically uses "thorns" (קוֹץ) to represent those in rebellion against the messianic king. Both Gen 3:18 and 2 Sam 23:6 associate "thorns" with rebellion. This further confirms that 2 Sam 23:1–7 is drawing upon creation language from Gen 1–3.

Further strengthening our contention that 2 Sam 23:1–7 is drawing upon creation language from Gen 1–3 is seen in how both 2 Sam 23:1–7 and Gen 1–3 contrast the "grass from the land" with the "thorns." Within Gen 1–3, when God makes the grass come up from the land, it is part of God's work in making "plants yielding seed, and fruit trees bearing fruit" (1:11). Thus, the grass from the earth is bound up with positive connotations. This is the case since God made it in his original creation and called it good. This is also the case because it is associated with the production of food that occurred before sin and rebellion entered the world (v. 12).

As we saw in chapter 2 of this book, after sin and rebellion came into the world through the serpent's influence, the Lord judged the man. On account of the man's rebellion, the days in which grass and food flourished disappeared and the ground instead produced "thorns and thistles" (3:18). On account of these thorns and thistles, food would no longer come from pain-free work, but rather the first man would only eat from the ground in pain (v. 17). Thus, the thorns are bound up with negative connotations. They are the result of the serpent's temptation, and God's judgment against sin. The text also associates them with the lack of the production of food. Within Gen 1–3 the grass and all of its original, good creation connotations serves as the opposite of the post-rebellion thorns and thistles.[73]

Likewise, we have seen in our exegesis of 2 Sam 23:1–7 that the grass that comes up from the land functions as the literary opposite of the thorns. The grass represents the flourishing subjects of the messianic king, and the thorns represent those subjects of "worthlessness" (בְּלִיַּעַל) incarnate, who are in rebellion against the messianic king. Second Samuel 23:1–7 not only alludes to the "grass" and the "thorns" of Gen 1–3, but it also contrasts these two botanical images with one another in a way that is reminiscent of Gen 1–3.

Yet there is another image from Gen 1–3 within 2 Sam 23:1–7, though it is only indirectly botanical. In 2 Sam 23:3–4, the righteous messianic king is like a sun shining in the morning. Since this king is like a sunrise, his

---

73. For one who likewise speaks of the thorns from Gen 3:18 as representing nature's corruption see Motyer, *The Prophecy of Isaiah*, 57.

righteous light ends the darkness of night. This is reminiscent of Gen 1:3: "God said, 'let there be light,' and there was light." God used this light to end darkness (v. 4), bring about the morning (v. 5), and give growth to the grass from the land (vv. 11–12a). Similarly, in Samuel the Messiah is like a morning sun ending the darkness of night. He shines down on the grass causing it to flourish. The confluence of this creation language drawn from Gen 1–3 within 2 Sam 23:3–7 seems intentional. David prophesied about the coming messianic king with creation language.

7.4.2. The Identity of Worthlessness (בליעל) in 2 Samuel 23:6–7

What then was David's purpose in alluding to Genesis in these different ways? To answer that question, we must first identify the "Worthless One" (בליעל; i.e., Belial) who stands in opposition against the messianic king in 2 Sam 23:1–7. In this section we will argue that the Worthless One in 2 Sam 23:6–7 is the serpent from Gen 3. To do this we will consider the identity of the Worthless One within the context of Samuel. Then, we will analyze 2 Corinthians's use of 2 Sam 23:1–7. Lastly, we will summarize our findings.

7.4.2.1. The Worthless One (בליעל) in 2 Samuel 23:1–7

Within 2 Sam 23:1–7 the messianic king is righteous, and we have seen that the one opposing him is a king who is personified "worthlessness" (בליעל). Firth went so far as to call this king "embodied wickedness."[74]

That this king is the embodiment of wickedness coheres nicely with identifying the king as the serpent from Gen 3. In chapter 2 of this book we considered the four different interpretations regarding the identity of the serpent: naturalistic, symbolic, *sensus plenior*, and messianic. Besides the naturalistic interpretation, the other three interpretations all understand the serpent to either represent evil or to embody evil. The symbolic view understood the serpent and his seed to be "the representatives of evil."[75] The *sensus plenior* view understood "the serpent [to symbolize] sin, death, and the power of evil."[76] The messianic interpretation understood the serpent to be the one that Scripture later identifies as Satan. He opposes God and his people. Those—like the present author—who adopt the messianic interpretation of Gen 3:15 are comfortable ascribing to the serpent the same

---

74. Firth, *1 & 2 Samuel*, 528.

75. Walton, *Genesis*, 226.

76. Wenham, *Genesis 1–15*, 81.

words with which Firth described the king of 2 Sam 23:6, namely "embodied wickedness."[77]

Another connection between the serpent of Gen 3 and the Worthless One is that both are royal figures opposing the Messiah. In chapter 2 we argued that the Genesis narrative presented the serpent as a ruler over a corrupted creation. Though God initially charged the first man and woman to exercise royal authority by subduing the earth and having dominion over the various animals (Gen 1:28), the serpent usurped the first man and woman's royal position. Instead of humanity exercising authority over the animals, the serpent exercised authority over the humans by leading them into rebellion against the Lord.[78] As Dempster argues, when this happened the "serpent [had] apparently won"[79] and the world suffered death and disorder under the serpent's reign. In order to undo the serpent's dominion, God promised to bring about a royal eschatological deliverer through the woman. This deliverer would bruise the serpent's head while the serpent would bruise the offspring's heel (3:15). We have already demonstrated that the Worthless One of 2 Sam 23:6–7 is a king who stands in opposition against the Messiah. This worthless king opposes the Messiah just as the serpent of Gen 3 is a royal figure whom God predicted would stand in opposition against the messianic seed of the woman.

Besides the worthless foe of 2 Sam 23:6–7 being a king and having the same character as the serpent, this king also has wicked, spiritual offspring. This is significant because we saw in chapter 2 of this book that the serpent also has wicked, spiritual offspring. While explaining that the Worthless One is the personification of evil, Firth mentions that this king has various non-physical sons and daughters within Samuel: "The personification is evident from the fact that in the noun's nine previous occurrences it always described someone as a son (1 Sam. 2:12; 10:27; 25:17), daughter (1 Sam 1:16) or man (1 Sam 25:25; 30:22; 2 Sam 16:7; 20:1; 22:5) of Belial."[80]

Firth's insight is important. This enemy who is personified worthlessness has sons, daughters, and subservient accomplices characterized by worthlessness within Samuel. Being sons and daughters of worthlessness makes them the seed of the Worthless One. Just as the serpent had wicked spiritual offspring like Cain, so too within Samuel this wicked king has offspring. Within Samuel the offspring of Belial are examples of those "thorns" in 2 Sam 23:6 who are subjects of the wicked king. It is for this reason that

77. Firth, *1 & 2 Samuel*, 528.

78. Beale, *A New Testament Biblical Theology*, 46.

79. Dempster, *Dominion and Dynasty*, 68.

80. Firth, *1 & 2 Samuel*, 528.

THE MESSIANIC HOPE OF THE NEW CREATION   167

those who are the offspring of Belial always oppose whoever happens to be the primary protagonist at that point in Samuel's narrative.[81] It is no coincidence either that one thing those we previously identified as serpentine all have in common is that they also opposed whoever was the primary protagonist within the Samuel narrative at that time.[82] The offspring of Belial and those characters constituting the serpent motif oppose whoever happens to be Samuel's primary protagonist at that point in the narrative because they are the seed of Belial, and Belial is the serpent that expresses enmity against the people of God.

An additional link between the serpent and the wicked king of 2 Sam 23:6–7 appears when one considers how the serpent relates to his wicked, spiritual offspring and the king relates to the thorns (i.e., his wicked, spiritual offspring). In both cases, the father is inseparably connected to his offspring such that the father can stand as a representative for his seed. Beale refers to this phenomenon as "corporate solidarity."[83]

We already saw that the serpent represents his seed in chapter 2 of this book. There we noted that Gen 3:15 surprisingly says the woman's (messianic) offspring will defeat the serpent itself. Given the parallelism between the woman and the serpent and between the woman's offspring and the serpent's offspring, one would have expected God to say that the woman's offspring would bruise the serpent's offspring. Instead the Lord said that the woman's offspring would bruise the serpent. By breaking the

81. The text of Samuel identifies those who oppose the primary protagonist within the narrative flow of Samuel as the seed of Belial. In 1 Sam 2:12—3:21 the narrative sets Eli's sons in opposition against Samuel, the boy. They are his priestly competition. For this reason, they are sons of Belial (1 Sam 2:12). Those who oppose the kingship of Saul in 10:27 are sons of Belial. Likewise, Nabal set his will against David, and for this the text calls him both a son (25:17) and a man of Belial (v. 25). The text also identifies those individuals who disagree with David's decision to share plunder with his men who stayed behind as men of Belial (30:22). Additionally, those who seek David's life are the seed of Belial. Sheba is a man of Belial (2 Sam 20:1), and David's enemies are poetically called torrents of Belial (22:5). Beside these seven instances, there are two times when misinformed characters errantly call Hannah and David the seed of Belial (1 Sam 1:16; 2 Sam 16:7).

82. Those we identified as serpentine were Nahash, the king of the sons of Ammon, Goliath, Hanun, Absalom, and Amasa. Nahash opposed Saul. Goliath sought to kill David. Hanun and Absalom desired to destroy David's kingdom. Amasa also sought to kill David since he was Absalom's leading general.

83. Though Beale's comments about corporate solidarity are regarding the Messiah, they can still apply to the serpent. See Beale, *Handbook on the New Testament Use of the Old Testament*, 96. See also Ellis, *Prophecy and Hermeneutic in Early Christianity*, 170–71.

expected parallelism, the author enables the serpent to stand in the place of its offspring demonstrating a fundamental unity between the serpent and its seed.[84]

In 2 Sam 23:6–7, the wicked king also stands as a representative for his subjects. In verse 6 after introducing this king, the verse immediately clarifies his identity by comparing him to a "thorn" (כקוץ). We know that the text understands this "thorn" as a collective singular because the verse then says "all of them" (כלהם; i.e., every "thorn") are driven away.[85] Thus, the Worthlessness One is a singular king, a thorn, and yet he represents all the thorns (i.e., his evil subjects). In 2 Sam 23:6–7 the Worthless One is a wicked, spiritual father who stands in corporate solidarity with his offspring just as the serpent is a wicked, spiritual father who stands in corporate solidarity with his offspring.

It is also significant that the text likens the king of worthlessness who stands in opposition against the Messiah to a thorn. We have previously seen that thorns were not part of God's original creation. They came into existence only after the serpent usurped the first man and woman's royal authority by leading them into rebellion. By leading humanity into rebellion, the serpent gained dominion and authority over God's previously good but now thorn-filled creation. Genesis 3 connected the serpent's dominion to a physical, thorn-filled domain, and 2 Sam 23:1–7 connects the Worthless One's reign to spiritual thorns.

7.4.2.2. The Worthless One (בליעל) in 2 Corinthians

The text of 2 Cor 6:14—7:1 links the Worthless One (i.e., Belial) of 2 Sam 23:6–7 to Satan. In this passage Paul argues that believers should not be yoked with "unbelievers" (v. 14a).[86] Thus, at first glance 2 Cor 6:14—7:1 divides humanity into two distinct groups much like we saw in 2 Sam 23:1–7. In both of these passages, the two groups are those who belong to the Messiah and those who belong to Belial. To demonstrate that believers should not be unequally yoked with unbelievers, Paul asks a series of questions. We will see that each question contains links with 2 Sam 23:1–7 prompting the

84. We previously mentioned that Sailhamer noticed that the serpent stands in the place of its seed and cannot be separated from them: "Though the 'enmity' may lie between two 'seeds,' the goal of the final crushing blow is not the 'seed' of the snake but rather the snake itself. . . . In other words, it appears that the author is intent on treating the snake and his 'seed' together, as one" (Sailhamer, *The Pentateuch as Narrative*, 107).

85. For other instances where קוץ functions as a collective singular see Gen 3:18; Isa 32:13; Hos 10:8.

86. Scholars dispute the identity of these unbelievers. See below for this discussion.

reader to identify Belial in 2 Cor 6:15 with Belial in 2 Sam 23:6–7. We will consider each question in turn.

Paul's first question appears in 2 Cor 6:14b, and it is as follows: "For what partnership has righteousness (δικαιοσύνη) with lawlessness?" Paul's point is that those who belong to the Messiah are not to partner with those who are lawless, the subjects of Belial (v. 15). Those of the Messiah are righteous and those of Belial are lawless. This distinction between the righteous ones of the Messiah and the lawless ones of Belial is reminiscent of the 2 Sam 23:4 wherein the Messiah's righteous (צדיק) reign is like a morning sun shining on his subjects, the grass, causing them to flourish. These subjects enjoy and benefit from righteousness revealing their righteous character. On the other hand, those who are the subjects of Belial, the thorns, are the opposite of the Messiah's righteous subjects. Being the opposite of those who flourish under righteousness, one can reasonably label them as lawless.

Paul next asks in 2 Cor 6:14c, "Or what fellowship has light with darkness?" Paul's point is that the Messiah's subjects are of the light, but the unbelievers who are of Belial are of the darkness. They therefore should not have fellowship with one another. Paul's contrast of the light with the dark is similar to 2 Sam 23:1–7. In those verses the Messiah's subjects were compared to grass that grows in the light of the Messiah's righteousness. We saw that by comparing the Messiah's light to a morning sun the text implied that his light brings about the end of darkness like the morning light of Gen 1:3–6 caused a division between day and night. Both 2 Sam 23:1–7 and 2 Cor 6:14c associate the Messiah's subjects with the light and Belial's subjects with darkness. Being even more specific, both passages use the Messiah's light to evoke creation imagery. We will see below that by evoking creation language, these passages associate the Messiah with the new creation.

Then in 2 Cor 6:15a, Paul identifies the leaders of the believers and unbelievers: "What accord has Christ with Belial?" Of course, Paul's point is that Christ has no accord with Belial. As 2 Sam 23:1–7 presented the Worthless One (i.e., Belial) as the Messiah's opposite, so too Paul presents Belial as the Christ's opposite.[87] Christ is the leader of the believers while Belial leads the unbelievers. In this verse commentators understand Belial to be Satan.[88]

A final contextual link worth noticing is that these elements in 2 Cor 6:14—7:1 mentioned above appear in the same order that one finds them in

---

87. That Belial (Βελιάρ) in 2 Cor 6:15 is spelled differently than an exact transliteration of the Worthless One (בליעל; Βελιάλ) of 2 Sam 23:6 is inconsequential. See Guthrie, 2 Corinthians, 300; Keener, 1–2 Corinthians, 194.

88. For those understanding Belial as Satan see Hughes, The Second Epistle to the Corinthians, 248; Barnett, The Second Epistle to the Corinthians, 347–48; Keener, 1–2 Corinthians, 193.

2 Sam 23:1–7. Paul inquires first about "righteousness" (2 Cor 6:14b), then about "light" (2 Cor 6:14c), and then about "Belial" (2 Cor 6:15a). Likewise, David's last words first mention "righteousness" (2 Sam 23:3), then "light" (2 Sam 23:4), and then finally "Belial" (2 Sam 23:6). That 2 Cor 6:14—7:1 not only shares these textual links with 2 Sam 23:1–7 but even mentions them in the same order further increases the likelihood that 2 Sam 23:1–7 serves as the background for 2 Cor 6:14—7:1.

Besides the contextual links we have already pointed out, there are lexical reasons for asserting that Paul's usage of "Belial" finds its OT background in the Worthless One of 2 Sam 23:6–7.[89] We have already seen that in 2 Sam 23:6, the Hebrew word for personified "worthlessness" is "Belial" (בליעל). Of the twenty-seven uses of בליעל in the OT,[90] only three texts use "worthlessness" (בליעל) as a substantival adjective standing for an evil figure like how Paul uses the word Belial in 2 Cor 6:15.[91] Of these three OT verses, only 2 Sam 23:6 presents a direct contrast between Belial and the Messiah. Thus, 2 Sam 23:1–7 and 2 Cor 6:14—7:1 are the only two passages in the Bible that contrast the Messiah with Belial, and both passages link the Messiah's subjects with righteousness and light and Belial's subjects with wickedness and darkness. It is apparent that Paul understands Belial of 2 Sam 23:6 to be Satan.

In 2 Cor 6:15b Paul then asks, "Or what portion does a believer share with an unbeliever?" Though Paul's overall point is clear enough—believers should not share a portion with unbelievers—there is dispute regarding the identity of these "unbelievers." Garland helpfully lays out the four main interpretations: (1) immoral or faithless Christians, (2) untrustworthy individuals, (3) Gentile Christians who do not keep Torah, and (4) false

---

89. Based on the potential links with Qumran theology, J. A. Fitzmyer has suggested that 2 Cor 6:14—7:1 is an interpolation that came from the Qumran community (see Fitzmyer, "Qumran and the Interpolated Paragraph in 2 Cor 6:14–7:1," 271–80). Though recognizing similarities between 2 Cor 6:14—7:1 and Qumran theology, Mark A. Seifrid writes, "The similarities between Paul and Qumran are remarkable, but so are the differences" (Seifrid, *The Second Letter to the Corinthians*, 289). Among these differences that Seifrid mentions are Paul's Christocentric thought and belief that the believing community is the Lord's temple. Interestingly, if one interprets 2 Sam 23:1–7 within the context of Samuel as we have done, then one can account for those theological distinctives missing in the Qumran community.

90. The verses containing בליעל are Deut 13:14 (ET v. 13); 15:9; Judg 19:22; 20:13; 1 Sam 1:16; 2:12; 10:27; 25:17, 25; 30:22; 2 Sam 16:7; 20:1; 22:5; 23:6; 1 Kgs 21:10, 13, 2 Chr 13:7; Job 34:18; Ps 18:5 (ET v. 4); 41:9 (ET v. 8); 101:3; Prov 6:12; 16:27; 19:28; Nah 1:11; 2:1 (ET 1:15).

91. The three texts that use "worthlessness" (בליעל) as a substantival adjective are 2 Sam 23:6; Job 34:18; Nah 2:1 (ET 1:15).

apostles.[92] Mark A. Seifrid strikes the right balance: "The warning against being unequally yoked is thus an admonition against common *labor* with unbelievers; it likely bears a special significance with respect to Paul's opponents in Corinth."[93] It is because Paul's command to not be unequally yoked is against common labor with unbelievers that various applications are legitimate,[94] but Seifrid is correct that Paul's focus is on the false apostles.

Noting how 6:14—7:1 lies between Paul's exhortation that the Corinthians would accept him and his teaching (6:11–13; 7:2–4), Craig S. Keener agrees with Seifrid's assessment.[95] He writes, "It is not difficult to envision Paul's conflict with his rivals here; if the Corinthians must be reconciled to Paul to be reconciled to God (5:20–6:13), they also must reject his rivals for their affection."[96] For Paul, the unbelievers are false apostles who are aligned with Belial, Satan, for whom Paul derives an OT background in 2 Sam 23:1–7. These false apostles are the thorns of 2 Sam 23:1–7, the subjects of Belial.

The next time Paul mentions Satan, Belial, and those aligned with him is in 2 Cor 11:3–15. As Keener says, "The conflict between Christ and Belial (6:15) appears in the conflict between Christ's ambassadors (4:5–6; 5:20) and the servants of Satan (11:14–15)."[97] What is most interesting is that in 2 Cor 11, Paul compares Satan to the serpent from Gen 3 (11:3–15). The reason that Paul compares Satan to the serpent is because Paul understands Satan to be the serpent (11:3–15).[98] As the serpent originally twisted God's word to deceive the first woman (v. 3),[99] Satan deceitfully twists God's word

---

92. Garland, *2 Corinthians*, 331–32.

93. Seifrid, *The Second Letter to the Corinthians*, 292, (emphasis his).

94. Two applications for Paul's command include the Corinthians not marrying non-Christians (see Wright, *Paul for Everyone*, 74), and not eating meat "offered to idols at pagan temples and in the homes of pagan associates" (Garland, *2 Corinthians*, 333).

95. Keener, *1–2 Corinthians*, 192–93.

96. Keener, *1–2 Corinthians*, 193.

97. Keener, *1–2 Corinthians*, 193.

98. Garland (*2 Corinthians*, 462) and Kruse (*2 Corinthians*, 241) understand the serpent in 2 Cor 11:3 to be Satan. Others, like Barnett (*The Second Epistle to the Corinthians*, 501–02) and Guthrie (*2 Corinthians*, 508) merely suggest that Paul draws an analogy between the serpent and Satan. That Paul understands the serpent to be Satan is evident from his allusion to Gen 3:15 in Rom 16:20 (see Seifrid, "Romans," 692; Schreiner, *Romans*, 804).

99. Second Corinthians 4:2 provides the reader with an additional connection between the serpent and false teaching (see Kruse, *2 Corinthians*, 139, 247; Garland, *2 Corinthians*, 462).

through his ministers, the false apostles (11:13).[100] Paul understands the one referred to as Belial in 2 Sam 23:1–7 to be Satan, who is the serpent from Gen 3.

Paul then asks a final question in 6:16 and tells the Corinthian church to cleanse themselves from every defilement in 7:1. In 6:16 Paul asks, "What agreement has the temple of God with idols?" Certainly, in Paul's mind the answer is "none," and he defends this unstated answer by arguing that the Corinthian church is the temple of the living God. He does this by either quoting or paraphrasing numerous OT texts including 2 Sam 7:14a in 2 Cor 6:18a.[101] That Paul understands 2 Sam 7 to refer to a spiritual eschatological temple is in keeping with our exegesis of 2 Sam 7 above, and his allusion to 2 Sam 7 further suggests that Paul has been alluding to 2 Sam 23:1–7 since we have seen how closely connected these two passages are.[102]

7.4.2.3. Summary of the Identity of the Worthless One (בליעל) in 2 Samuel 23:6–7

We have adduced numerous links between the Worthless One of 2 Sam 23:6–7 and the serpent of Gen 3. Within the context of Samuel, we saw that the Worthless One of 2 Sam 23:6–7 personifies or represents evil as the serpent did. Concerning the serpent and Worthless One's positions, both

100. Keener (1–2 Corinthians, 193) further buttresses his position that the false apostles, who are the servants of Satan, in 11:14–15 are the unbelievers who belong to Belial in 6:14–15 by pointing out that the false apostles bear a false "light" and "righteousness" in 11:14–15 in contrast to the believers who are of the light and righteousness in 6:14.

101. Barnett, The Second Epistle to the Corinthians, 354. The other texts that Paul either quotes or paraphrases are Lev 26:12 and Ezek 37:27 in 2 Cor 6:16b; Isa 52:11 and Ezek 20:34 in 2 Cor 6:17; Isa 43:6 in 2 Cor 6:18b (see Balla, "2 Corinthians," 770–71).

102. The tight connection between 2 Sam 7:11b–17 and 23:1–7 encourages the interpreter to consider how the subjects of the Messiah from each passage relate to each other. We argued above that the subjects (i.e., house) of the Messiah from 7:16 also function as the house/temple of the Lord. Does this imply then that the subjects of the Messiah (i.e., the grass) in 23:1–7 are also the temple of the Lord? This is certainly possible since the Messiah's subjects are presented as being part of a new creation (for a defense of this see below), and Genesis presents God's original creation as a temple (see Beale, The Temple and the Church's Mission, 77; Beale and Kim, God Dwells Among Us, 17–28). Within Samuel, then, the subjects of the Messiah would be God's building (i.e., temple) and field (i.e., grass). Interestingly, the apostle Paul refers to Christians as God's field and building in 1 Cor 3:9. In this passage the building is the temple (see Blomberg, 1 Corinthians, 37–39; Fee, The First Epistle to the Corinthians, 144, n. 364). This increases the likelihood that Paul understands the field to be another metaphor for the temple.

figures are royal and rule over a dominion. Regarding these dominions, both the Worthless One and the serpent rule over thorns. The mention of "thorns" in verse 6 was just one of at least three different allusions back to Gen 1–3. That 2 Sam 23:1–7 repeatedly alludes to the early chapters of Genesis further invites the reader to consider the relationship between the Worthless One and the serpent and their relationship to the larger theme of creation. On account of the significance that the Genesis narrative attaches to the "thorns" of Gen 3:18, we suggested that both the Worthless One and the serpent exercise authority over a creation that has been corrupted through humanity's sinful rebellion against the Lord. With respect to their parentage, both the serpent and the Worthless One have wicked, spiritual offspring whom they represent in corporate solidarity. Lastly, both Genesis and Samuel presented the serpent and the Worthless One as the adversary whom the Messiah will defeat.

Though 2 Sam 23:1–7 did not explicitly call the Worthless One the serpent, the similarities were striking. Given Samuel's overall expectation that God's anointed one will defeat the serpent—whether that be Nahash, Goliath, Hanun, Absalom, or Amasa—the reader has been set up to expect the ultimate anointed one, the son of David, to likewise defeat the serpent. Thus, the larger context encourages the reader to identify the Worthless One as the serpent from Gen 3. The similarities between the Worthless One and the serpent only strengthen this identification.

We then argued that the apostle Paul's OT background for Belial in 2 Cor 6:15 was the Worthless One of 2 Sam 23:6–7. This was evident because the only two passages in the Bible that display a contrast between Belial and the Messiah are 2 Sam 23:1–7 and 2 Cor 6:14—7:1. In addition to this, in both passages those aligned with the Messiah are of the light and righteousness while those of Belial are lawless and of the dark. Also, both passages associate the Messiah and his subjects with creation language. By implication, both passages inform the reader that Belial and his subjects are of the old, corrupted creation. In addition, Paul's allusion to 2 Sam 7:14 in 2 Cor 6:18 further strengthens our contention that 2 Sam 23:1–7 serves as Paul's background in 2 Cor 6:14—7:1 because 2 Sam 23:5 alludes back to 2 Sam 7. Furthermore, Paul proceeds in 2 Cor 11 to again discuss Belial and his subjects. Here, Belial is clearly Satan, and Satan is the serpent from Gen 3. Thus, within Second Corinthians, Paul interprets the Worthless One of 2 Sam 23:6–7 to be Satan, the serpent from Gen 3.

That Paul interprets the Worthless One (i.e., Belial) in this way further strengthens our conclusion that the Worthless One is the satanic serpent from Gen 3. Like Paul, we have sufficient warrant to understand the Worthless One of 2 Sam 23:6–7 to be the serpent from Gen 3 on account of the larger serpent motif of Samuel and the numerous textual and conceptual links between the Worthless One and the serpent found in 2 Sam 23:1–7.

7.4.3. The Significance of 2 Samuel 23:1–7 within Samuel

We are now in a position to pull together the various threads so as to affirm the second half of this book's thesis: Samuel presents David's messianic seed as the one who will reign as king in a new creation and defeat all opposition—including the serpent.

Second Samuel 23:1–7 contains a contrast between the ideal king and the Worthless One. We understood the ideal king to be David's messianic son, and we have identified the Worthless One as the serpent from Gen 3. Second Samuel 23:1–7 refers to the serpent's subjects as "thorns" and the Messiah's subjects as "grass." The "thorns" and "grass" respectively correspond to the seed of the serpent and those aligned with the seed of the woman from Gen 3. That the Messiah defeats the serpent and his subjects is evident in 2 Sam 23:7. The Messiah is the man who sets the serpent and his offspring ablaze. Second Samuel 23:1–7 presents the Messiah as the one who will reign as king and defeat all opposition against the Lord.

Second Samuel 23:1–7 also presents David's messianic son as reigning during the time of the new creation. We have demonstrated that 2 Sam 23:1–7 not only mentions key figures from Gen 1–3 (i.e., the seed of the woman, the serpent, and its seed), but it also contains allusions to both God's good creation from Gen 1 and the corrupted creation of Gen 3. These allusions are the morning sun (2 Sam 23:4), grass coming up from the earth (v. 4), and thorns (v. 6). When one rightly understands their significance, it becomes apparent that 2 Sam 23:1–7 presents the Messiah as one who reigns in a new creation.

The first allusion was the morning sun of Gen 1:3–5. We have already demonstrated that 2 Cor 6:14's light and darkness imagery derives from the depiction of the Messiah in 2 Sam 23:3–4 as one who brings light like the morning sun. Concerning this light Seifrid wrote, "Paul then moves to creational language. . . . God's saving work in Christ brings a new creation, including the re-creation of the human being (5:17). . . . He directly recalls his description of his own conversion as God creating light out of darkness within his heart (4:6)."[103]

---

103. Seifrid, *The Second Letter to the Corinthians*, 292. It is also worth noting that Seifrid connects the light of 6:14 to the new creation language of 4:6. This is the case because 4:6 depends upon the new creation language of Isa 9:1–7 (see Meyer, *The End of the Law*, 108–09). We have already seen that Isa 9:1–7 is dependent in some measure

That Seifrid links the creation language in 6:14 with the new creation is significant for our purposes. The apostle Paul understands the light of the Messiah in 2 Sam 23:3–4 to be the light of the new creation. As the light shone into the darkness making morning and evening in God's original creation (Gen 1:3–5), so too will the Messiah shine like the sun bringing about the morning and ending the darkness of night (2 Sam 23:3–4).

That the Messiah reigns in a new creation is also evident in how 2 Sam 23:1–7 alluded to the grass of the earth from God's original, good creation and the thorns from the corrupted creation (3:18). As the grass sprouted from the earth after God made light (Gen 1:11–12), once again the grass will sprout and flourish in the form of the Messiah's prospering subjects. As thorns came about from the serpent enticing the first man and woman to rebel against the Lord (3:18), so the Messiah will defeat the serpent and remove every thorn ridding his domain from all evil and rebellion against the Lord. Once again, God's creation will be without thorns. God's creation has been made anew.

Samuel is not the only book to connect the new creation with the removal of thorns. Isaiah 55:13a anticipates the day when "the cypress will come up instead of the thorn bush (הנעצוץ) and the myrtle will come up instead of the nettle" (AT). Isaiah's language here communicates the same reality expressed in Isa 65:17 when the Lord "creates a new heavens and a new earth and the former things shall not be remembered or come up in one's mind" (AT).[104] That Isaiah, which has already shown dependence on 2 Sam 23:1–7, also connects the cessation of thorns with the new creation increases the likelihood that Samuel is depicting a new creation.

To sum it up, 2 Samuel 23:1–7 is the climax of the serpent motif within Samuel. Prior to this passage Samuel has been heightening the reader's expectations for one who will finally overcome the serpent. At the book's conclusion, the author finally informs us who will defeat the serpent. It was not Saul who failed to live righteously after beating Nahash the serpent. It was not David, though he looked like the serpent-slaying seed of the woman when he initially lived righteously after defeating Goliath the serpent. Like Saul before him, after David beat Hanun, the serpentine seed of Nahash, he

---

on 2 Sam 23:1–7. This further supports our claim that 2 Cor 6:14—7:1 finds its OT background in 2 Sam 23:1–7.

104. Regarding Isa 55:12 Motyer writes, "But the ultimate reality is the new earth, creation released from the bondage of corruption." He then describes the lack of thorns in verse 13 as "Genesis 3:18 put into reverse" (see Motyer, *Isaiah*, 347). Also, though Brueggemann does not explicitly call this world without thorns in Isa 55:12–13 the new creation, he does write that it "bespeaks the healing of all creation" (see Brueggemann, *Isaiah 40–66*, 163).

failed to practice justice and righteousness. Instead of resisting temptation, he sinned with Bathsheba like Eve sinned with the forbidden fruit. David "saw" that Bathsheba was "good" in his eyes, and so he "took" her. Like Eve, he sinned as one who falls prey to the temptation of the serpent. As Genesis promised that Eve would have a seed who would eventually defeat the serpent, so too Samuel teaches that one day the Lord would raise up David's messianic seed.

At Samuel's conclusion, we learn that the seed of David—whom the NT identifies as Jesus of Nazareth (Matt 1:1; Mark 10:47)—is this king who conquers the serpent, which Samuel understands to be embodied wickedness. In this way, all rebellion against the Lord will end and unlike Adam, Eve, Saul, and David, there is no indication within Samuel that the Messiah will fall to the serpent's God-defying ways. This priest-king succeeds where Adam, the first priest-king, failed.[105]

In conjunction with the Messiah's victory over the serpent, 2 Sam 23:1–7 presents the Messiah as one who reigns over a new creation. A corrupted creation replaced God's original creation through the serpent leading the first man and woman into rebellion. Though this new creation over which the Messiah reigns is like the original creation of Gen 1, it differs from it because it is superior in at least two ways. First, unlike what we see in Gen 1–3, this time the ruler will not be the first man, Adam. The ruler will be God's messianic priest-king. Second, in this new creation the Messiah will have defeated the serpent, and so no opposition will exist.

7.5. SUMMARY

Our goal in this chapter was to demonstrate that Samuel teaches that its Messiah is the seed of the woman who will reign in the new creation and that he would defeat all opposition including the serpent. To do this, we first located 2 Sam 23:1–7 within its larger context and exegeted the passage. We argued that Samuel's author has intentionally placed 2 Sam 23:1–7 in a structural location that is messianically significant. Upon exegeting the passage, we noted that David—following Balaam's messianic prophecies—anticipated that one day his messianic seed will reign in righteousness for the good of his subjects. When the Lord raises this seed up, he will fulfill his covenant with David and cause a complete salvation to grow and blossom. We then supported our findings by pointing out that Psalms, Isaiah,

105. For Adam as a priest-king see Beale, *The Temple and the Church's Mission*, 66–70.

Jeremiah, Zechariah, and Malachi drew upon language and imagery in 2 Sam 23:1–7 and consistently applied it to the Messiah.

Finally, we revisited David's messianic prophecy in 2 Sam 23:1–7 in hopes of understanding the significance of the passage's creation language and the identity of the Worthless One. Our investigation of the passage's creation language yielded three primary allusions to Gen 1–3. These allusions were the dawning of the morning sun, grass growing from the earth, and thorns. We understood the cumulative force of these allusions to mean that Samuel expects the Messiah to reign over a new creation that is without any of the previous creation's corruption.

We were also capable of determining the identity of the Worthless One of 2 Sam 23:6–7. Based on numerous links between the serpent from Gen 3 and the Worthless One, Paul's interpretation of the Worthless One in 2 Corinthians, and Samuel's larger serpent motif, we deduced that the Worthless One is the serpent.

That the Messiah will defeat the serpent coheres nicely with Samuel's serpent motif, and it makes sense of how the Messiah will be able to reign in a new creation. Since the serpent was responsible for bringing about the corruption of God's original creation, it seems reasonable that the Messiah's victory over the serpent and his offspring would coincide with a new creation. This Messiah, the seed of David, is both a royal king and a faithful priest who causes salvation to sprout, and he eternally reigns for the well-being of all of his subjects. As we have seen, the Samuel narrative contains a serpent motif which is significant because through it Samuel presents the seed of David as the promised seed of the woman from Gen 3:15 who will defeat the serpent and reign as king in the new creation for the flourishing of his people.

8

CONCLUSION

8.1. SUMMARY

CHAPTER 1 OF THIS book served as an introduction. It overviewed every serpentine reference scholars have suggested within Samuel. It then laid out the guiding questions of this book. These questions were (1) whether Samuel's references to various "serpents" constitute a literary motif and (2) what the probable significance of this motif might be. Based on these questions, the book's thesis was that Samuel contains a serpent motif and that this motif's significance within Samuel is to present the seed of David as the promised seed of the woman from Gen 3:15 who will defeat the serpent and reign as king in the new creation.

In chapter 2 we considered the serpent's role in Gen 3 in order to enable one to responsibly determine when a passage alludes to the serpent. In this process we determined that the serpent is God's greatest enemy, and the seed of the woman is the royal eschatological deliverer. We also determined that the seed of the serpent are all who oppose the seed of the woman and any who oppose those that the text presents as types of the coming seed of the woman. Following Dempster, we inferred that God's promise to send the seed of the woman includes not just a pledge to defeat the serpent but also to restore the world and humanity to an Edenic-like state, a new creation. We then investigated the serpent's insurrection and the Lord's judgment against all involved in the insurrection. In these sub-sections we produced a list of the various words, images, and concepts that an author could use to allude to the serpent's dealings.

The remainder of the chapter demonstrated these findings by doing a brief biblical theology of the serpent in the OT and NT based on the list of words, images, and concepts that allude to the serpent. In the OT we looked at the serpent in the Law, Prophets, and Writings, and in the NT we looked at this serpent motif in the Gospels, Pauline Epistles, General Epistles, and Revelation. In all of these portions of Scripture, we detected a serpent motif that derived from Gen 3. We concluded the chapter by asking if Samuel would also contain a serpent motif that connects the serpent's defeat to the seed of the woman bringing about a new creation.

In chapter 3 we argued that Samuel presents Goliath as a serpent by considering Goliath's introductory description, death, and Hab 3:13–14's interpretation of David defeating Goliath. While observing Goliath's introductory description, we noted that Goliath wore scale armor like a scaly sea serpent. We also saw that Ezek 29:1–6 contained several links with the David and Goliath narrative, all of which further suggested that Goliath had serpentine associations. We then saw that the Samuel narrative four different times said that Goliath had "bronze" (נחשת) military equipment. We argued that the author most likely fixated on Goliath's "bronze" (נחשת) equipment to associate him with the serpent (נחש) through a play on words.

The text continued to portray Goliath as a serpent in his death. Against the majority of scholars, we tentatively concluded that David struck with the stone not Goliath's forehead but rather his greave. Since "forehead" (מצח) and "greave" (מצח) are homonyms, we suggested that the author wrote with intentional ambiguity. Upon questioning why the author would write with this ambiguity, we suggested that the author did this because he wanted the reader to consider if David's stone did crush Goliath's forehead much like Genesis had promised that the royal eschatological deliverer would one day bruise the serpent's head. Through this ambiguity, the author associated Goliath's death with the serpent's promised defeat. If this study in incorrect and the stone actually struck Goliath's head, then that would be an ever clearer link between Goliath and the serpent from Gen 3:15. That Samuel says that Goliath fell face down also reminded us of the serpent's judgment of eating the dust from Gen 3:14. Lastly, David used Goliath's own sword to remove Goliath's head. Like the serpent, Goliath's demise came from a blow to the head.

Lastly, we understood Hab 3:13–14 to be a poetic interpretation of David's victory over Goliath. This was significant because many scholars understood Hab 3:13 to poetically describe the defeat of a sea serpent or a dragon. Similarly, we noted that Hab 3:13–14 described Goliath's death with language reminiscent of the serpent's judgment from Gen 3:15. We concluded that Habakkuk saw in Goliath's defeat a foreshadowing of when God's final anointed one would defeat the serpent and all aligned with it once and for all.

In chapter 4 we analyzed every passage within Samuel that mentions the name Nahash, the Hebrew word for serpent. We concluded that Samuel consistently presents those who are named Nahash or are associated with one named Nahash as serpentine if they oppose Israel. The first example of this within Samuel is in 1 Sam 11. By presenting Saul as though he were the woman's seed from Gen 3, this text presents Nahash, the king who reigns over the sons of Ammon, as a serpent. In 2 Sam 10, Nahash's name reappears. In this instance the text casts his son, Hanun, as the serpent's seed. Like the serpent from Gen 3, Hanun opposed the woman's seed by shamefully exposing the nakedness of certain individuals from Israel.

The last text to reference the name Nahash was 2 Sam 17:25–27. In these verses the narrative mentions two individuals who descended from men named Nahash. Amasa was one of these individuals. We understood Amasa's descent from Nahash to be the text's signal that Amasa is serpentine. To support this, we noted that Amasa opposed David by aligning with Absalom like Goliath and Hanun had previously opposed David. We also observed that the text depicted Amasa's death as the death of a serpent in 20:10–12.

The second individual in 17:25–27 who descended from a man named Nahash was Shobi. He was the son of Nahash, the king of the sons of Ammon, and Hanun was his brother. He arrived to aid David and his men as they escaped from Absalom, who is deceitful like the serpent. We noted that the narrative does not present Shobi as the seed of the serpent because he helped David. We understood this positive portrayal of Shobi to encourage the reader to see Shobi as a contrast to Amasa. In only a few verses the text communicated that Amasa the Israelite descends from a man named Nahash and is a serpent seeking David's destruction under Absalom's leadership while Shobi the Gentile descends from a man named Nahash and is not a serpent because he seeks David's well-being. This use of irony informs the reader that it is not one's lineage that determines whether or not one is serpentine but whether or not one opposes the Lord's anointed.

In chapter 5 we sought to relate the different serpent stories within Samuel to each other. We noted that after Saul defeated Nahash the serpent, the narrative began to present him in a decidedly negative way by highlighting his disobedience and foolishness. Unlike Saul, when David defeated Goliath, he walked uprightly for a time. In this way, the narrative presented David as a messianic model. He defeated the serpent, and he lived righteously for an extended period of time. Despite David's greatness, he too eventually failed to live a morally upright life. Like we saw with Saul, immediately after David defeated Hanun, the narrative informed the reader of David's affair with Bathsheba and how he murdered Uriah. The narrative shows Saul and David's failure to live faithfully after they defeated Nahash and Hanun in order to demonstrate that these two kings were not the seed of the woman. David falls so far that toward Samuel's conclusion, it is not David who slays the serpents (i.e., Amasa and Absalom) but—shockingly—Joab. David is not the promised seed from Gen 3:15. We concluded with the understanding that as Saul was a foil for David, so too David must be a foil for someone else: his seed.

Chapter 6 attempted to demonstrate that Samuel presents the promised seed of David in 2 Sam 7:11b–17 as the promised seed of the woman who will defeat the serpent. In order to accomplish this, we argued that Solomon did not fulfill the expectations of the Davidic covenant within Samuel nor do other books present him as the ultimate son of David who fulfills the Davidic covenant. Rather, the promised seed of David is the Messiah, who is the faithful priest from 1 Sam 2:35 in whom no evil would ever be found. Thus, Samuel presents the seed of David as a priest-king. This messianic priest-king will fulfill the Abrahamic covenant. This means that he will defeat the serpent because the Lord intended the Abrahamic covenant to restore the blessing on humanity that the first man and woman lost because of the serpent's temptation.

In chapter 7, we attempted to demonstrate that Samuel explicitly links the Messiah's victory over the serpent with his reign over the new creation. On account of our exegesis of 2 Sam 23:1–7, we understood this passage to climax Samuel's serpent motif by predicting the son of David's victory over the serpent and its subjects. As a result of his victory, David's son would reign over the new creation. This son causes salvation to grow and branch out, and he eternally reigns for the well-being of all of his subjects.

8.2. MAJOR CONTRIBUTIONS OF THIS STUDY

The present author understands this book to primarily make two contributions. First, this book presents the most detailed examination of Samuel's serpent motif. Though some (Hamilton, Leithart, Ronning) have noted serpentine elements within Samuel, none have concentrated specifically on the serpent within Samuel.

Second, the present author is not aware of another work that has sought to explain how Samuel's serpent motif operates on a literary level within the book. Though others have briefly suggested that Nahash, Hanun, Amasa, and Goliath are serpentine, no one else has explained in length how these stories relate to each other or to the book's larger message. This study has sought to remedy this gap by suggesting that Samuel's serpent motif fits within the broader theme of messianic new creation.

8.3. PROPOSALS FOR FURTHER INVESTIGATION

One could expand and/or enhance this book by further investigating at least four different areas. First, this book said little about the Spirit's work. It was by the Spirit that both Saul and David defeated serpents. Likewise, the NT presents Jesus as the man of the Spirit who defeats the serpent. What does this suggest—if anything at all—about the first man's failure to defeat the serpent in the garden? How do the Spirit of God and the serpent's defeat relate to each other?

Second, we noted that Saul and David's respective victories over Nahash and Goliath were integral in their process of becoming king. After Saul defeated Nahash, the nation recognized him as king, and after David defeated Goliath, the nation began to recognize him as their future king. What then is the role of defeating the serpent and reigning as king, and how might Jesus's reign as king relate to this? Third, the present author noticed that both the OT and the NT frequently allude to the serpent by using "deception" language. Does all "deception" language allude to the serpent to one degree or another? Also, what is the Messiah's role in defeating deception? Fourth, Ronning has surveyed much of the serpent material throughout both Testaments. Still, one can only see so much, and the present study on Samuel has expanded Ronning's findings in Samuel. Doing additional serpent studies in other books would be an exciting endeavor.

8.4. PASTORAL APPLICATION

This book has shown that Samuel contains a messianic literary strategy dependent on Gen 3:15 that runs throughout most of Samuel. Jesus has plainly stated that the OT centers on him (Luke 24:44), and our study in Samuel has affirmed his interpretation. From Saul's victory over Nahash in 1 Sam 11 to David's prophecy in 2 Sam 23:1–7, Samuel anticipates that the seed of David will defeat evil and reign as king in the new creation. By understanding how Samuel uses its various serpent stories to create a literary strategy that climaxes in the Messiah's work, pastors can preach Samuel both messianically and textually. May pastors preach Jesus as the Messiah from Samuel who saves his people from the serpent's curse by defeating the serpent and reigning forever as king in the new creation for the good of his people.

BIBLIOGRAPHY

Abasili, Alexander Izuchukwu. "Was It Rape?: The David and Bathsheba Pericope Re-examined." *Vetus Testamentum* 61 (2011) 1–15.

Ackroyd, Peter R. *The Second Book of Samuel.* Cambridge Bible Commentary on the New English Bible. Cambridge: Cambridge University Press, 1977.

Albright, W. F. "The Psalm of Habakkuk." In *Studies in Old Testament Prophecy,* edited by H. H. Rowley, 1–18. Edinburgh: T & T Clark, 1950.

Alexander, T. Desmond. *From Eden to the New Jerusalem: An Introduction to Biblical Theology.* Grand Rapids: Kregel, 2008.

———. "Further Observations on the Term 'Seed' in Genesis." *Tyndale Bulletin* 48 (1997) 363–67.

———. "Messianic Ideology in the Book of Genesis." In *The Lord's Anointed: Interpretation of Old Testament Messianic Texts,* edited by R. S. Satterthwaite, Richard S. Hess, and Gordon J. Wenham, 19–39. Grand Rapids: Baker, 1995.

Allen, David L. *Lukan Authorship of Hebrews.* New American Commentary Studies in Bible and Theology 8. Nashville: Broadman & Holman, 2010.

———. "Substitutionary Atonement and Cultic Terminology in Isaiah 53." In *The Gospel According to Isaiah 53: Encountering the Suffering Servant in Jewish and Christian Theology,* edited by Darrel L. Bock and Mitch Glaser, 171–90. Grand Rapids: Kregel, 2012.

Allen, Leslie C. *Jeremiah: A Commentary,* The Old Testament Library. Philadelphia: Westminster, 2008.

Alt, Albrecht. *Essays on Old Testament History and Religion.* Translated by R. A Wilson. Oxford: Blackwell, 1967.

Alter, Robert. *The David Story: A Translation with Commentary of 1 and 2 Samuel.* New York: Norton, 1999.

Amit, Yaira. *The Book of Judges: The Art of Editing.* Translated by Jonathan Chipman. Vol. 38. Leiden: Brill, 1999.

Anderson, A. A. *2 Samuel.* Word Biblical Commentary 32. Dallas: Word, 1989.

Arnold, Bill T. *1 & 2 Samuel.* The NIV Application Commentary. Grand Rapids: Zondervan, 2003.

Avioz, Michael. "The Motif of Beauty in the Books of Samuel and Kings." *Vetus Testamentum* 59 (2009) 341–59.

Aubert, Bernard. *The Shepherd-flock Motif in the Miletus Discourse (Acts 20:17–38) Against Its Historical Background.* Studies in Biblical Literature. New York: Lang, 2009.

Auld, A. Graeme. *I & II Samuel: A Commentary.* 1st ed. The Old Testament Library. Louisville: John Knox, 2011.

Auld, A. Graeme, and Craig Y. S. Ho. "The Making of David and Goliath." *Journal for the Study of the Old Testament* 56 (1992) 19–39.

Baldwin, Joyce G. *1 and 2 Samuel.* Tyndale Old Testament Commentaries. Downers Grove, IL: InterVarsity, 2008.

Balla, Peter. "2 Corinthians." In *Commentary on the New Testament Use of the Old Testament,* edited by G. K. Beale and D. A. Carson, 753–83. Grand Rapids: Baker Academic, 2007.

Barker, Kenneth L., and Waylon Bailey. *Micah, Nahum, Habakkuk, Zephaniah: An Exegetical and Theological Exposition of Holy Scripture.* The New American Commentary. Nashville: Broadman & Holman, 1998.

Barnett, Paul. *The Second Epistle to the Corinthians.* New International Commentary on the New Testament. Grand Rapids: Eerdmans, 1997.

Baron, David. *Commentary on Zechariah: His Visions and Prophecies.* Grand Rapids: Kregel Publications, 1918.

Beale, G. K. *The Book of Revelation.* New International Commentary on the New Testament. Grand Rapids: Eerdmans, 1999.

———. "Eden, the Temple, and the Church's Mission in the New Creation." *Journal of the Evangelical Theological Society* 48 (2005) 1–31.

———. *Handbook on the New Testament Use of the Old Testament: Exegesis and Interpretation.* Grand Rapids: Baker Academic, 2012.

———. *A New Testament Biblical Theology: The Unfolding of the Old Testament in the New.* Grand Rapids: Baker Academic, 2011.

———. *The Temple and the Church's Mission: A Biblical Theology of the Dwelling Place of God.* New Studies in Biblical Theology 17. Downers Grove, IL: InterVarsity, 2004.

———. *We Become What We Worship: A Biblical Theology of Idolatry.* Downers Grove, IL: InterVarsity, 2008.

Beale, G. K., and Mitchell Kim. *God Dwells Among Us: Expanding Eden to the Ends of the Earth.* Downers Grove, IL: InterVarsity, 2013.

Bergen, Robert D. *1, 2 Samuel: An Exegetical and Theological Exposition of Holy Scripture.* The New American Commentary. Nashville: Broadman and Holman, 1996.

Bewer, Julius A. "Notes on 1 Sam 13:21; 2 Sam 23:1; Psalm 48:8." *Journal of Biblical Literature* 61 (1942) 45–49.

Biddle, Mark E. "Ancestral Motifs in 1 Samuel 25: Intertextuality and Characterization." *Journal of Biblical Literature* 121 (2002) 617–38.

Billington, Clyde E. "Goliath and the Exodus Giants: How Tall Were They?" *Journal of the Evangelical Theological Society* 50 (2007) 489–508.

Blenkinsopp, J. "2 Sam. XI and the Yahwist Corpus." In *Volume Du Congès Genève 1965,* 15:44–57. Supplements to Vetus Testamentum. Leiden: Brill, 1966.

Block, Daniel I. "Bny 'mwn : the Sons of Ammon." *Andrews University Seminary Studies* 22 (1984) 197–212.

―――. *The Book of Ezekiel: Chapters 25–48*. New International Commentary on the Old Testament. Grand Rapids: Eerdmans, 1998.

―――. *Judges, Ruth: An Exegetical and Theological Exposition of Holy Scripture*. The New American Commentary. Nashville: Broadman & Holman, 1999.

Blomberg, Craig L. *1 Corinthians*. The NIV Application Commentary. Grand Rapids: Zondervan, 1994.

Boda, Mark J. *The Book of Zechariah*. New International Commentary on the Old Testament. Grand Rapids: Eerdmans, 2016.

Borgman, Paul. *David, Saul, and God: Rediscovering an Ancient Story*. Oxford: Oxford University Press, 2008.

Brettler, Marc Zvi. *The Book of Judges*. Old Testament Readings. London: Routledge, 2002.

―――. "The Composition of 1 Samuel 1–2." *Journal of Biblical Literature* 116 (1997) 601–12.

―――. *The Creation of History in Ancient Israel*. London: Routledge, 1998.

Bruce, F. F. *The Gospel of John: Introduction, Exposition and Notes*. Grand Rapids: Eerdmans, 1983.

Brueggemann, Walter. *David and His Theologian: Literary, Social, and Theological Investigations of the Early Monarchy*. Edited by K. C. Hanson. Eugene, OR: Cascade, 2011.

―――. *David's Truth: In Israel's Imagination and Memory*. 2nd ed. Minneapolis: Fortress, 2000.

―――. *First and Second Samuel*. 1st ed. Interpretation: A Bible Commentary for Teaching and Preaching. Louisville: Westminster John Knox, 1990.

―――. *Isaiah 40-66*. Westminster Bible Companion. Louisville: Westminster John Knox, 1998.

Calvin, John. *Jeremiah*. Translated by John Owen. Vol. 3. Calvin's Commentaries. Grand Rapids: Eerdmans, 1950.

Camery-Hoggatt, Jerry. *Irony in Mark's Gospel: Text and Subtext*. Society for New Testament Studies 72. Cambridge: Cambridge University Press, 1992.

Camp, Philip G. "David's Fall: Reading 2 Samuel 11–14 in Light of Genesis 2–4." *Restoration Quarterly* 53 (2011) 149–58.

Carlson, Rolf August. "David, the Chosen King: A Traditio-Historical Approach to the Second Book of Samuel." Stockholm: Almqvist & Wiksell, 1964.

Carroll, John T. *Luke*. The New Testament Library. Louisville: Westminster John Knox, 2012.

Carson, D. A. *The Gospel According to John*. Grand Rapids: Eerdmans, 1991.

Cartledge, Tony W. *1 & 2 Samuel: Bible Commentary*. Macon, GA: Smyth & Helwys, 2001.

Catastini, Alessandro. "4Q Sama: 11 Nahash il 'Serpente.'" *Henoch* 10 (1988) 17–49.

Charlesworth, James H. "Revealing the Genius of Biblical Authors: Symbology, Archaeology, and Theology." *Communio Viatorum* 46 (2004) 124–40.

Childs, Brevard S. *Introduction to the Old Testament as Scripture*. 1st American ed. Philadelphia: Fortress, 1979.

―――. *Isaiah*. Louisville: Westminster John Knox, 2001.

Chisholm, Robert. B., Jr. *1 & 2 Samuel*. Teach the Text Commentary Series. Grand Rapids: Baker, 2013.

————. "Forgiveness and Salvation in Isaiah 53." In *The Gospel According to Isaiah 53: Encountering the Suffering Servant in Jewish and Christian Theology*, edited by Darrel L. Bock and Mitch Glaser, 191–212. Grand Rapids: Kregel, 2012.

Clements, Ronald E. *Jeremiah*: Interpretation: A Bible Commentary for Teaching and Preaching. Louisville: Westminster John Knox, 1989.

Cole, Dennis R. *Numbers: An Exegetical and Theological Exposition of Holy Scripture*. The New American Commentary. Nashville: Broadman & Holman, 2009.

Cole, Robert L. *The Shape and Message of Book III: Psalms 73–89*. Journal for the Study of the Old Testament Supplement Series 307. Sheffield: Sheffield Academic, 2000.

Collins, C. J. "A Syntactical Note (Genesis 3:15): Is the Woman's Seed Singular or Plural?" *Tyndale Bulletin* 48 (1997) 139–48.

Collins, C. John. *Genesis 1–4: A Linguistic, Literary, and Theological Commentary*. Phillipsburg, NJ: Presbyterian & Reformed, 2006.

Collins, John Joseph. *Daniel*. Edited by Frank M. Cross. Hermeneia. Minneapolis: Fortress, 1993.

Cross, Frank Moore. *Canaanite Myth and Hebrew Epic: Essays in the History of the Religion of Israel*. 9th ed. Cambridge: Harvard University Press, 1997.

D'Angelo, Mary Rose. *Moses in the Letter to the Hebrews*. SBL Dissertation Series 42. Missoula, MT: Scholars, 1979.

Davidson, Richard M. "Did King David Rape Bathsheba?: A Case Study in Narrative Theology." *Journal of the Adventist Theological Society* 17 (2006) 81–95.

Dearman, J. Andrew. *Jeremiah, Lamentations*. The NIV Application Commentary. Grand Rapids: Zondervan, 2002.

Decker, Aaron J. "Multivalent Readings of Multivalent Texts: 1 Samuel 10:27 and the Problem of Textual Variants in the Interpretation of Scripture." *Currents in Theology and Mission* 41 (2014) 412–16.

deClaissé-Walford, Nancy L. *The Book of Psalms*. New International Commentary on the Old Testament. Grand Rapids: Eerdmans, 2014.

Deem, Ariella. "And the Stone Sank into His Forehead: A Note on 1 Samuel 17:49." *Vetus Testamentum* 28 (1978) 349–51.

Deenick, Karl. "Priest and King or Priest-king in 1 Samuel 2:35." *Westminster Theological Journal* 73 (2011) 325–39.

Dempster, Stephen G. *Dominion and Dynasty: A Biblical Theology of the Hebrew Bible*. New Studies in Biblical Theology 15. Downers Grove, IL: InterVarsity, 2003.

DeRouchie, Jason S. "The Blessing-commission, the Promised Offspring, and the Toledot Structure of Genesis." *Journal of the Evangelical Theological Society* 56 (2013) 219–47.

————. "Counting Stars with Abraham and the Prophets: New Covenant Ecclesiology in OT Perspective." *Journal of the Evangelical Theological Society* 58 (2015) 445–85.

————. "The Heart of YHWH and His Chosen One in 1 Samuel 13:14." *Bulletin for Biblical Research* 24 (2014) 467–89.

DeRouchie, Jason S., and Jason C. Meyer. "Christ or Family as the 'Seed' of Promise?: An Evaluation of N. T. Wright on Galatians 3:16." *The Southern Baptist Journal of Theology* 14 (2010) 36–48.

Diffey, Daniel S. "David and the Fulfilment of 1 Samuel 2:35: Faithful Priest, Sure House, and a Man after God's Own Heart." *Evangelical Quarterly* 85 (2013) 99–104.

Dillard, Raymond B. *2 Chronicles*. Word Biblical Commentary 15. Waco, TX: Word, 1987.

Dorsey, David A. *The Literary Structure of the Old Testament: A Commentary on Genesis–Malachi*. Grand Rapids: Baker Academic, 1999.

Dragga, Sam. "In the Shadow of the Judges: The Failure of Saul." *Journal for the Study of the Old Testament* 38 (1987) 39–46.

Driver, S. R. *Notes on the Hebrew Text of the Books of Samuel*. 2nd ed. Glasgow: Oxford University Press, 1960.

Duguid, Iain M. *Ezekiel*. The NIV Application Commentary. Grand Rapids: Zondervan, 1999.

Dumbrell, William J. "The Content and Significance of the Books of Samuel: Their Place and Purpose within the Former Prophets." *Journal of the Evangelical Theological Society* 33 (1990) 49–62.

———. "'In Those Days There Was No King in Israel, Every Man Did What Was Right in His Own Eyes': The Purpose of the Book of Judges Reconsidered." *Journal for the Study of the Old Testament* 25 (1983) 23–33.

Ellis E. E. *Prophecy and Hermeneutic in Early Christianity: New Testament Essays*. Grand Rapids: Eerdmans, 1971).

Eschelbach, Michael A. *Has Joab Foiled David?: A Literary Study of the Importance of Joab's Character in Relation to David*. Studies in Biblical Literature. New York: Lang, 2005.

Eslinger, Lyle M. *House of God Or House of David: The Rhetoric of 2 Samuel 7*. Journal for the Study of the Old Testament Supplement Series 164. Sheffield: Sheffield Academic, 1994.

———. *Kingship of God in Crisis: A Close Reading of 1 Samuel 8–12*. Edited by David M. Gunn. Bible and Literature. Decatur, GA: Almond, 1987.

Eves, Terry L. "One Ammonite Invasion or Two : 1 Sam 10:27–11:2 in the Light of 4QSama." *Westminster Theological Journal* 44 (1982) 308–26.

Fee, Gordon D. *The First Epistle to the Corinthians*. Revised edition. New International Commentary on the New Testament. Grand Rapids: Eerdmans, 2014.

Firth, David G. *1 & 2 Samuel*. Apollos Old Testament Commentary. Downers Grove, IL: InterVarsity, 2009.

Fitzmyer, Joseph A. *The Gospel According to Luke I–IX: Introduction, Translation, and Notes*. The Anchor Bible 28. New York: Doubleday, 1982.

———. "Qumran and the Interpolated Paragraph in 2 Cor 6:14–7:1." *Catholic Biblical Quarterly* 23 (1961) 271–80.

Flanagan, James W. "Court History or Succession Document? A Study of 2 Samuel 9–20 and 1 Kings 1–2." *Journal of Biblical Literature* 91 (1972) 172–81.

Fokkelman, J. P. *The Crossing Fates*. Vol. 2 of *Narrative Art and Poetry in the Books of Samuel*. Assen, Netherlands: Van Gorcum, 1986.

———. *King David*. Vol. 1 of *Narrative Art and Poetry in the Books of Samuel*. Assen, Netherlands: Van Gorcum, 1981.

———. *Throne and City*. Vol. 3 of *Narrative Art and Poetry in the Books of Samuel*. Assen, Netherlands: Van Gorcum, 1990.

———. *Vow and Desire*. Vol. 4 of *Narrative Art and Poetry in the Books of Samuel*. Assen, Netherlands: Van Gorcum, 1993.

Fyall, Robert. *Now My Eyes Have Seen You: Images of Creation and Evil in the Book of Job*. New Studies in Biblical Theology 12. Downers Grove, IL: InterVarsity, 2002.

Garland, David E. *2 Corinthians: An Exegetical and Theological Exposition of Holy Scripture*. The New American Commentary. Nashville: Broadman and Holman, 1999.

———. *A Theology of Mark's Gospel: Good News About Jesus the Messiah, the Son of God*. Biblical Theology of the New Testament. Grand Rapids: Zondervan, 2015.

Garland, David E., and Diana S. Richmond Garland. "Bathsheba's Story: Surviving Abuse and Loss." *Family and Community Ministries* 21 (2008) 22–33.

Garsiel, Moshe. *The First Book of Samuel: A Literary Study of Comparative Structures, Analogies and Parallels*. Jerusalem: Revivim, 1985.

———. "The Story of David and Bathsheba: A Different Approach." *The Catholic Biblical Quarterly* 55 (1993) 244–62.

Gaster, T. H. "Notes on 'the Song of the Sea.'" *Expository Times* 48 (1936) 45.

Gehrke, Ralph David. *1–2 Samuel*. Concordia Commentary. St. Louis: Concordia, 1968.

Gentry, Peter J., and Stephen J. Wellum. *Kingdom through Covenant: A Biblical-Theological Understanding of the Covenants*. Wheaton, IL: Crossway, 2012.

George, Mark K. "Yhwh's Own Heart." *The Catholic Biblical Quarterly* 64 (2002) 442–59.

Gilmour, Rachelle. "Reading a Biblical Motif: Gifts of Listed Food Provisions in the Books of Samuel." *Australian Biblical Review* 61 (2013) 30–43.

Goldingay, John. *Psalms: Psalms 42–89*. Baker Commentary on the Old Testament: Wisdom and Psalms 2. Baker Academic, 2007.

———. *Psalms: Psalms 90–150*. Baker Commentary on the Old Testament: Wisdom and Psalms 3. Grand Rapids: Baker Academic, 2008.

Gordon, Robert P. *I & II Samuel: A Commentary*. Library of Biblical Interpretation. Grand Rapids: Zondervan, 1986.

Gray, John. *I and II Kings: A Commentary*. 2nd Revised edition. The Old Testament Library. Philadelphia: Westminster John Knox, 1971.

Greene, Harry W. *Snakes: The Evolution of Mystery in Nature*. 1st ed. Berkeley: University of California Press, 2000.

Gunn, David M. "Narrative Patterns and Oral Tradition in Judges and Samuel." *Vetus Testamentum* 24 (1974) 286–317.

Guthrie, George H. *2 Corinthians*. Baker Exegetical Commentary on the New Testament. Grand Rapids: Baker Academic, 2015.

Hamilton, James. "The Skull Crushing Seed of the Woman: Inner-Biblical Interpretation of Genesis 3:15." *Southern Baptist Theological Journal* 10 (2006) 30–55.

Hamilton, James M., Jr. *God's Glory in Salvation through Judgment: A Biblical Theology*. Wheaton, IL: Crossway, 2010.

———. "The Seed of the Woman and the Blessing of Abraham." *Tyndale Bulletin* 58 (2007) 253–73.

———. "The Typology of David's Rise to Power: Messianic Patterns in the Book of Samuel." *The Southern Baptist Journal of Theology* 16 (2012) 4–25.

Halpern, Baruch. "The Constitution of the Monarchy in Israel." Scholars, 1981.

Hamilton, Victor P. *The Book of Genesis 1–17*. New International Commentary on the Old Testament. Grand Rapids: Eerdmans, 1990.

Harvey, John E. "Tendenz and Textual Criticism in 1 Samuel 2–10." *Journal for the Study of the Old Testament* 96 (2001) 71–81.

Harrington, Daniel J., and Anthony J. Saldarini. *Targum Jonathan of the Former Prophets*. The Aramaic Bible 10. Wilmington, DE: Glazier, 1987.

Hays, J. Daniel. "The Height of Goliath: A Response to Clyde Billington." *Journal of the Evangelical Theological Society* 50 (2007) 509–16.

———. "Reconsidering the Height of Goliath." *Journal of the Evangelical Theological Society* 48 (2005) 701–14.

Heiser, Michael S. "Why Would Jesus Compare Himself to a Snake." Logos Bible Software Blog. 27 September 2019. https://blog.logos.com/2018/06/the-healing-serpent.

Hertzberg, Hans Wilhelm. *I and II Samuel: A Commentary*. Translated by J. S. Bowden. Philadelphia: Westminster John Knox, 1964.

Hess, Richard S. "Equality With and Without Innocence: Genesis 1–3." In *Discovering Biblical Equality: Complementarity Without Hierarchy*, edited by Ronald W. Pierce, Rebecca Merrill Groothuis, and Gordon D. Fee, 2nd ed., 79–95. Downers Grove, IL: InterVarsity, 2005.

Hill, John. "*The Book of Jeremiah (MT) and Its Early Second Temple Background*." In *Uprooting and Planting: Essays on Jeremiah for Leslie Allen*, edited by John Goldingay, 153–71. The Library of Hebrew Bible/Old Testament Studies 459. New York: T&T Clark, 2007.

Hossfeld, Frank-Lothar, and Erich Zenger. *Psalms 2: A Commentary on Psalms 51–100*. Edited by Klaus Baltzer. Translated by Linda M. Maloney. Hermeneia. Minneapolis: Fortress, 2005.

———. *Psalms 3: A Commentary on Psalms 101–150*. Edited by Klaus Baltzer. Translated by Linda M. Maloney. Hermeneia. Minneapolis: Fortress, 2011.

Howard, David M. *Joshua: An Exegetical and Theological Exposition of Holy Scripture*. The New American Commentary. Nashville: Broadman & Holman, 1998.

Howard, George E. "The Twelve Prophets." In *A New English Translation of the Septuagint*. Oxford: Oxford University Press, 2007.

Huey, F. B. *Jeremiah, Lamentations: An Exegetical and Theological Exposition of Holy Scripture*. The New American Commentary. Nashville: Broadman & Holman, 1993.

Hughes, Philip E. *The Second Epistle to the Corinthians*. New International Commentary on the New Testament. Grand Rapids: Eerdmans, 1962.

Humphreys, W. Lee. "The Rise and Fall of King Saul: A Study of an Ancient Narrative Stratum in 1 Samuel." *Journal for the Study of the Old Testament* 18 (1980) 74–90.

———. "The Tragedy of King Saul: A Study of the Structure of 1 Samuel 9–31." *Journal for the Study of the Old Testament* 6 (1978) 18–27.

Israelstam, Rev. J., and Judah J. Slotki. trans. *Midrash Rabbah: Leviticus*. 3rd ed. London: Socino, 1983.

Jackson, Jared J. "David's Throne: Patterns in the Succession Story." *Canadian Journal of Theology* 11 (1965) 183–95.

Janzen, David. "The Condemnation of David's 'Taking' in 2 Samuel 12:1–14." *Journal of Biblical Literature* 131 (2012) 209–20.

Jobling, David. "Saul's Fall and Jonathan's Rise: Tradition and Redaction in 1 Sam 14:1–46." *Journal of Biblical Literature* 95 (1976) 367–76.

Johnson, Benjamin J M. "Reconsidering 4QSam^a and the Textual Support for the Long and Short Versions of the David and Goliath Story." *Vetus Testamentum* 62 (2012) 534–49.

Kaiser, Walter C., Jr. "The Identity and Mission of the Servant of the Lord." In *The Gospel According to Isaiah 53: Encountering the Suffering Servant in Jewish and*

Christian Theology, edited by Darrel L. Bock and Mitch Glaser, 87–107. Grand Rapids: Kregel, 2012.

———. *Malachi: God's Unchanging Love*. Grand Rapids: Baker, 1984.

———. *The Messiah in the Old Testament*. Revised edition. Grand Rapids: Zondervan, 1995.

Keddie, Gordon J. *Dawn of a Kingdom*. Welwyn Commentary Series. Welwyn: Evangelical, 1988.

Keener, Craig S. *1-2 Corinthians*. New Cambridge Bible Commentary. Cambridge University Press: Cambridge, 2005.

Keil, C. F., and F. Delitzsch. *Biblical Commentary on the Books of Samuel*. Translated by James Martin. Commentaries on the Old Testament. Grand Rapids: Eerdmans, 1950.

Kessler, John. "Sexuality and Politics: The Motif of the Displaced Husband in the Books of Samuel." *The Catholic Biblical Quarterly* 62 (2000) 409–23.

Keys, Gillian. *The Wages of Sin: A Reappraisal of the "Succession Narrative."* Journal for the Study of the Old Testament Supplement Series 221. Sheffield: Sheffield Academic, 1996.

Klein, Ralph W. *1 Chronicles: A Commentary*. Edited by Thomas Krüger. Hermeneia. Minneapolis: Fortress, 2006.

———. *1 Samuel*. Word Biblical Commentary 10. Waco, TX: Word, 1983.

———. *2 Chronicles: A Commentary*. Edited by Paul D. Hanson. Hermeneia. Minneapolis: Fortress, 2012.

Klement, Herbert H. "Structure, Context and Meaning in the Samuel Conclusion (2 Sa. 21–24)." *Tyndale Bulletin* 47.2 (November 1, 1996) 367–70.

Kline, Meredith G. *Kingdom Prologue: Genesis Foundations for a Covenantal Worldview*. Eugene, OR: Wipf & Stock, 2006.

Klink III, Edward W., and Darian R. Lockett. *Understanding Biblical Theology: A Comparison of Theory and Practice*. Grand Rapids: Zondervan, 2012.

Knowles, Michael P. "Serpents, Scribes, and Pharisees." *Journal of Biblical Literature* 133 (2014) 165–78.

Knutson, Brent F. "Literary Genres in PRU IV." In *Ras Shamra Parallels: The Texts from Ugarit and the Hebrew Bible*, edited by Loren Raymond et al., 2:170–73. Analecta Orientalia: Commentationes Scientificae de Rebus Orientis Antiqui 50. Rome: Pontificium Institutum Biblicum, 1975.

Koehler, Ludwig, Walter Baumgartner, and Johann Jakob Stamm. *The Hebrew and Aramaic Lexicon of the Old Testament, 2 Volume Set*, edited and translated by M. E. J. Richardson. Study Edition 1. Leiden: Brill Academic, 2001.

Köstenberger, Andreas J. "John." In *Commentary on the New Testament Use of the Old Testament*, edited by G. K. Beale and D. A. Carson, 415–512. Grand Rapids: Baker Academic, 2007.

———. *Salvation to the Ends of the Earth: A Biblical Theology of Mission*. New Studies in Biblical Theology 11. Downers Grove, IL: InterVarsity, 2002.

Kruse, Colin G. *2 Corinthians*. Revised edition. Tyndale New Testament Commentary. Downers Grove, IL: InterVarsity, 2015.

———. *Paul's Letter to the Romans*. Pillar New Testament Commentary. Grand Rapids: Eerdmans, 2012.

Kruse, Heinz. "Psalm 132 and the Royal Zion Festival." *Vetus Testamentum* 33 (1983) 279–97.

Kuhn, Karl A. "The Point of the Step-Parallelism in Luke 1–2." *New Testament Studies* 47 (2001) 38–49.

Kuruvilla, Abraham. "David V. Goliath (1 Samuel 17): What Is the Author Doing with What He Is Saying?" *Journal of the Evangelical Theological Society* 58 (2015) 487–506.

Lane, William L. *Hebrews 1–8*. Word Biblical Commentary 47A. Dallas: Word, 1991.

Leithart, Peter. *A Son to Me: An Exposition of 1 & 2 Samuel*. Moscow, ID: Canon, 2003.

Levenson, Jon D. "A Technical Meaning for N'm in the Hebrew Bible." *Vetus Testamentum* 35 (1985) 61–67.

Lewis, Joe O. "An Asseverative לא in Psalm 100₃." *Journal of Biblical Literature* 86 (1967) 216.

Long, V. Philips. *The Reign and Rejection of King Saul: A Case for Literary and Theological Coherence*. SBL Dissertation Series 118. Atlanta: Scholars, 1989.

Longman, III, Tremper. "The Divine Warrior: The New Testament Use of an Old Testament Motif." *Westminster Theological Journal* 44 (1982) 290–307.

———. "Literary Approaches to the Old Testament." In *The Face of Old Testament Studies: A Survey of Contemporary Approaches*, edited by David W. Baker and Bill T. Arnold, 97–115. Grand Rapids: Baker, 1999.

———. *Psalms: An Introduction and Commentary*. Tyndale Old Testament Commentaries. Downers Grove, IL: InterVarsity, 2014.

Lucas, Ernest C. *Daniel*. Apollos Old Testament Commentary. Leicester: InterVarsity, 2002.

Lunn, Nicholas P. "Patterns in the Old Testament Metanarrative: Human Attempts to Fulfill Divine Promises." *The Westminster Theological Journal* 72 (2010) 237–49.

Lyke, Larry L. *King David with the Wise Woman of Tekoa: The Resonance of Tradition in Parabolic Narrative*. Journal for the Study of the Old Testament Supplement Series 255. Sheffield: Sheffield Academic, 1997.

Martin, John A. "Studies in 1 and 2 Samuel, Pt 1: the Structure of 1 and 2 Samuel." *Bibliotheca Sacra* 141 (1984) 28–42.

Matthews, Kenneth. *Genesis 1–11:26: An Exegetical and Theological Exposition of Holy Scripture*. The New American Commentary. Nashville: Broadman & Holman, 1996.

McCarter, P. Kyle., Jr. *I Samuel*. The Anchor Bible. New York: Doubleday, 1980.

———. *II Samuel*. The Anchor Bible. New York: Doubleday, 1984.

McDonough, Sean M. "'And David Was Old, Advanced in Years': 2 Samuel XXIV 18–25, 1 Kings I 1, and Genesis XXIII–XXIV." *Vetus Testamentum* 49 (1999) 128–31.

McGill, Kevin Rayfield. "The Foil Relationship of David and Saul in 1 Samuel 18." ThM thesis, Dallas Theological Seminary, 2006.

McKane, W. *I & II Samuel: Introduction and Commentary*. Torch Bible Commentaries. London: SCM, 1963.

McLean, Paul D. "The Kaige Text of Reigns." In *A New English Translation of the Septuagint*. Oxford: Oxford University Press, 2007.

McNamara, Martin, and Michael Maher. *Targums Neofiti 1 and Pseudo-Jonathan: Exodus*. Edited by Robert Hayward. Vol. 2. The Aramaic Bible. Collegeville, MN: Liturgical, 1994.

McKeown, James. *Genesis*. The Two Horizons Old Testament Commentary. Grand Rapids: Eerdmans, 2008.

Meyer, Jason C. *The End of the Law: Mosaic Covenant in Pauline Theology*, New American Commentary Studies in Bible and Theology 6. Nashville: Broadman & Holman, 2009.

Meyers, Carol L., and Eric M. Meyers. *Haggai, Zechariah 1–8*, 25B. New York: Doubleday, 1995.

Mitchell, Alan C. *Hebrews*. Sacra Pagina, 13. Collegeville, MN: Liturgical, 2007.

Mitchell, David C. *The Message of the Psalter: An Eschatological Programme in the Book of Psalms*. Sheffield: Sheffield Academic, 1997. Repr., Newton Mearns, UK: Campbell, 2017.

Molin, George. "What Is a Kidon." *Journal of Semitic Studies* 1 (1956) 334–37.

Moo, Douglas J. *The Epistle to the Romans*. New International Commentary on the New Testament. Grand Rapids: Eerdmans, 1996.

Morales, L. Michael. *Who Shall Ascend the Mountain of the Lord? A Biblical Theology of the Book of Leviticus*. New Studies in Biblical Theology 37. Downers Grove, IL: InterVarsity, 2015.

Morrison, Craig E. *2 Samuel*. Berit Olam: Studies in Hebrew Narrative & Poetry. Collegeville, MN: Liturgical, 2013.

Motyer, J. Alec. *Isaiah*. Tyndale Old Testament Commentaries. Downers Grove, IL: InterVarsity, 1999.

———. *The Prophecy of Isaiah: An Introduction & Commentary*. Downers Grove, IL: InterVarsity, 1993.

Muilenburg, J. "The Form and Structure of Covenantal Formulations." In *Essays in Honour of Millar Burrows*. Leiden: Brill, 1959.

Mulder, Martin J. *1 Kings*. 1 Kings 1–11. Historical Commentary on the Old Testament 1. Leuven: Peeters, 1998.

Nicol, George G. "The Alleged Rape of Bathsheba: Some Observations on Ambiguity in Biblical Narrative." *Journal for the Study of the Old Testament* 73 (1997) 43–54.

Niditch, Susan. *Judges*. The Old Testament Library. Louisville: Westminster John Knox, 2008.

Noble, Paul R. "Esau, Tamar, and Joseph: Criteria for Identifying Inner-biblical Allusions." *Vetus Testamentum* 52 (2002) 219–52.

Noll, K. L. *The Faces of David*. Sheffield, England: Sheffield Academic, 1997.

O'Brien, Peter T. *The Letter to the Hebrews*. Pillar New Testament Commentary. Grand Rapids: Eerdmans, 2010.

O'Connell, Robert H. *The Rhetoric of the Book of Judges*. Leiden: Brill, 1996.

Olley, John W. "'The Many': How Is Isa 53, 12a to Be Understood?" *Biblica* 68 (1987) 330–56.

Olmo Lete, Gregorio del. "David's Farewell Oracle (2 Samuel 23:1–7): A Literary Analysis." *Vetus Testamentum* 34 (1984) 414–38.

O'Neal, G. Michael. *Interpreting Habakkuk as Scripture: An Application of the Canonical Approach of Brevard S. Childs*. Studies in Biblical Literature 9. New York: Lang, 2007.

Ortland, Raymond C., Jr. "Male-Female Equality and Male Headship: Genesis 1–3." In *Recovering Biblical Manhood and Womanhood*, edited by John Piper and Wayne Grudem, 2nd ed., 95–112. Wheaton, IL: Crossway, 2006.

Osborne, Grant R. *Matthew*. Exegetical Commentary on the New Testament. Grand Rapids: Zondervan, 2010.

Oswalt, John N. *The Book of Isaiah: Chapters 1–39*. New International Commentary on the Old Testament. Grand Rapids: Eerdmans, 1986.

———. *The Book of Isaiah: Chapters 40–66*. New International Commentary on the Old Testament. Grand Rapids: Eerdmans, 1998.

———. *Isaiah*. NIV Application Commentary. Grand Rapids: Zondervan, 2003.

Payne, David F. "Apologetic Motifs in the Books of Samuel." *Vox Evangelica* 23 (1993) 57–66.

Petersen, David L. *Haggai and Zechariah 1–8: A Commentary*. 1st ed. The Old Testament Library. Philadelphia: Westminster, 1984.

Petterson, Anthony R. *Behold Your King: The Hope for the House of David in the Book of Zechariah*. The Library of Hebrew Bible/Old Testament Studies 513. New York: T&T Clark, 2009.

Pohl IV, Williiam C. "A Messianic Reading of Psalm 89: A Canonical and Intertextual Study." *Journal of the Evangelical Theological Society* 58 (2015) 507–26.

Polzin, Robert. *Samuel and the Deuteronomist: A Literary Study of the Deuteronomic History Part Two: 1 Samuel*. 1st ed. Bloomington: Indiana University Press, 1993.

Postell, Seth D. *Adam as Israel: Genesis 1–3 as the Introduction to the Torah and Tanakh*. Eugene, OR: Pickwick, 2011.

Postel, Seth D., Eitan Bar, and Erez Soref. *Reading Moses, Seeing Jesus: How the Torah Fulfills Its Goal in Yeshua*. Expanded 2nd ed. Wooster, OH: Weaver, 2017.

Prague, Filip Čapek. "David's Ambiguous Testament in 1 Kings 2:1–12 and the Role of Joab in the Succession Narrative." *Communio Viatorum* 52 (2010) 4–26.

Rad, Gerhard von. *Genesis*. Revised edition. The Old Testament Library. Philadelphia: Westminster John Knox, 1973.

Richardson, H. Neil. "A Critical Note on Amos 7$_{14}$." *Journal of Biblical Literature* 85 (1966) 89.

———. "Last Words of David: Some Notes on 2 Samuel 23:1–7." *Journal of Biblical Literature* 90 (1971) 257–66.

Roberts, J. J. M. *Nahum, Habakkuk, and Zephaniah*. The Old Testament Library. Louisville: Westminster John Knox, 1991.

Robertson, O. Palmer. *The Books of Nahum, Habakkuk, and Zephaniah*. The New International Commentary on the Old Testament. Grand Rapids: Eerdmans, 1990.

———. *The Flow of the Psalms: Discovering Their Structure and Theology*. Phillipsburg, NJ: Presbyterian & Reformed, 2015.

Robinson, Gnana. *Let Us Be Like the Nations: A Commentary on the Books of 1 and 2 Samuel*. International Theological Commentary. Grand Rapids: Eerdmans, 1993.

Rofé, Alexander. "The Battle of David and Goliath." In *Judaic Perspectives on Ancient Israel* Rdited by Jacob Neusner, Baruch A. Levine, and Ernest S. Frerichs. Eugene, OR: Wipf & Stock, 2004.

Ronning, John L. "The Curse on the Serpent (Gen 3:15) in Biblical Theology and Hermeneutics." PhD diss., Westminster Theological Seminary, 1997.

Roth, Wolfgang M. W. "You Are the Man: Structural Interaction in 2 Samuel 10–12." *Semeia* 8 (1977) 1–13.

Rost, Leonhard. *Succession to the Throne of David*. Translated by M. D. Rutter and D. M. Gunn. Sheffield: Almond, 1982.

Rudman, Dominic. "The Patriarchal Narratives in the Books of Samuel." *Vetus Testamentum* 54 (2004) 239–49.

Runions, J. Ernest. "Exodus Motifs in First Samuel 7 and 8: A Brief Comment." *The Evangelical Quarterly* 52 (1980) 130–31.

Rydelnik, Michael. *The Messianic Hope: Is the Hebrew Bible Really Messianic?* New American Commentary Studies in Bible and Theology 9. Nashville: Broadman & Holman, 2010.

Sailhamer, John H. "Biblical Theology and the Composition of the Hebrew Bible." In *Biblical Theology: Retrospect and Prospect*, 25–37. Downers Grove, IL: InterVarsity, 2002.

———. *NIV Compact Bible Commentary*. Grand Rapids: Zondervan, 1999.

———. *Introduction to Old Testament Theology: A Canonical Approach*. Grand Rapids: Zondervan, 1995.

———. *The Meaning of the Pentateuch: Revelation, Composition and Interpretation*. Downers Grove, IL: InterVarsity, 2010.

———. *The Pentateuch as Narrative: A Biblical-Theological Commentary*. Grand Rapids: Zondervan, 1995.

Sasson, Jack M. "Reflections on an Unusual Practice Reported in ARM X:4." *Orientalia* 43 (1974) 409–10.

Satterthwaite, Philip E. "'No King in Israel': Narrative Criticism and Judges 17–21." *Tyndale Bulletin* 44 (1993) 75–88.

Scheumann, Jesse R. "A Biblical Theology of Birth Pain and the Hope of the Messiah." ThM thesis, Bethlehem College & Seminary, 2014.

———. "Mothers of Offspring in 1–2 Kings: A Messianic Hope in David's Line." *Tyndale Bulletin* 65 (2014) 37–55.

Schreiner, Thomas R. *The King in His Beauty: A Biblical Theology of the Old and New Testaments*. Grand Rapids: Baker Academic, 2013.

———. *Romans*, Baker Exegetical Commentary on the New Testament. Grand Rapids: Baker Academic, 1998.

Seifrid Mark A. *The Second Letter to the Corinthians*. Pillar New Testament Commentary. Grand Rapids: Eerdmans, 2014.

———. "Romans." In *Commentary on the New Testament Use of the Old Testament*, edited by G. K. Beale and D. A. Carson, 607–694. Grand Rapids: Baker Academic, 2007.

Shepherd, Michael B. "Daniel 7:13 and the New Testament Son of Man." *The Westminster Theological Journal* 68 (2006) 99–111.

———. *Daniel in the Context of the Hebrew Bible*. Studies in Biblical Literature 123. New York: Lang, 2009.

———. *The Text in the Middle*. Studies in Biblical Literature 162. New York: Lang, 2014.

Simon, Maurice. *Midrash Rabbah: Esther & Song of Songs*. 3rd ed. London: Socino, 1983.

Smith, Gary V. *Isaiah 40–66: An Exegetical and Theological Exposition of Holy Scripture*, The New American Commentary. Nashville: Broadman & Holman, 2009.

Smith, Henry Preserved. *A Critical and Exegetical Commentary on the Books of Samuel*. International Critical Commentary 25. Edinburgh: T&T Clark, 2009.

Smith, Ralph L. *Micah–Malachi*. Word Biblical Commentary 32. Waco, TX: Word, 1984.

Smith, Richard G. *The Fate of Justice and Righteousness during David's Reign: Narrative Ethics and Rereading the Court History According to 2 Samuel 8:15–20:26*. The Library of Hebrew Bible/Old Testament Studies 508. New York: T&T Clark, 2009.

Soggin, J. Alberto. *Judges: A Commentary*. The Old Testament Library. Philadelphia: Westminster John Knox, 1981.

Sternberg, Meir. *The Poetics of Biblical Narrative: Ideological Literature and the Drama of Reading*. First Midland Book ed. Bloomington, IN: Indiana University Press, 1987.

Sweeney, Marvin A. *The Twelve Prophets*. Berit Olam 2. Collegeville, MN: Liturgical, 2000.

Talmon, S. *The "Desert Motif" in the Bible and in Qumran Literature*. Harvard University Press, 1966.

Tate, Marvin E. *Psalms 51–100*. Word Biblical Commentary 20. Waco, TX: Word, 1990.

Thompson, J. A. *The Book of Jeremiah*, 1st ed. New International Commentary on the Old Testament. Grand Rapids: Eerdmans, 1980.

Tov, Emmanuel. "The Composition of 1 Samuel 16–18 in Light of the Septuagint." In *The Greek and Hebrew Bible: Collected Essays on the Septuagint*, 333–62. Leiden: Brill, 1999.

Turner, Kenneth J. *The Death of Deaths in the Death of Israel: Deuteronomy's Theology of Exile*. Eugene, OR: Wipf & Stock, 2011.

Tsumura, David Toshio. *The First Book of Samuel*. New International Commentary on the Old Testament. Grand Rapids: Eerdmans, 2007.

VanGemeren, Willem A. *Psalms*. Rev. ed. The Expositor's Bible Commentary 5. Grand Rapids: Zondervan, 2008.

Vannoy, J. Robert. *Covenant Renewal at Gilgal: A Study of 1 Samuel 11:14–12:25*. Cherry Hill, NJ: Mack, 1978.

Veijola, Timo. *Das Königtum in der Beurteilung der Deuteronomistischen Historiographie: eine Redaktionsgeschichtliche Untersuchung*. B 198. Helsinki: Suomalainen Tiedeakatemia, 1977.

Waltke, Bruce K., and Charles Yu. *An Old Testament Theology: An Exegetical, Canonical, and Thematic Approach*. Grand Rapids: Zondervan, 2007.

Walsh, Jerome T. *1 Kings*. Berit Olam. Collegeville, MN: Liturgical, 1996.

Walton, John H. *Genesis*. The NIV Application Commentary. Grand Rapids: Zondervan, 2001.

Weiser, Artur. *The Psalms*. Translated by Herbert Hartwell. The Old Testament Library. Louisville: Westminster John Knox, 1962.

Wellhausen, Julius. *Der Text Der Bücher Samuelis Untersucht*. Göttingen: Vandenhoeck & Ruprecht, 1871.

Wenham, Gordon John. *Genesis 1–15*. Word Biblical Commentary 1. Waco, TX: Word, 1987.

Wesselius, J. W. "Joab's Death and the Central Theme of the Succession Narrative (2 Samuel 9–1 Kings 2)." *Vetus Testamentum* 40 (1990) 336–51.

Wesselius, Jan-Wim. "A New View on the Relationship Between the Septuagint and Masoretic Text in the Story of David and Goliath." In *Early Christian Literature and Intertextuality*, edited by Craig A. Evans and H. Daniel Zacharias, 15:5–26. Library of New Testament Studies 392. London: T&T Clark, 2009.

Westermann, Claus. *Genesis 1–11: A Commentary*. Translated by John J. Scullion S.J. Minneapolis: Augsburg, 1987.

Whiston, William. trans. *The Works of Josephus*. New Updated Edition. Hendrickson, 1987.

Wijk-Bos, Johanna W. H. van. *Reading Samuel: A Literary and Theological Commentary*. Macon, GA: Smyth & Helwys, 2011.

Williamson, H. G. M. *1 and 2 Chronicles*. New Century Bible Commentary. Grand Rapids: Eerdmans, 1982.

———. *Israel in the Books of Chronicles*. Cambridge: Cambridge University Press, 1977.

Wilson, Gerald Henry. *The Editing of the Hebrew Psalter*. SBL Dissertation Series 76. Chico, CA: Scholars, 1985.

Wolf, Herbert. *Haggai & Malachi: Rededication and Renewal*. Everyman's Bible Commentary. Chicago: Moody, 1976.

Wong, Gregory T. K. "A Farewell to Arms: Goliath's Death as Rhetoric Against Faith in Arms." *Bulletin for Biblical Research* 23 (2013) 43–55.

———. "Goliath's Death and the Testament of Judah." *Biblica* 91 (2010) 425–32.

Wright, Christopher J. H. *The Message of Jeremiah*, The Bible Speaks Today. Downers Grove, IL: InterVarsity, 2014.

Wright, N. T. *Paul for Everyone: 2 Corinthians*. 2nd ed. Louisville: Westminster John Knox, 2004.

Yarbrough, Robert W. *1, 2, and 3 John*. Baker Exegetical Commentary on the New Testament. Grand Rapids: Baker Academic, 2008.

Younger, K. Lawson., Jr. *Judges/Ruth*. The NIV Application Commentary. Grand Rapids: Zondervan, 2002.

Printed in Great Britain
by Amazon

16267736R00122